The Thucydidean Turn

Bloomsbury Studies in Classical Reception

Bloomsbury Studies in Classical Reception presents scholarly monographs offering new and innovative research and debate to students and scholars in the reception of Classical Studies. Each volume will explore the appropriation, reconceptualization and recontextualization of various aspects of the Graeco-Roman world and its culture, looking at the impact of the ancient world on modernity. Research will also cover reception within antiquity, the theory and practice of translation, and reception theory.

Also available in the Series:
Alexander the Great in the Early Christian Tradition: Classical Reception and Patristic Literature, Christian Thrue Djurslev
Antipodean Antiquities, edited by Marguerite Johnson
Classics in Extremis, edited by Edmund Richardson
Frankenstein and its Classics, edited by Jesse Weiner, Benjamin Eldon Stevens and Brett M. Rogers
Greek and Roman Classics in the British Struggle for Social Reform, edited by Henry Stead and Edith Hall
Greeks and Romans on the Latin American Stage, edited by Rosa Andújar and Konstantinos P. Nikoloutsos
Homer's Iliad and the Trojan War: Dialogues on Tradition, Jan Haywood and Naoíse Mac Sweeney
Julius Caesar's Self-Created Image and Its Dramatic Afterlife, Miryana Dimitrova
Once and Future Antiquities in Science Fiction and Fantasy, edited by Brett M. Rogers and Benjamin Eldon Stevens
Reading Poetry, Writing Genre, edited by Silvio Bär and Emily Hauser
Sex, Symbolists and the Greek Body, Richard Warren
The Codex Fori Mussolini, Han Lamers and Bettina Reitz-Joosse
The Classics in Modernist Translation, edited by Miranda Hickman and Lynn Kozak
The Gentle, Jealous God, Simon Perris
Translations of Greek Tragedy in the Work of Ezra Pound, Peter Liebregts
Victorian Epic Burlesques, Rachel Bryant Davies

The Thucydidean Turn

(Re)Interpreting Thucydides' Political Thought Before, During and After the Great War

Benjamin Earley

BLOOMSBURY ACADEMIC
LONDON • NEW YORK • OXFORD • NEW DELHI • SYDNEY

BLOOMSBURY ACADEMIC
Bloomsbury Publishing Plc
50 Bedford Square, London, WC1B 3DP, UK
1385 Broadway, New York, NY 10018, USA
29 Earlsfort Terrace, Dublin 2, Ireland

BLOOMSBURY, BLOOMSBURY ACADEMIC and the Diana logo are trademarks of Bloomsbury Publishing Plc

First published in Great Britain 2020
This paperback edition published in 2021

Copyright © Benjamin Earley, 2020

Benjamin Earley has asserted his right under the Copyright, Designs and Patents Act, 1988, to be identified as Author of this work.

For legal purposes the Acknowledgements on p. xvi–xvii constitute an extension of this copyright page.

Cover design: Terry Woodley
Cover image © Marguerite Rami

All rights reserved. No part of this publication may be reproduced or transmitted in any form or by any means, electronic or mechanical, including photocopying, recording, or any information storage or retrieval system, without prior permission in writing from the publishers.

Bloomsbury Publishing Plc does not have any control over, or responsibility for, any third-party websites referred to or in this book. All internet addresses given in this book were correct at the time of going to press. The author and publisher regret any inconvenience caused if addresses have changed or sites have ceased to exist, but can accept no responsibility for any such changes.

A catalogue record for this book is available from the British Library.

A catalog record for this book is available from the Library of Congress.

ISBN: HB: 978-1-3501-2371-7
PB: 978-1-3501-9464-9
ePDF: 978-1-3501-2372-4
eBook: 978-1-3501-2373-1

Series: Bloomsbury Studies in Classical Reception

Typeset by RefineCatch Limited, Bungay, Suffolk

To find out more about our authors and books visit www.bloomsbury.com and sign up for our newsletters.

To my Grandmother

Contents

Preface	ix
Acknowledgements	xiv

1	Introduction: Defining the Thucydidean Turn	1
	A short history of labelling Thucydides	6
	The proliferation of labels	11
	Thucydides today	14
	The value of the Thucydidean turn today: Psychology, realism and time	17
	The structure of this book	18
2	Thucydides: Between Science and Tragedy	23
	Thucydides from rational to tragic	27
	From *Historicus* to *Mythistoricus*	34
	The politics and ethics of *Mythistoria*	40
	Conclusion: Reception and influence	47
3	Thucydides, Realism and Political Psychology	53
	Before the Great War	55
	Thucydides the imperialist	61
	Greek political thought and modernity	63
	Thucydides and political psychology	69
	Thucydides: Man and scholar	75
	Conclusion: A new Thucydidean paradigm?	78
4	Thucydides, Realism and the Great War	81
	Abbott, Thucydides and the Great War	85
	Thucydides and historical realism	91
	Thucydides and political realism	97
	Self-interest in Thucydides	101
	Fear in international relations	103
	Conclusion	107

5	Thucydides, Historical Change and Contemporaneity	109
	Thucydides and the cycle of civilizations	113
	Toynbee on Cornford and the 'impersonal forces' of history	122
	The contemporaneity of Thucydides	125
	Conclusion: A Thucydidean turn?	130
6	Learning to Tolerate Thucydides	131
	The moral and political principles of Thucydides	135
	Thucydides the Realpolitiker	141
	The speeches as political thought	145
	Political psychology and historical change	149
	Thucydides the imperialist	152
	Conclusion: The morality of the city and man	154
7	Epilogue: American Thucydides(s)	159
	Wars ancient and modern: Thucydides in America	161
	Thucydidean turn(s)	167
	The value of the (British) Thucydidean turn	171
Notes		175
Bibliography		197
Index		221

Preface

This book has four main aims. The first is to offer a comprehensive account of the principal texts in the British reception of Thucydides in the early twentieth century (specifically the period from 1900 to 1939). This account is important because it is only then that Thucydides' role begins to shift from that of a historiographical colleague and model to that of the archetypal political thinker, theorist and philosopher in the scholarly imagination. I have labelled this moment the 'Thucydidean turn' because it is characterized by individual scholars discovering Thucydides' contemporary relevance under the influence of the Boer War and the Great War. I discuss in turn and at length the writings of key British thinkers in this 'turn' to Thucydides, namely Francis Cornford, George Abbott, Alfred Zimmern, Arnold Toynbee and Enoch Powell. While there was important material produced on the continent, for example by Eduard Schwartz and Albert Thibaudet, it was in Britain that the contemporary relevance of Thucydides was most keenly felt and had the most impact on subsequent scholarship. No such survey of this critical moment in the reception history of Thucydides has yet been attempted. Neville Morley's monograph *Thucydides and the Idea of History* (2013) is, of course, a classic in the field, and I cannot hope to emulate his range or scholarship, but this work focuses almost exclusively on Thucydides in the history of historiography. Greater light has been thrown on Thucydides and the history of political thought in various essays written for collected volumes edited by Morley with Kathleen Harloe (2012) and later with Christine Lee (2015).[1] However, these individual essays have tended to focus on the reception of Thucydides' thought within the writings of one particular author or a discrete period. Little has been written on the transition between Thucydides as the father of historiography and Thucydides as the father of International Relations, as he is often known today. I claim, therefore, that the turn is a moment of crucial importance in the reception history of Thucydides.

The second aim is to offer a reconsideration of the reception of Thucydides in the history of International Relations.[2] My analysis of the turn also marks a significant departure from previous thought on the place of Thucydides in the history of that discipline. In many standard histories of International Relations, Thucydides, alongside Machiavelli, Hobbes, Kant and others, is held up as a practitioner of the discipline before its formal establishment in 1919 (see, for example, Knutsen 1997; Donnelly 2000). More recently, Jeanne Morefield (2014) and Edward Keene (2015) have pointed to the important place of Alfred Zimmern and Arnold Toynbee in the transmission of knowledge about Thucydides from Classics to International Relations. Both men began by studying Classics but found themselves key figures in the establishment of the latter discipline following the carnage of the Great War. Recent scholarship has, therefore, done much to improve our knowledge of the passing of Thucydides from one discipline to the other. What is much less well known is how Classicists themselves were opening up new avenues of research and producing new interpretations in the wake of the Boer War and the Great War and how important this work would prove to subsequent Thucydidean scholarship. This book will fill that lacuna. It will argue that under the influence of these wars a number of British thinkers turned to Thucydides' account of necessity in human affairs, political psychology and realism to make sense of their own shattered world. These paradigms of interpretation came to dominate the twentieth- and twenty-first-century reception of Thucydides in both Classics and International Relations. The emergence of the British turn to Thucydides was, therefore, necessary for the subsequent establishment of the Athenian historian as one of the greatest thinkers in the American tradition of International Relations after the Second World War.

My third aim is to analyse and critically engage with the arguments of these British scholars for the contribution that they might make to Thucydidean scholarship today. I have pursued this aim in two ways. First, I have explored how certain interpretations have influenced subsequent scholarship down to today. For example, how Cornford's idea of Thucydides as a tragedian influences scholarship for the subsequent century or so. Second, I have compared and contrasted early twentieth-century interpretations with those current today. For example, Powell's depiction of Thucydides as a Realpolitiker was almost entirely forgotten after the Second World War but shows significant similarities (and differences) with contemporary realist interpretations of the *History*. While each of the scholars I study in this book read Thucydides in unique ways, there is an overarching theme which unites them: the relationship between political psychology (of both the individual and the *polis*) and historical change. Cornford's tragic and Powell's Realpolitik interpretation both point, in different ways, to the importance of various iterations of political psychology in Thucydides. Both scholars, however, also point to the number of connections between political psychology and the causes of the Peloponnesian War, the conduct of the *poleis* while engaged in the conflict, and the rise and fall of states. These interpretations speak in important ways to the recent interest in the emotions (Visvardi 2015; Fragoulaki 2016), the ways in which different actors display different psychologies in Thucydides (Lebow 2001; Zumbrunnen 2015), and the ongoing debate over necessity and change in the *History* (Ostwald 1988; Meier 2005; Rusten 2015; Jaffe 2017a; Hoekstra and Fisher 2017). I hope, therefore, that the interpretations of Cornford, Zimmern, Abbott, Toynbee and Powell will all prove interesting to scholars working today at the coalface of Thucydidean scholarship.

My fourth aim is to think critically about the contribution that classical reception studies can make to the study of Thucydides in International Relations and Political Science.[3] It is, perhaps, unfair today to draw too sharp a distinction between the study of Thucydides in Classics and the social sciences. Although the disciplinary boundaries remain somewhat rigid, it is possible to point to a number of philologically astute studies of Thucydides in political science. One thinks immediately of works by Clifford Orwin, Gregory Crane, Arlene Saxonhouse, Ned Lebow and most recently Seth Jaffe. These studies, and the methodology of the political sciences in general, have had a profound effect on the work of classicists such as Josiah Ober and Ryan Balot and vice versa. One could also point to the prominent place of political science voices in the recent *Oxford Handbook to Thucydides* (2017).[4] Nevertheless, as Thauer and Wendt (2016) remind us, there is still much work to be done to ensure that both disciplines do not speak to each other with crossed purposes. One possible solution, I submit, is to consider the connections and congruencies between the intellectual histories of both traditions. Ideas of necessity and political psychology in the *History* are common to many, perhaps all, studies of Thucydides no matter their disciplinary origin. My account of the turn, I hope, will remind Classicists, International Relations Scholars and Political Scientists of the common roots of their respective disciplines' interest in Thucydides.

One of the gravest difficulties in Thucydidean scholarship, it appears to me, is breaking new ground and asking new questions. Classics, International Relations and Political Science can all sometimes appear to be locked in a scholarly Groundhog Day, refighting old battles with only the occasional new twist. The prominence of the realist and neorealist reading of Thucydides has prompted spirited and very well thought out rejoinders from Political Scientists such as Orwin, Crane, Price, Saxonhouse, Lebow and Jaffe, but I believe that the fact that this debate is still playing out today suggests that we are still going over old ground. The same is true in Classics where, for example, Martha Taylor and

Edith Foster have questioned Thucydides' attitude to Pericles and the Athenian Empire. This is all-important work that has offered much insight into Thucydides' thought and world, but I would question whether it has really pushed the field in new directions. As early as J. P. Mahaffy, writing in 1874, scholars have questioned whether Thucydides could really have possessed such a brutal apolitical view of politics, or whether he really could have been so realist. Similarly, debates over Thucydides' attitude to Pericles and the Athenian Empire are at least as old as Dionysius of Halicarnassus. This book is not intended to suggest new questions or new debates that could redefine Thucydidean scholarship. Rather, its aim is to demonstrate the roots of the debates that are currently playing out and their intellectual history. It is hoped that this will allow scholars to see more clearly how their readings fit into transhistorical conversations on Thucydides. In particular, it will identify continuities and discontinuities in approaches to Thucydides over the past one hundred years or so. It is, of course, impossible to step outside of this conversation. Previous readings and interpretations are always with us. Nevertheless, I hope, a better understanding of the place of earlier readings of Thucydides in our reactions to the text today will help scholars formulate new interpretations rooted in the fascinating history of Thucydidean studies.

This endeavour will hopefully stop any tendency to reinvent the wheel. By that, I mean to challenge readers to think critically about how their own reading of the text builds upon, incorporates and departs from previous interpretations. The author of this monograph recently attended an excellent workshop on reading, researching and performing Thucydides today. After hearing an afternoon's worth of fascinating papers, many participants remarked that they were struck by an 'emerging' focus on the literary qualities of the text, oral as well as written, and the varied ways that Thucydides' skill defined and allowed different readings, aesthetic responses and performances. This tendency is, I believe, to be applauded but would be augmented by a reference to the reception history of the text. As we shall in the readings studied in this book, early twentieth-century British scholars were very much alive to the literary qualities and challenges of the multivocality of Thucydides (Mara 2008), which in turn had a profound effect on how they interpreted and presented his political thought. Even scholars such as George Abbott and Enoch Powell, who presented Thucydides as a realist and a Realpolitiker respectively, rooted their interpretations in a reading based upon Thucydides' skill as a writer. Moreover, a major theme of this book is the way in which the changing political and scholarly world affected Thucydidean scholarship. I have been at pains throughout this book to point out how reactions to Thucydides were shaped by individual experiences of the Great War and the terrible and unstable peace that followed it. Modern scholars, I hope, will look at my reading of Cornford, Zimmern or Powell and see the origins and early history of psychological and realist interpretations of the text, which in turn will enable them to position their own work in a tradition of scholarship that extends back far beyond the 1960s.

Acknowledgements

This project would not have been possible without the help and support of a small army of friends and colleagues. I would like to start by thanking the institutions that have given my work such a warm home: namely, the Friedrich Meinecke Institut at the FU Berlin, the Hebrew University of Jerusalem and the Center for Hellenic Studies in Washington, DC. In particular, I would like to thank Maximilian Sutulin (FU) and Lanah Koelle (CHS) for their constant good humour and patience. Much of the material presented in this book is based on archival research, which would not have been possible without the assistance of staff at the Bodleian, Oxford, Trinity College Archive, Cambridge, St John's College Archive, Cambridge, and Churchill College Archive, Cambridge. Few pleasures in life quite match the thrill of discovering previously forgotten documents, but I would have found very little indeed without the help and guidance of the staff at those collections. This book would not have been possible without the patience and expertise of my publisher Bloomsbury Academic; I would like to thank Alice Wright and particularly Lily Mac Mahon for all their help and guidance in turning this manuscript into a book. Finally, I must mention the anonymous reviewer of this book who provided invaluable insight into the International Relations tradition of reading Thucydides and saved me from many linguistic infelicities. Any mistakes, of course, remain my own.

On a more personal level, I have learnt more about Thucydides from conversations with knowledgeable friends than I believe would have been possible through a lifetime's reading of dusty tomes in old libraries. In particular, Robert Pitt provided a warm welcome to Athens, great scholarly insight into the Greek historian, and excellent company. In Bristol and Berlin, Seth Jaffe asked probing questions and pertinent provocations, which has helped steer the path of this project in its early and later stages. While in Washington, Mark Fisher lent me collegial company, a much-needed reminder that the ancient symposium lives on today, and a penetrating insight into the minutiae of Thucydidean scholarship that has greatly benefitted both my ideas and the arguments presented in this book. And finally, Hans Kopp with whom I shared an office in Berlin, welcomed me to his home, introduced me to the delights of German brewing, helped me navigate the labyrinthine corridors of German academic administration and taught me a great detail about Thucydides and his reception in the traditions of German scholarship. My knowledge, thoughts and arguments have been sharpened immeasurably by my friendship with these four scholars.

Academically, the roots of this project extend back to my PhD at the University of Bristol under Neville Morley. Neville is a model supervisor who not only imparted academic wisdom but also knowledge of the dark arts necessary to complete a research project successfully. He went above and beyond the call of duty on many occasions, for which I thank him sincerely. After Bristol, I began a postdoctoral research fellowship jointly hosted at the FU Berlin and Hebrew University of Jerusalem as part of a larger project on *Thucydides and Political Order*. At Jerusalem, Professor Christian Thauer supervised me. He also showed me one of the most fascinating and perplexing countries that I have ever visited. At Berlin, Professor Christian Wendt provided the warmest welcome imaginable to a great city. Christian tested my ideas and shaped my thinking in crucial ways. It is no understatement to say that without his support this project would never have seen the light of day.

Finally, I would like to acknowledge the personal debts I have incurred in researching and writing this book. In Cambridge, Alex Summers and Richard Faulks reminded me that there is more to life than scholarship and their company and good humour provided a welcome respite from the travails of studying Thucydides. However, it is to my family that I owe the most sincere thanks. From Bristol onwards, Melissa Gammons has been my constant companion. She has borne with amusement and love my long periods of absence and my scholarly trials and tribulations, all the while carrying out her own highly successful research into the fundamentals of life. My interest in ancient history was first encouraged by my mother. It must have seemed strange to her that people who had been dead for two thousand years suddenly fascinated me but she supported my interest and nurtured it materially and spiritually. Without her constant belief and support I never would have pursued my passion this far, nor would I have been able to write this book. For these reasons, I owe her a debt that I can never truly repay. Lastly, I would like to thank my grandmother. Like my mother, she supported my slightly insane obsession with ancient history with love and care. It is a great regret to me that she is not here today to see this book finished; however, I hope that it will prove a suitable memorial.

1

Introduction: Defining the Thucydidean Turn

In an engagingly written and provocative book, titled *Destined for War? Can America and China Escape Thucydides's Trap*, the Harvard political scientist and policy-maker Graham Allison has argued that Thucydides offers 'the most frequently cited one liner in the study of international relations' when he claimed that 'it was the rise of Athens and the fear that this instilled in Sparta that made war inevitable' (Allison 2017b: xiv). The 'trap' has given greater public prominence to Thucydides than the Greek historian has ever enjoyed in the past. Allison first publicly floated his idea in a 2012 article for the *Financial Times*, before expanding it into a 2015 article for *The Atlantic*, which he then worked up into a 2017 article in *Foreign Policy*, before it became a book. As a concept, the trap has introduced Thucydides to the wider world of contemporary policy making. Allison's book has endorsements from politicians and generals such as Joe Biden, Henry Kissinger, Ban Ki-Moon and David Petraeus, among other such luminaries. Across the Pacific Ocean, the trap has been referenced and analysed by Malcolm Turnball, the ex-Australian premier, and even by China's President Xi Jinping (see, for example, Rachman in the *Financial Times*, 19 February 2018). One could perhaps even imagine that in the corridors of power in the White House the trap has introduced Donald Trump to Thucydides and the *History of the Peloponnesian War*,[1] particularly as Steve Bannon was a well-known Thucydideophile. It is tempting to believe from the sudden prominence of Allison's trap that Thucydides matters to current geopolitics. Perhaps uniquely so for a text written almost two and a half thousand years ago, it suddenly feels like Thucydides has something specific, useful and applicable to say to our modern situation beyond vague apothegms and bits of advice. Allison helpfully summarizes what he believes that lesson to be:

> While others identified an array of contributing causes to the Peloponnesian War, Thucydides went to the heart of the matter. When he turned the spotlight on 'the rise of Athens and the fear that this instilled in Sparta,' he identified a

primary driver at the root of some of history's most catastrophic and puzzling wars. Intentions aside, when a rising power threatens to displace a ruling power, the resulting structural stress makes a violent clash the rule, not the exception. It happened between Athens and Sparta in the fifth century BCE, between Germany and Britain a century ago, and almost led to war between the Soviet Union and the United States in the 1950s and 1960s.

Allison 2017b: xv

Thucydides is, for Allison, the originator of the idea that it is very difficult for a rising power and an established power to avoid war. Allison has identified sixteen cases that he believes are analogous to the Thucydides trap in modern history, in all but four of which war ensued.[2] There are obvious dangers to reducing a text as rich as the *History* to such a simple formula. However, for the scholars of classical reception the most pressing question is what role is Thucydides himself playing in all of this? The cynic might imagine that Thucydides is merely a convenient hook from which Allison can hang his own theory. Thucydides has just enough cultural cachet to be known among the reading public, even if only by name, but he is not so familiar that the idea of the trap itself appears passé or crass. In other words, Thucydides lends the gravitas of ancient wisdom to Allison's book, but he is not truly integral to the argument. Indeed his presence might easily have been replaced by, for example, Sun Tzu or Machiavelli. Another commentator might suggest that Allison sought out Thucydides because the Greek historian is a writer for troubled times and is suddenly relevant now that the post-Cold War certainty of a unipolar American international order is fast disappearing. Moreover, the Greek debt crisis, Brexit and the rise of populism has halted, perhaps permanently, the progress of the European project. In the US, the comparative loss of international power and prestige following the wars in Iraq and Afghanistan and the emergence of a new culture war has severely damaged the country's confidence and assertiveness. On the other side of the Pacific, the rise of China's economy (even if that rise is now beginning to stall) has heralded in a new era of political order that the international community has not yet learnt to accommodate. In short, we live in a world full of uncertainty and tumult that appears able, at a moment's notice, to erupt into conflict and catastrophe. At such a troubled moment, Allison may have felt compelled to return to Thucydides because he seemingly describes a similar moment of great uncertainty and incipient calamity in the closing decades of the fifth century BC.

Thucydides, in short, is a text for troubled times. This is the same Thucydides who so powerfully appeals to soldiers in the trenches, to sailors at sea, to policy-makers looking to avoid catastrophe and, notably, to Thomas Hobbes, fearful of the propensity of the English to factional strife and imperial overreach (Hoekstra 2016). This is perhaps the same Thucydides that W. H. Auden (2007) invoked during the opening days of the Second World War when he claimed that 'Exiled Thucydides knew' about the political power of speech, about democracy, about dictators, about how war can drive enlightenment away, and, most hauntingly that 'We must suffer them all again.' For Auden, Thucydides provides a hard succour in the form of knowledge of how bad things can get and how, tragically, such events will occur again and again. Auden's poetic thought here touches on elements of Allison's trap concept but also displays a significant difference. Auden suggests that history is moving forward in a cycle: what was true in Thucydides' day will somehow prove irresistibly true for future generations. Sitting in a New York dive bar, Auden imagined that the pain and suffering of the Peloponnesian War were about to be revisited on the world again and there is nothing that anyone could do to stop it. Thucydides, therefore, identified a political problem that has recurred repeatedly throughout history. For Allison, however, it is possible to break the cycle of Thucydidean history that is now beginning to re-emerge in the US–China relationship. Thucydides challenges his readers to recognize that the Peloponnesian War was not inevitable by explaining how a series of contingent events led to the trap being sprung and war breaking out. Allison believes that in four out of sixteen historical cases war was avoided. He published his own book, he maintains, in an attempt to ensure that the US and China create the fifth incidence thereby escaping the trap and avoiding war.

There is, however, another reason that Allison may have chosen to model his ideas of the trap around Thucydides. The Greek historian is incredibly important in the discipline of International Relations, and to a lesser extent in Political Science, in the US. Since the 1950s and 1960s until today, Thucydides has been a staple of International Relations reading lists across the US. He is often considered to be the founder of the discipline itself, or at least of the so-called realist tradition (Boucher 1998), and a small industry has emerged that mines Thucydides' text for new interpretations relevant to theoretical debates or contemporary policy issues (Doyle 1990; Bagby 1995; Welch 2003; Lebow 2003; Forde 2012; Johnson 2015). Allison has used Thucydides to create a theoretical framework through which to understand a difficult and pressing contemporary political problem. However, Allison's Thucydides also represents a new intervention into these debates. He claims that his vision of Thucydides is the correct and only interpretation of the *History*, largely ignoring all previous scholarship. However, Allison's idea of the trap resembles closely, at first glance at least, the idea of power transition theory that has been debated within International Relations since A. F. K. Organski's pioneering 1958 work, *World Politics*. Far from superseding previous scholarship, Allison appears to build upon and profit from it. As already mentioned, Thucydides himself offers a notoriously rich and varied work that presents a multitude of different actors, visions of political life and varied motivations, articulated through carefully crafted speeches married to a well-written narrative depiction of the events of the war. It is far from certain, therefore, that the true import of Thucydides' lengthy text can ever be reduced to a single line, epithet or idea such as Allison's Thucydides trap.

Allison's reduction of Thucydides' thought to the notion of the trap represents the culmination of a tendency in Thucydidean studies that has defined the field for at least the past century: namely, the belief that it is possible to encapsulate Thucydides' thoughts and views in a single label, epithet, name or saying. Many scholars have recently baulked at Allison's reduction of Thucydides to the idea of the trap as unsophisticated (Chan 2019; Kirshner 2018; Lewbow and Tomkins 2016). Allison has reduced Thucydides' lengthy description of the causes of the Peloponnesian War to a single sentence, a single word even, and therefore much has been lost in such a pithy summation of a great work. Yet, as I hope to show in this chapter, readers of Thucydides have been reducing him to a label or a sound bite for a very long time. For sure, those labels maybe backed up with hundreds of pages of analysis worked out over a monograph or multi-volume commentary, but ultimately scholars have felt the need again and again to neatly package and present Thucydides' thought. Scholars today are familiar with many iterations of Thucydides: Thucydides the political historian, Thucydides the historical scientist, Thucydides the tragedian, Thucydides the realist, Thucydides the constructivist, the Straussian Thucydides, and most recently Thucydides the prospect theorist. The Thucydides trap, then, is just another iteration of this near constant tendency within the fields of Classical Studies, International Relations and Political Science. It is in the application of these many labels, I believe, that we discover the clearest articulation of various scholars' own ideas of the essence of Thucydides 'political thought'. I use that last term cautiously because it is difficult to pin down precisely what it means. The term is loaded in the sense that all texts represent political thought in so far as they are produced within the matrix of a particular society's power structures, which they either reproduce or contest. Thucydides, however, goes far beyond this bare minimum and explicitly claims to offer his readers an account of man, human nature, the *polis*, the state, and the movements and change that affect them all, in the guise of an accurate (*akribeia*, ἀκρίβεια) account (*xunegrapse*, ξυνέγραψε, 1.1) of the Peloponnesian War fought between Athens and Sparta. The structure of the text resists easy characterization as history, political science or philosophy, while at the same time inviting these categories. Thucydides himself claims to offer transhistorical truths (1.22), but then recedes into the authorial background, only occasionally offering his authorial voice, thereby challenging readers to uncover his true teaching. Reacting to this challenge, scholars have aimed to contain (we might almost say creatively reimagine) Thucydides' thought in a single label, name or sound bite. The questions I aim to pursue here are simple: when did scholars first begin the attempt to present Thucydides' 'political thought' in such ways? Why? Moreover, in what ways has this attempt shaped Thucydidean studies today? And what have we forgotten?

In this chapter, I offer a history of the various labels and epithets that readers and scholars have applied to Thucydides.[3] I do this to explore the significance of the Thucydidean turn (roughly 1900–39) in the broader history of the reception of the text. If I was to define the turn as simply an awakening to the value of Thucydides' thought then we could point to individual turns stretching back through early modern Europe to antiquity. Instead, my aim, in this chapter, is to explore issues of continuity and change in the reception of Thucydides from antiquity to the present day in order to contextualize the significance of the twentieth-century turn. I will argue below that many still current interpretations have very long histories and frequently recur again and again, albeit in slightly different forms. However, the early twentieth century is significant, crucial even, because it is only then that, almost at once, a number of different labels are applied to Thucydides, leading to a scholarly debate of incredible importance. The turn played out in the shadow of the Great War and gave scholars today many of the labels that are still routinely applied to Thucydides. This debate established Thucydides as a tragedian, a scientist, a political psychologist, a realist, a contemporary and a Realpolitiker. The sheer number of labels that appear, and the depth and breadth of the scholarship that support them, mark the turn as perhaps the most significant moment in the formation of the many Thucydides(s) that we still read today. I will end this chapter by drawing readers' attention to the relationship between Thucydides' depiction of political psychology, reality and historical time, themes that run through almost all early twentieth-century readings of the *History* and therefore unite this book.

Before continuing, however, I would like to first point out that the use of labels and epithets to encapsulate Thucydides' thought is an entirely understandable reaction to the nature of the *History*. Thucydides explains in a famous passage (1.22) that he is writing because he hopes that future readers will judge his work as an aid to the interpretation of the future. For Thucydides, the past (that is to say his account of the Peloponnesian War) is likely to resemble the future in the course of human things (*kata to anthropinon*, κατὰ τὸ ἀνθρώπινον). In this manner, he hopes that his *History* will become a possession for all time (*ktema es aiei*, κτῆμά ἐς αἰεὶ). The difficulty is that Thucydides never tells his readers precisely what lessons or insights his *History* contains and he rarely offers comments on events in his own voice (cf. his comment on the rule of the five thousand at 8.97). What then is the intelligent reader that Thucydides envisaged to do? Faced with a mass of complicated narrative and conflicting orations, I argue, readers have naturally attempted to define and capture Thucydides' thought through the use of labels as a useful summation of a complicated and often challenging work.

A short history of labelling Thucydides

The use of labels and epithets to encapsulate a particular interpretation of Thucydides began, as I far I can tell, in the first century BC. In that century, the Roman jurist and man of letters Cicero (106–43 BC) claims that while Thucydides had disposed of battles and events in a masterful manner, his 'Attic' style was not the right fit for Roman orators (*Orator* 9.30–32) because it was too long-winded and obscure to be serviceable as a rhetorical model. In these brief comments,[4] Cicero is passing a political, as well as aesthetic, judgement on Thucydides through the label Attic. Rhetoric mattered in ancient Rome. The student who mastered this subject could carry debates in the Senate, win court cases and fire up armies for battle. Cicero claims that Thucydides was useful for those who wished to know of the past, or who were looking for a model to write contemporary history, but he was not suitable for aspiring generals and politicians because of his supposed long windedness and obscurity. Nevertheless, the very fact that Cicero felt compelled to argue against the Roman 'Atticists' proves that Thucydides' rhetorical style held political value in at least some quarters in Republican Rome. The use of the term 'Attic' is the first time Thucydides' thought, and indeed his style, is subsumed within a label.

It is in the early modern period, however, that Thucydides' name begins to proliferate in European political debates. Kinch Hoekstra (2012) has noted that as early as the sixteenth century, around a hundred years after Lorenzo Valla first translated the *History* into Latin, Thucydides' name began to crop up in debates over war and peace. As in the reception of Tacitus, red and black ideas of Thucydides were occasionally used by scholars and statesmen to condemn or justify expansionary warfare. Red interpretations focused on Thucydides' depiction of republican government and black on his presentation of power politics. However, Thucydides' first English translator from the Greek, Thomas Hobbes (1588–1679), is the first to apply explicitly a label to Thucydides. Hobbes is also one of the few early modern commentators to contemplate seriously how a reader might raise the *History* above the level of a source of historical examples to suggest concrete examples of the ways in which Thucydides' thought might prove relevant today, indeed, the ways in which the *History* might prove universal to all states. Hobbes labels Thucydides the 'most politic historiographer that ever writ' (1989: xii) because through his accurate and truthful description of events, Thucydides demonstrated the danger of tumultuous republican governments, and the benefits of a strong stable government embodied in one man, in this case Pericles. For Hobbes, this is a universal truth that applies to all states, which he went on to expound at greater length in *Leviathan*. Hobbes does not use Thucydides to provide simple parallels with a specific situation and neither is he mined for vignettes, quotations or sound bites to support a particular argument. Rather, what Hobbes imagined Thucydides had to say about government, that he was in effect a monarchist, is held to be a universally valid assertion. In making this claim, Hobbes is holding Thucydides up as one of the few ancient writers who argues against republicanism and the discord at home and wars abroad that this form of government engendered. In Hobbes' estimation, Thucydides was not only a 'politic historiographer' but also a 'monarchist'. The former label has survived better than the latter.

Hobbes was followed in his attempt to encapsulate Thucydides' political thought in a label by writers in the age of Enlightenment such as the abbé de Mably (1709–85), a French philosophe and republican. Mably writes in his *Two dialogues, concerning the manner of writing history* that:

> I well know that whilst I read, the other day, the History by Thucydides, I thought that I perceived, amidst the just relation of the wild and foolish passions of the Greeks, the portraiture of those which agitate the present states of Europe, and which will cast us into wretched servitude, as they enslaved the Grecian Republics, if, at some future period, another Philip of Macedon should rise against us.
>
> Mably 1769: x–xi

Mably was writing during a difficult time in European politics. Britain and France were at war for much of the eighteenth century. Increase in manufacture, the development of trade and the expansion of overseas empires were making the European states richer but also giving them the necessary means to expand their militaries. Wars were becoming more frequent and brutal. Against this dark backdrop, Mably worried about interstate politics and clearly found in Thucydides an echo of the passions and forces that were driving Britain and France toward war in his own day. We might also point to the only eighteenth-century French translator of Thucydides, Pierre Charles Levesque (1736–1812), a protégée of Mably, who labelled Thucydides, in preference to Tacitus, 'the historian of politics' and the author of the one text which every citizen of a free state should read (Levesque 1795: xvii). Or even to the British premier Lord Chatham who gave special instructions that his son William Pitt should read Thucydides 'at College, thereby testifying to his belief in the value of the historian as a teacher of statesmanship' (Pitt 1840: 295). In other words, the idea that Thucydides was in some sense political and relevant was beginning to attach itself to his name with increasing frequency. He was becoming an ancient guide to modern politics. This development should not surprise us. Throughout the early modern period, the Athenian historian's star was rising as a literary model and trustworthy historian (Morley 2013). Moreover, while Renaissance readers had found little of value in the *History* as a source of moral exemplars and *magistra vitae*, the increasing strain between the European nation states and the rise of republican and democratic governments in the eighteenth century made Thucydides' text appear increasingly relevant to certain commentators fearful of overseas wars and sedition at home. It is during unsettled moments that Thucydides becomes particularly relevant. This tendency, of course, is entirely in sympathy with Thucydides' claim at 1.22 that he wrote the history in the expectation that it might prove 'useful' (*ophelima*, ὠφέλιμα) to future readers living through the same or similar events to those of the Peloponnesian War.

Following the French Revolution and the destruction of the Napoleonic Empire, the use of ancient historians, including Thucydides, as sources of political thought and moral exemplars was becoming increasingly unfashionable. The horrors of Jacobinism, civil war and class conflict had demonstrated to many European intellectuals that the pursuit of ancient virtue in the modern nation state led only to disorder and bloodshed. It is, therefore, unsurprising at the end of the eighteenth and the beginning of the nineteenth century to find increasingly critical attitudes toward Athenian democracy (Roberts 1997; Sachs 2016) in British, French and German writings on the ancient world such as William Mitford's (1744–1827) *History of Greece* (written between 1788 and 1810 and cited in the bibliography as Mitford 2010). Attitudes hardened in the post-

Revolutionary period when academics such as Volney (1757–1820) began teaching students that ancient texts such as Herodotus and Thucydides could only describe the realities of ancient politics and had little to offer the modern world (Volney 1800).[5] In a famous paper given in 1819, Benjamin Constant (1767–1830) even drew a sharp distinction between the liberty of the ancients and the moderns, declaring the latter superior to the former (Constant 1988). Thucydides' relevance was seemingly under attack from incipient notions of historicism. It is in Germany, however, that we find the greatest and most long-lasting effect of the French Revolution on Thucydidean studies. Many German states suffered greatly in the Revolutionary and Napoleonic wars, enduring both occupation and the spread of revolutionary ideals, which inevitably led to civil disorder and conflict. In the years that followed the Battle of Waterloo in 1815, many German scholars turned their thoughts to the differences, rather than the universalizing similarities, between different historical periods. The work of Hegel (1770–1831) opened the door to the emergence of historicism in the distinctly modern sense, by drawing attention to the way social and cultural phenomena were determined by historical circumstance (Beiser 1993). Accordingly, the ancient historians, including Thucydides, were increasingly read for what they could tell us about their own culture, society and politics and not because they might offer apothegms and examples for the modern day. Ulrich Muhlack (2011; cf. Süßmann 2012; Meister 2013, 2015) has pointed out that this turn to historicism represents a political choice on the part of German academics to deny the applicability of ancient thought to modern realities following the horrors of the Revolution and the French occupation of German lands.

Concurrent with the emergence of historicism, Thucydides became known in the nineteenth century as the greatest historiographical model to survive from antiquity. Particularly in the first half of that century, he was taken as an exemplary figure of his craft who practised careful accuracy in his historical researches and was taken by many German historicists as a totemic figure. Famously, Leopold von Ranke's (1795–1886) dictum that history should describe the past as it really was (*wie es eigentlich gewesen*) is almost certainly a nod to Thucydides' famous methodological statement at 1.22 (quoted in Fitzsimons 1980). Although by the second half of the century, many historians were distancing their aims from those of ancient historiographers, including Thucydides (Süßmann 2012). Thucydides was therefore rarely given a label in the nineteenth century, except as an historian or occasionally as an historical scientist. His thought, however, did find its way into British debates over the nature and viability of democracy, particularly in the thought of Grote and Mill

(Potter 2012; cf. Lianeri 2015 on Grote's reception of Thucydides' historiography), but mostly for his account of ancient Athens rather than as a guide for the future constitutional arrangements of Britain. A notable exception to this picture is Friederich Nietzsche (1844–1900), the noted German philologist and philosopher, who is, I believe, the first commentator to apply the term realist to Thucydides at the turn of the nineteenth century. Nietzsche was particularly taken with the Athenian historian,[6] and believed that he owed Thucydides a great debt in the field of moral psychology (Scott 2011). In the *Twilight of the Idols* (1887) he writes:

> My recreation, my predilection, my *cure* for all Platonism has always been *Thucydides*. Thucydides. Thucydides, and, maybe, Machiavelli's prince are most closely related to me by their unconditional will to fabricate nothing and to see reason in *reality* – *not* in 'reason,' and still less in 'morality' ... There is no cure more fundamental than Thucydides for the miserable prettification of the Greeks into an ideal, which the 'classically educated' youth brings with him into life as the reward for his prep-school training. One has to turn Thucydides over line by line and read his background thoughts as clearly as his words: there are few thinkers so rich in background thoughts. In him, the *culture of the sophists*, which means the *culture of the realists*, reaches its perfect expression: this invaluable movement in the midst of the Socratic schools' moralistic and idealistic swindle, which was then breaking out on every side. Greek philosophy as the *décadence* of Greek instinct; Thucydides as the great summation, the final appearance of that strong, strict, hard factuality that was a matter of instinct for older Hellenes. *Courage* in the face of reality is, in the final analysis, the point of difference between natures such as Thucydides and Plato. Plato is a coward in the face of reality – *consequently* he flees into the ideal; Thucydides has control over *himself* – consequently he also has control over things.
>
> Nietzsche 1997: 87–8

In this remarkable passage, we can see that Nietzsche, reading against the grain of many contemporary scholars, was attracted to Thucydides precisely because he was a realist: a term with which Thucydides is often associated today and, as we shall see in this book, grew in prominence in Britain during the first half of the twentieth century. In a recent paper, Morley (2018a) has suggested that scholars should be careful to distinguish between the reception of Thucydides' empirical realism, which is part of his literary and historical style, and the hardheaded but quite different assertion that Thucydides himself is a proponent of a doctrinal political realism. Empirical realism refers to the fact that Thucydides does not flinch from reporting the gruesome details of the war or presenting human nature as it really is, or at least as he believed it to be. Doctrinal realism, by contrast, is the belief that Thucydides himself endorsed a view of politics unencumbered with concern for ethical norms, morality or customs as we find in, for example, the speech of the Athenian ambassadors in the Melian dialogue (see, in particular, 5.105). These two realisms often, of course, shade into each other. Readings of doctrinal realism are often rooted in an appreciation of Thucydides' empirical realism. Nietzsche, I believe, is clearly leaning to the side of doctrinal realism in this passage. He views Thucydides as the 'cure' to idealism and to Plato. Moreover, Thucydides is specifically pointed to as the summation of the older Greek philosophy of the sophists or the realists. For his readers at the end of the nineteenth century, Nietzsche's labelling of Thucydides must have been an unexpected and provocative gambit. He removes Thucydides from his traditional realm as the prince of historians and places him, instead, in a commanding position in the history of philosophy.

The proliferation of labels

Nietzsche's labelling of Thucydides as a 'realist' makes the German philosopher, as in so many other things, ahead of the proverbial curve. We have now reached the first half of the twentieth century in this potted history of the reception of Thucydides. It is this period, this book argues, that is the crucial period in Thucydides' reception history because it leads directly to the position that the Athenian historian occupies in academia and political debate today. It is also during this period that many of the labels still associated with Thucydides today first emerged. The reception of Thucydides in the early twentieth century is different because it is only then that the Greek historian began to be presented, gradually at first, as the single most important exponent of ancient political thought still relevant today. Raising Thucydides' work beyond the level of an exemplar of a certain type of historiography (although he still regularly fulfilled this role) to see the historian himself as a timeless political thinker created a number of problems. Scholars debated exactly how to speak of Thucydides: was he a political thinker, scientist, psychologist, theorist or even a philosopher? In short, what label most neatly encapsulated Thucydides' overall intellectual project and could best put his thought to good use. More difficult still was understanding what 'the political' might mean when discussing Thucydides. Clearly his work describes in detail the machinations of various Greek states during the time of the Peloponnesian War, the causes of that war and its course, as well as providing the views of various characters though his recreated speeches. Thucydides also occasionally provides his own critical account of events, for example during his account of the stasis on Corcyra (3.82) or his narrative description of the effect of the plague on Athens. There is no easy answer to how a future commentator should use this varied mass of material to access the thinking of the 'real' Thucydides. One effect of the complexity of Thucydides' thought was to add to the air of impartiality, detachment and accuracy that his text imparted. Thucydides could not be classified as simply a democrat, an oligarch, an imperialist, a proponent of war or a pacifist. Instead, the complexity of his work invited readers to try to understand his own political philosophy.

This book does not mean to suggest that there is a linear history, in which Thucydides develops from a scientific historian in the nineteenth century to a political thinker, theorist or scientist in the twentieth. Rather, this book will suggest that the first half of the twentieth century produced a number of esoteric interpretations of the *History of the Peloponnesian War*, deeply influenced by the experience of the Boer Wars and particularly the Great War. These esoteric views each offered differing interpretations of Thucydides' thought. In sum: the turn to Thucydides is not some monolithic movement. Rather, it is the shattering of old orthodoxies and the creation of a noisy debate, the contours of which are still very much with us today.

The proliferation of Thucydidean labels and epithets in and of themselves would not, I believe, be sufficient to create the turn. However, they are the product of the increasing centralization of Thucydides studies within the academy. Already in 1812-13, we find Victor Cousin (1792-1867),[7] the noted French philosopher, preparing a doctorate on Thucydides. He was followed by Ranke in the 1820s (for an account of Ranke's early life, see Boldt 2019: chapter 1). Throughout the rest of the nineteenth century, particularly in Germany, Thucydides became more and more frequently an object of study among historians, Classicists and social scientists such as Wilhelm Roscher (Morley 2012). In Britain, academic monographs are not devoted exclusively to Thucydides before Jane Ellen Harrison's *Primitive Athens as described by Thucydides* (1904) and Francis Cornford's *Thucydides Mythistoricus* (1907). These works are followed by essays by J. A. K. Thomson (1913), William Hutton (1916) and T. R. Glover; monographs by Alfred Zimmern (1911, 1928), G. B. Grundy (1911), Walter Lamb (1914), George Abbott (1925) and Charles Cochrane (1929); a fellowship dissertation by Powell (1936); and, finally, references to Thucydides across the voluminous writings of Arnold Toynbee, to mention only the most prominent examples of academics reading Thucydides as a source of historical information, for sure, but also as a political thinker and philosopher. In other words, in terms of output alone, Thucydides becomes a major feature of the British academy in the first half of the twentieth century. These scholars also give us the idea of Thucydides as a tragedian, a realist, a psychologist, a scientist, a Realpolitiker.

Accompanying this increasing academic interest in Thucydides is a rise in his presence in British literary culture. For example, David Mitrany (1888–1975), a British scholar, historian and political theorist, wrote to the *Guardian* in 1925 to remind the editors that Thucydides 1.34, the claim that Corinthians were at fault for not offering up their dispute with Corcyra to arbitration, lends support to the 'famous definition of aggression as the refusal to use peaceful means for settling a dispute'. After quoting this Thucydidean passage, Mitrany writes, 'There we have it, four centuries B.C., the complete thing, presumption at all. How slow we have been to learn! The passage occurs in the 34th chapter of the First Book of the Phoenician War' (Mitrany 1925: 7). The mistake – Phonecian instead of Peloponnesian – reminds us that while scholarly disputants such as Mitrany could easily draw parallels between Thucydides and modern politics, among people who transcribed telegraphs or who worked as copy editors for newspapers (it is not clear which) facility with the *History*, or indeed with ancient history of any kind, could not be expected. Despite the error, however, Mitrany's letter itself is precise. It points to a particular passage in Thucydides' text and offers a reasonable translation of the Greek. In these years, Thucydides enjoyed more and more attention, both within and outside the academy. However, knowledge of the *History* was usually restricted to a small number of scholars, journalists and policy-makers, mostly university educated. Thucydides never achieved popular appeal among the great reading public but his name was increasingly well known.

Part of the reason for this increase in interest in Thucydides and its change in quality among the university educated was, this book claims, the increasing British anxiety over their imperial project following the Boer Wars and the complicated forces and emotions unleashed by the Great War. Another reason related to changing academic circumstances. Classics had long enjoyed a preeminent position in British education. Throughout the nineteenth and into the twentieth century it remained the core of the curriculum in the great private schools and also at Oxford and Cambridge. A classical education was the preserve of the elite and conferred a mark of distinction. However, ominous clouds loomed on the horizon. In an increasingly industrial world, the physical and natural sciences were becoming of ever-greater importance (Livingstone 1921; Murray 1921). The Great War served to emphasize that Britain needed

Engineers, Chemists and Physicists as much, if not more, than she needed Classicists. Moreover, Classicists were starting to feel that their field was threatened by internal developments within the humanities and the establishment of the social sciences. At Oxford, the study of Latin and Greek was (and still is) known as *Literae Humaniores*, a Latin phrase that suggests facility in ancient literature represented facility in human literature as such (Stray 2013). Most fellows at Oxbridge colleges were elected in the classical languages, and those subjects formed the core of most undergraduate education. However, the argument that to understand Homer, Euripides, Plato, Virgil, Seneca and the rest represented an education in the humanities, one might even say humanity *tout court*, was difficult to sustain in an increasingly complicated and interconnected world. Surely, a firm grasp of modern history and politics was essential to understand the great political shifts that were shaking modern Europe and that had led to the outbreak of the Great War. In the new world of complicated political causes and action, facility in German and French, not to mention languages such as Russian or Hindi, must surely be more useful than Latin or Greek (Toynbee 1921a). Moreover, the development of increasingly complicated societies, both domestically and internationally, led to a growing need for students who understood the modern disciplines of sociology and economics. It was these concerns that led to the creation of the discipline of International Relations and, slightly later, the undergraduate degree in Philosophy, Politics, and Economics at Oxford, which was intended to function as a 'modern' version of *Literae Humaniores*.

Thucydides today

The significance of this earlier British turn to the subsequent high esteem in which Thucydides finds himself in US International Relations and Political Science departments today is a tricky issue. The labels employed by these British writers survived into later US readings of Thucydides. However, it would be difficult to claim that after the Second World War there was a wholesale importation of British ideas into American universities. The idea of a 'turn' (without using that precise term) to Thucydides has been previously debated in the field of International Relations, where thoughtful practitioners of that discipline have asked at what moment and why did their subject first come to view Thucydides as an intellectual predecessor or even a colleague (Tritle 2006; Ruback 2015, 2016; Forde 2012; Lebow 2012; Keene 2015). The answer to this question is complex and multifaceted. Thucydides, along with Machiavelli and Thomas Hobbes, is one of the most commonly cited 'founders' of International Relations. One might say a practitioner of the discipline before its creation in the academy.

However, to return to the application of labels to Thucydides it is clear that during the late 1940s and 1950s political scientists such as Louis J. Halle were already hailing the Athenian historian as a realist (Keene 2015). At the University of Chicago, Leo Strauss was producing a very intricate and powerful dissection of Thucydides that defies easy characterization (cited in the bibliography as Strauss 1978). Nevertheless, over subsequent years his vision of Thucydides, along with those of many of his students, would be named Strassian (Jaffe 2015; Keedus 2016). During the years of conflict in Vietnam a number of scholars in the US found in Thucydides an account of both the horrors of war and the way that bipolar international politics functioned (Lebow and Strauss 1991) or, indeed, could go horribly wrong that they thought reflected the current geopolitical situation (cf. Connor 2013: 7). Easy, yet painful, comparisons were drawn between the ever-rising civilian death toll in Indochina and particular Thucydidean passages, for example the massacre at Mycalessus or the Melian dialogue, while the comparison between the democratic US as Athens, a democracy with a blue water navy, and the communist USSR as militaristic Sparta with a superior land power came easy to many commentators (Sawyer 2013; Bloxham 2018). It is also during the 1960s that military staff colleges begin to teach Thucydides, most prominently the Naval Staff College in Annapolis, where a paper on the Greek historian was offered to aspiring naval officers (Stradis 2015).

From the 1980s onwards, the most commonly applied label to Thucydides is that of political realist. In that decade and subsequently a cottage industry began to emerge among US International Relations scholars of classifying Thucydides as a political realist of one kind or another, often based upon a reading of only certain portions of the text, particularly Cleon's speech in the Mytilene debate or the Athenian portions of the Melian dialogue. Ruback (2015) has gone so far as to suggest that many appropriations of Thucydides in International Relations are simply banal and superficial references to the ancient master. These references have led to the formation of a 'Thucydides industry' which has seen a production line of papers produced in the last forty years or so and a 'Thucydides function' which refers to scholars' often shallow attempt to use Thucydides as a centre to the discipline. I believe, however, that under the broad label of a realist stretches a formidable body of scholarship. Realism as a label covers a multiplicity of specific views that are held together by a shared belief that international politics forms an anarchic system in which each state seeks to gain power over its peers. The application of this term to Thucydides meant that the labels attaching themselves to the Athenian historian were becoming ever more specialized and opaque. Classical realists (Morgenthau 1948; Aron 2003; Halle 1955) have found in Thucydides support for their view that human nature inevitably leads to anarchy and competition by taking, for example, the Athenian claim that fear, honour and profit (1.75) led them to gain and retain their empire as the view of the Greek historian (Milner 1991; Ahrensdorf 2000). Neorealists, or structural realists (Waltz 2010, 2018; Gilpin 1981), by way of contrast have found in the *History* support for their view that international relations are characterized by anarchy and continual conflict because there is no law or force above the nation state or, in the case of Thucydides, above the *polis* (Shimko 1992; Bagby 1995; Eckstein 2017).

Realist interpretations of Thucydides are by no means universally accepted. In International Relations, there has been something of a backlash, with scholars such as Jonathan Monten (2006) denying the label, Daniel Garst (1989) arguing that neo-realists define power too narrowly, and David Welch (2003) even imploring his colleagues, somewhat tongue-in-cheek, to stop reading Thucydides altogether (cf. Bagby 1994; Ober 2001).[8] More robust criticism has come from the field of political theory where a number of monograph-length studies have done much to correct egregious mistakes and misreadings. Gregory Crane (1998) argues that Thucydides describes a number of realist interpretations of politics, through the mouths of his various actors. However, Thucydides only describes this political world without fully endorsing it. Rather, his work represents a lament for the lost hegemony of ancestral *nomos* (the titular ancient simplicity) in the face of the harsh realities of power politics. In the same vein, Paul Rahe (1995) sees Thucydides as an historian who presents a clear-eyed depiction of power politics at work but who is personally critical of realism and the excesses to which it inevitably leads. While Steven Forde (1995, 2004) and Clifford Orwin (1994), writing from a Straussian perspective, have attempted to reintroduce ideas of justice into the debate over Thucydides' politics. Most notably, Ned Lebow (2001) has presented a complicated vision of Thucydides, which challenges readers to recognize different 'layers' to the text, which Thucydides sign posted through deliberate repetition, omissions and inconsistencies. On the surface level, then, Thucydides is a political realist, but in the deeper levels of his text, he presents the tragedy of the rise and fall of Athens and a tension between *nomos* (law, convention, νόμος) and *phusis* (nature, φύσις). Lebow's layered reading allows him to reintroduce notions of law, justice, morality and emotion into the realist reading of Thucydides. We should also add to this list the recent seminal study by Seth Jaffe (2017a) which has refocused attention on the complicated roles of necessity (*anangke*, ἀνάγκη) and causation in book 1 of the *History*. These studies are, by and large, intelligent, well argued and rooted in a thorough philological knowledge of the text. However, one could argue that they simply replace the labels that are applied to Thucydides from realist to, say, Straussian, constructivist (Lebow 2003) or even prospect theorist (Ober and Perry 2014). The difference is that these labels are now based upon considerably more impressive scholarship and a greatly more nuanced reading of Thucydides.

The value of the Thucydidean turn today: Psychology, realism and time

The turn, in my reading, represents a critical moment in the reception of Thucydides. Specifically, it is the years between 1900 and 1939 that Thucydidean labels begin to proliferate and it is then that they begin to be backed up by increasingly complicated academic arguments. However, there is another value to studying the turn: its merit as scholarship. The readings that I uncover in this book will, I hope, act as a provocation to current readers of Thucydides. In two recent collected volumes, Thauer and Wendt provocatively argue that there needs to be greater rapprochement between Classicists and social scientists in Thucydidean scholarship. There was a brief period during the late 1980s when such a coming together appeared to be on course, culminating in the volume edited by Lebow and Strauss (1991), but the two disciplines have grown steadily further apart over the course of the 1990s and the 2000s.[9] For Thauer and Wendt, the best way to foster interdisciplinary collaboration is through talking and the identification of common ground. In their case, they point to a series of conferences at which participants were allowed to speak on whatever subject they wished. From these papers, it emerged that the problem of political order in Thucydides is an area of common concern (cf. Lebow 2016; Thauer 2016). This book will also, inevitably, speak to the issue of Thucydides and political order. As the scholars I survey toiled in the shadow of the Great War they could not but help consider the role of man, the *polis*, the tribe, allies, the *koine* and a whole host of other institutions and orders in the *History*. However, they were much more concerned with the relationship between Thucydides' 'realist' depiction of human nature (or psychology) and historical change. This problem, I believe, could similarly act as a site of common interest between Classicists and social scientists. Realism then initially referred to literary realism. However, following the carnage of the Great War, realist readings began to become increasingly politicized as scholars such as Alfred Zimmern (Chapter 3) and G. F. Abbott (Chapter 4) found in Thucydides' depiction of the psychology of the Greeks similar psychologies at play in contemporary Europe. The interplay between realism, psychology and its role in the causes of war and the decline of states becomes a key interpretative theme of many of the works surveyed in this book.

This focus on psychology is hardly surprising. The role of human nature in Thucydides has formed one of the main causes of disagreement between realist and neorealist scholars and their critics in recent decades (Orwin 2017). Meanwhile, Classicists, taking their cue from the wider humanities, have become increasingly interested in recent years in the complicated role of emotion in the *History* (Visvardi 2015; Fragoulaki 2016; Wohl 2017). An exploration of how British scholars in the early twentieth century, having experienced the trauma of war and the terrors of the long peace, saw human nature and psychology in Thucydides, therefore, provides not simply a genealogy of current debates but also, potentially, important ideas and perspectives that may perhaps open up new horizons in Thucydidean scholarship. It also sheds light on the careers and preoccupations of Cornford, Zimmern, Abbott, Toynbee and Powell and provides a unique window on the history of Classics as a discipline during a time of great upheaval in both politics and scholarship. Let us now turn to the structure of the remainder of this book.

The structure of this book

This book's structure follows chronologically, as far as possible, the writings of these British scholars. It begins by analysing the influence of the Boer Wars on readings of Thucydides in Chapter 2 and the first half of Chapter 3, before considering in greater depth the effect of the Great War in the remaining chapters.

In the second chapter, I consider F. M. Cornford's *Thucydides Mythistoricus*. I take this book to mark the beginning of the Thucydidean turn in Britain. I argue that Cornford's 1907 work followed the earlier work of Jebb and Shorey in asking whether Thucydides' Greek was actually capable of describing the true causes of the Peloponnesian War because it lacked the vocabulary and grammar of the modern disciplines of sociology, economics and psychology. Instead, Cornford suggests that Thucydides attempted to write an accurate and rational account of the war, stripping away the religious interpretations of his contemporaries and leaving only the earlier tragic mode of thought that formed the bedrock for all of Greek culture. Thucydides, thereby, emerged as a tragic writer who described how humans were constrained by the 'irrational' forces of history; forces, which I will argue, Cornford thought might still be at work in his own day. The final section of this chapter will consider Cornford's influence on later readings of the *History* from the mixed early reviews, to Charles Cochrane's 1929 riposte that Thucydides was, in fact, a 'scientific' writer, to the modern search for the 'tragic' in Thucydides in the writings of today's scholars such as Lebow and Crane, among others.

The third chapter seeks to understand the place of Thucydides in the thought of Alfred Eckhard Zimmern, a prominent British Classicist, liberal thinker and International Relations scholar. It will explore how Zimmern's conception of Thucydides changed from his pre-war work, *The Greek Commonwealth* (1911), to his post-war career as a professor of International Relations at Aberystwyth and later at Oxford, which would lead to the establishment of the new discipline in the UK and exert considerable influence on its development in the US. Before the war, Zimmern focused on Thucydides as a 'realist', who described how the 'war spirit' (a bundle of political passions, including fear and greed) led Athens into wars of expansion and eventually caused her moral and political decline, thereby drawing attention to the relationship between human nature and historical change. After the war, however, Zimmern shifted his attention to focus on Thucydides' idea of 'political psychology' or his method of describing how local circumstance and experience shaped the psychologies of each individual *poleis* in the text. Zimmern believed that modern scholars should attempt to emulate Thucydides' methodology to understand better the psychological states of the post-Great War nation states of Europe, which, he argued, would prove key to the success of his new discipline and the establishment of world peace. Zimmern would later explicitly argue that Thucydides the realist political psychologist represented the first scholar of international politics.

The fourth chapter examines the influence of the Great War on readings of Thucydides, particularly through that of G. F. Abbott as an exemplar. In 1925, Abbott published *Thucydides: A Study in Historical Reality*, the first English language attempt, I will argue, to cast Thucydides as a political realist. Abbott's vision of Thucydides as a realist drew the reader's attention to the emotions/psychologies of fear, honour and greed that are still prominent in International

Relations discussions of the *History* today. However, Abbott's book also raised a broader problem. If Thucydides is relevant to students of politics today because he describes an unchanging human nature dominated by those same passions, then what room is there for historical change? Are we to imagine that human nature has not changed in 2,500 years as material and political circumstances have changed so significantly? Moreover, what might historical change look like within the *History* itself? For example, do the passions that govern Athens' actions shift over time in Thucydides' view? Abbott offers no easy answers to these questions. Instead, he works within a paradigm that emerged during the Great War, which emphasized the parallels between the 1914–18 conflict and the Peloponnesian War. As scholars pondered the greatest historical upheaval of their time, they turned to Thucydides for a sense of certainty and immutability in a time of great change.

The fifth chapter charts the place of Thucydides in the thought of Arnold Toynbee, a pupil of Zimmern and a noted public intellectual in Britain and the US. Toynbee's published output on history and international relations is enormous. However, Thucydides is often present in his thoughts on both history and politics. In particular, the Athenian historian provoked in Toynbee a feeling that 431 BC and 1914 were parallel years, that the outbreak of both conflicts marked a key moment in the history of Greek and Western civilization respectively. This chapter focuses on Toynbee's reception of Thucydides as a contemporary. It argues that Toynbee was not simply attracted to Thucydides' depiction of human nature and change when he drew the parallel between the two conflicts. Rather, he imagined that the moments really were contemporaneous in the sense that they marked the same point in the overall life cycle of a civilization. Thucydides' description of this moment, therefore, is useful for those moderns clever enough to heed his message and attempt to avoid the calamity that engulfed the Greek world.

The sixth chapter excavates a forgotten reading of Thucydides by Enoch Powell from the archives of Churchill College, Cambridge. Powell is best known today as a serious philologist and as an editor of the *Oxford Classical Text* edition of Thucydides. However, in the archive two remarkable essays demonstrate that he had thought deeply about the effect of contemporary politics on Thucydidean studies and the intricacies of the political world that Thucydides paints in the *History*. The first essay is a paper Powell delivered at the Classical Association AGM in 1936 on the effect of the Great War on Thucydidean studies. In it, he argues that the conflict had led to an unprecedented seventeen years of scholarship but that was now threatened by the rise of pacifism in the English-speaking world and Nazism and fascism on the continent. The second essay is a substantial paper that Powell wrote as a prize essay while still an undergraduate then expanded as part of his application for a fellowship at Trinity College, Cambridge. This essay is on the moral and ethical thought of Thucydides. It claims that the Athenian historian is a Realpolitiker. This claim denies any role for morality in Thucydides' depiction of interstate politics. It further claims that for Thucydides, human nature and psychology can be understood in terms of a number of emotions, particularly fear and greed, which defined politics both then and now. Powell combines this vision of an unchanging human nature with an account of how Thucydides explains shifts and developments in political orders and power.

The seventh chapter, which forms the epilogue and conclusion to this book, looks at the reception of the turn to Thucydides in the US and Canada, and the legacy of the British readings surveyed in this book in the post-Second World War world. It will explain that throughout the early twentieth century, Thucydides' name became increasingly current in US studies of politics and international law, without reaching quite the levels of ubiquity that it enjoys today. During the Second World War, in particular, scholars became increasingly open to parallels between the Peloponnesian War and modern conflicts. At the same time, there are clear similarities and differences between the interpretation of Thucydides in the US and the British readings outlined in this book. Both US and British readings, I will further argue, had only marginal influence on the subsequent 'realist' turn to Thucydides associated with Louis J. Halle, Hans Morgenthau and Kenneth Waltz. This creates a problem of intellectual genealogy: is there a direct connection between the Thucydidean turn and interpretations of Thucydides today? Rather than argue for a direct connection or influence, I will, instead, suggest that the turn should be viewed on its own terms as the moment at which Thucydides' role in the academy began to shift from historian to political philosopher. Accompanying this moment the labels applied to the text began to multiply and proliferate, creating an aura around the text that made Thucydides a prime candidate for later International Relations scholars and political scientists looking for an ancient sage and predecessor. American scholars were working in the wake of the British turn, if not yet explicitly engaging with all of its scholarship in the 1930s, 1940s and 1950s.

2

Thucydides: Between Science and Tragedy

In 1907, the British publisher Edward Arnold released Francis Macdonald Cornford's (1874–1943) *Thucydides Mythistoricus*. Cornford's book is only the second English-language monograph to take Thucydides as its exclusive object of study and is near unique in the fact that it is a book from before the Great War still regularly cited today.[1] It is a well written analysis of the role of the mythical and tragic in Thucydides' thought that, if it occasionally takes its arguments too far (Kelly 1990), asks fundamental questions about Thucydides' worldview, his idea of human nature, and the portrayal of historical change in the *History*. *Mythistoricus* also represents a watershed moment in the reception history of Thucydides and is the beginning of the turn to the Greek historian among British academics. Before Cornford, British scholars generally knew Thucydides as a great 'scientific historian' (Pires 2006; Muhlack 2011; Morley 2012, 2013; Meister 2013, 2015). After *Mythistoricus*, this view could no longer be taken as read but had to be defended more fully or even rejected. This moment, however, does not represent the automatic enthronement of Thucydides as the first great political historian, philosopher and theorist in the traditions of thinking on international relations. Instead, it is an iconoclastic moment that challenged long held assumptions about what Thucydides was attempting to do in his work and how successful he had been in doing it. As Cornford notes in the first sentence of the book, 'the epithet *Mythistoricus* may seem to carry a note of challenge, or even of paradox'. The title certainly pointed to the controversial and demanding contents of the book's arguments. Thucydides had claimed in his own voice that he had deliberately excluded the mythic element from his work (1.22), yet Cornford claimed that 'by Mythistoria I mean history cast in a mould of conception, whether artistic or philosophic, which, long before the work was even contemplated, was already inwrought into the very structure of the author's mind' (1907: vii). In other words, Cornford was attempting to argue that, far from being the great rationalistic (even scientific) writer in masterful command of his material, Thucydides was in fact conditioned by Greek religion and mythology to see the world in a certain way. Just as modern scholars had been conditioned to see the world through the prism of 'Darwinian biology and by the categories of mechanical and physical science' (1907: viii). In penning this argument, Cornford was offering an incredible provocation: if Thucydides' words and thoughts had been fundamentally conditioned by the world in which he lived, then so too might modern views of the world be constrained by their own intellectual milieu (Gerson 1998).

Cornford's work has proven influential, if divisive, in the traditions of Thucydidean scholarship in both Classics and Political Science. A century-long debate has emerged over whether readers should emphasize Thucydides' supposed rationality and accuracy or instead focus on the literary, moral and tragic qualities of his work (Hesk 2015: 219–24). In short, can we label Thucydides as a tragedian? Scholars such as Abbott (1925), Cochrane (1929), Bluhm (1962), Adcock (1963), Pires (2007) and Meister (2015)[2] have argued against Cornford that Thucydides' rationalism and realism heralds the birth of the genre of 'scientific history', characterized by the accurate recording of events and the deep probing of the causes of events in order to delineate rules and patterns of history. In a different vein, although still emphasizing Thucydides' rationality, Forde (1995), Ober (2006), Crane (1998), Bagby (2000) and de Romilly (2012) have pointed to Thucydides' pivotal role in the emergence of 'political science', arguing that Thucydides' rational mind led him to become a highly engaged political historian who used the Peloponnesian War to highlight general truths about human society and politics. Others, however, have continued to emphasize Thucydides' tragic qualities in thought, ethics and literary presentation (Parry 1981; Romilly 1977; Pouncey 1980; Macleod 1983; Euben 1990; Orwin 1994; Rood 1998; Bedford and Workman 2001; Lebow 2001, 2003; Stahl 2003; Shanske 2006; Joho 2017).[3] This debate about Thucydides and science has become increasingly divided as the different camps attempt to hold the Athenian historian up as the founding figure for the author's preferred approach to politics. In recent years, this debate has merged into the more general disagreement between positivists and postmodernists (Connor 1977, 2013; Lebow 2001), who are naturally drawn to the opposing rationalist and mythic camps. Both sides still cite Cornford regularly, if not ubiquitously, as the cause of this schism. Cornford's assertion that Thucydides is a mythic writer, therefore, maybe said to represent a kind of Kuhnian paradigm: his book represents the first serious challenge to notions of Thucydides as a rationalist, realist and scientific writer and so cannot be easily ignored or dismissed. Scholars today cannot go back to scholarship as it was before Cornford.

At the same time, scholarly interest in the tension between the rational and the tragic Thucydides has, I believe, obscured Cornford's main theme in *Mythistoricus*: the survival of ritual and tragedy in Greek thought from its beginnings, through the rise of the sophists, to the fourth-century philosophers. Cornford was attempting to disabuse British scholarship of two shibboleths: that Greek thinkers produced their great insights independently of the world around them and that the only valid question to ask of the ancient historians is that of trustworthiness. Cornford presents these difficulties in a memorable turn of phrase in his preface:

> The history of philosophy is written as if Thales had suddenly dropped from the sky, and, as he bumped the earth, ejaculated, 'Everything must be made of water!' The historians are examined on the point of 'trustworthiness' – a question which it is the inveterate tendency of Englishmen to treat as a moral question; and, the certificate of honesty once awarded, their evidence is accepted as if they had written yesterday.
>
> Cornford 1907: x

Cornford challenges us to ask, do we believe that Thucydides too fell from the sky with a bump to sweep away mythical Herodotean historiography and enlighten the world with his new more trustworthy methodology of political history? The answer, of course, is no. Instead, Cornford offers readers a different question through which to understand Thucydides: where in the progress of Greek thought from ritual, to sophistry, to science and philosophy is he best understood?[4] This was not an entirely new question. Jebb (1907) and Shorey (1893) had already asked in the late nineteenth century whether the Greek language of Thucydides' day was capable of conveying his rational analysis of contemporary politics. Cornford, however, pushed the issue further than ever before by asking whether Thucydides' own thought, as conditioned by the intellectual climate of his day, was capable of understanding historical causality and political events in a rational or scientific way. By placing Thucydides firmly in his own historical and intellectual setting, Cornford hoped to problematize the widely held view of his achievements in the discipline of political history.

Cornford's concern with the evolution of Greek thought and the place of the great thinkers within this grand sweep of history was not limited to Thucydides, but would go on to define his life's work in Greek philosophy and letters. He would revisit the same themes in, for example, *From Religion to Philosophy* (1912, cited as Cornford 2018), *The Origin of Attic Comedy* (1994), 'Mysticism and science in the Pythagorean tradition' (1922) and *Greek Religious Thought from*

Homer to Alexander (1923). W. K. C. Guthrie, Cornford's student and literary executor, recalled that in later life Cornford often remarked 'that it sometimes seemed to him as if he had been all his life writing one and the same book' (in Cornford 1967: viii). The hypothetical book Cornford referenced asked what modern assumptions underpinned scholarly reactions to the writings of the ancient Greeks and, instead, offered a thorough analysis of the world in which the Greeks lived, their thoughts and feelings, and the intellectual atmosphere that nurtured them to better understand the undercurrents that shaped their work. The intellectual atmosphere that Cornford highlights in the case of Thucydides is Aeschylean drama. He posits that in books four to seven, Thucydides, subconsciously, had applied the different psychological states of *hubris*, *ate* and *nemesis* (ὕβρις, ἄτη, νέμεσις) to Athens as the 'main character' in a history which closely followed a pattern familiar from Aeschylus' tragedies.

In this chapter, in addition to discussing Cornford's role in the Thucydidean turn, I also wish to ask, have we truly understood the import of his arguments? It may seem odd to begin a study of the canonization of Thucydides as a relevant international relations thinker with a reading that emphasized the Greek historian's fundamental antiquity. However, Cornford's readers today must be cautious of assuming that he did not find Thucydides' thought stimulating, and even illuminating, when read with the contemporary world in mind. By raising the issue of the tragic and mythic worldview, Cornford asked whether Thucydides' characters, even Athens herself, were ever truly free to make their own decisions, or conversely, were these political actors stuck in some inescapable pattern? By extension, Cornford was also asking his readers whether they, ensnared in a still different worldview, could similarly take charge of their own destinies. In other words, how did Thucydides engage with historical necessity (*anangke*, ἀνάγκη) and what lessons might his insight hold for the present day? I do not mean to imply, by posing this question, that Cornford took as the main subject of his work the role necessity plays in Thucydides. Rather, Cornford's Aeschylean and tragic analysis of the role psychological states and external forces play in Thucydides leads him to ask fundamental questions about the role of choice and fate in the *History* and, by extension, in modern politics.[5]

Cornford himself would later emphasize just how acutely his reaction to the British Empire and Boer Wars affected his interpretation of Thucydides. Was Britain, Cornford wondered, similarly locked in a tragic pattern of history comparable to the Athens of the Peloponnesian War? *Mythistoricus*, therefore, represents the beginning of the turn to Thucydides in two ways. First, it poses the problem of the relationship between tragedy and rationalism that would become an incredibly important aspect of the turn in the years around the Great War and which is still present in Thucydidean scholarship today. Second, Cornford was the first writer of the twentieth century to consider what Thucydides' political outlook was beyond simply interrogating the text for support or condemnation of democracy or empire. He asked how the Greek historian conceived of human nature, chance, change and choice in the *History* as elements that were only explicable when considered in Thucydides' fifth-century BC context.

Thucydides from rational to tragic

Before we consider in detail Cornford's arguments, let us turn first to his early life and education. F. M. Cornford was born at Eastbourne, Sussex, in 1874, the son of the Reverend James Cornford and Mary Emma Macdonald.[6] His parents ensured that he received the best education possible in the Classics at St Paul's School in London, where he excelled in both Greek and Latin. From St Paul's he went up to Trinity College, Cambridge, in 1894, in the footsteps of his father, where he won an Open Minor Scholarship, obtained a first class in both parts of the classical tripos in 1895 and 1897, and was bracketed equal in the chancellor's medal for that year. The Cambridge of his time profoundly shaped Cornford's view of the Greeks; it nourished him intellectually and connected him to broader cultural conversations over university politics, the state of Britain and the world, and the philosophical innovations that were taking hold in the late Victorian and Edwardian periods.

It is during his time at Trinity that the first influences on Cornford's later writings on Thucydides begin to emerge. His teachers appear to have inculcated in him a desire to offer reinterpretations of the Greek texts that treated their authors as artists and, at the same time, products of their own historical moment. Henry Jackson (1839–1921), then praelector in Ancient Philosophy at Trinity and later Regius Professor of Greek, began teaching Cornford in his second year. Jackson was a great humanist and Plato scholar who impressed on the young man the need for wit in his writings as well as the importance of ancient philosophy as an intellectual pursuit. Outside of Trinity, Arthur Headlam (1862–1947) at King's College London called upon Cornford to help him with his translations of Aeschylus. The Greek dramatist, as has already been noted, is an important presence in *Mythistoricus* and it is, no doubt, at this moment that Cornford really began to meditate deeply on these plays and the manner in which they expressed the thoughts and sentiments of the classical age. Finally, and most importantly, Cornford was taught by Arthur Woollgar Verrall (1851–1912), College Lecturer in Classics at Trinity, and a figure identified as a great influence in the preface to *Mythistoricus*. Cornford writes that Verrall's presence in *Mythistoricus* is 'somewhat indefinite, but still profound' (Cornford 1907: xi). He continues that Verrall, at a time when the Classics were used either as an engine of moral discipline in the teaching of grammar or to an add an air of elegance to the profane leisure of a deanery, was the first to show that the modern mind could 'achieve a real and burning contact with the living minds of Greece' (Cornford 1907: xi). In other words, Verrall was instrumental in awakening in the young Cornford the notion that the ancient Greeks were living breathing people who could be interrogated and profitably engaged with through a profound and sympathetic reading of their literature. Cornford's own words point to the emotional force and significance of this revelation:

> From his [Verrall's] books and lectures many of my generation first learnt that the Greeks were not blind children, with a singular turn for the commonplace, crying for the light of Christian revelation; and I am conscious, moreover, that in this present attempt to understand, not the syntax, but the mind, of Thucydides, I am following, for part of the way, a path which first opened before me when, in the breathless silence of his lecture-room, I began to understand how literary art could be the passion of a life.
>
> Cornford 1907: xii

Verrall's influence is not necessarily simply the illumination of Thucydides, but a wholesale scholarly, almost spiritual, approach to the literary and intellectual study of ancient Greek thought itself. Verrall implored his students not to view the Greeks through a Christian lens but to make the effort, imaginative as well as philological, to understand them on their own terms. Such a revelation must have made a deep impression on the young Cornford. His words here seem to recall a scholarly revelation, almost a road to Damascus moment, in the 'breathless silence' of Verrall's lecture room. Some inkling of the concrete lessons that Verrall had to teach may be gleaned from his published works, particularly his 1895 study, *Euripides the Rationalist: A Study in the History of Art and Religion*.[7] The title of this work suggests that Verrall was thinking along the lines of a tension between rationalism and religion and offers the real possibility that Cornford was already studying and discussing this issue as an undergraduate. However, there are important differences between Verrall's presentation of Euripides and Cornford's subsequent analysis of Thucydides and other writers. Where Cornford aimed to emphasize the influence of the mythic and the tragic on Thucydides as part of the evolution of Greek thought itself, Verrall sought to emphasize the rational side of Euripides' thought. He argued that the ancient Greek dramatist adopted a rational worldview to the extent that he did not even believe in the Olympian gods and, indeed, that his plays were covert attacks on the Hellenic Pantheon only the most intelligent readers and viewers were meant to uncover. It is not known how Cornford reacted to this specific argument, but it is clearly somewhat at odds with his focus on Thucydides, another alleged rationalist, and the relationship he posits to Aeschylean drama.[8] Nevertheless, what clearly emerges from Verrall's writings is the idea that Euripides was a living and breathing human being who produced art that could, and should, be understood by the intelligent modern mind as more than a philological storehouse of the rules of Greek grammar. The idea that the Classics represent something greater than grammatical exercises and literary models is a thought that surely inspired Cornford and stayed with him for the rest of his life. More than this, Verrall also left Cornford with the notion that questions were worth asking even if previous scholarship had considered certain notions sacrosanct and subsequent ideas rendered one's answers obsolete. *Euripides the Rationalist*, like *Mythistoricus*, caused quite a stir when it was first published because many believed that Verrall was pushing his arguments too far. Cornford remembered that Verrall would similarly ask difficult questions in his lectures, before offering contentious answers only for those answers to be abandoned if one of the students could make well-argued points contradicting them.[9]

Cornford's affection for writing controversial works almost cost him his future as a university academic early in his career. After graduation in 1897, family financial difficulties meant that he nearly became a school teacher. Gambling that he could get a fellowship before his financial problems become unbearable, he applied to Trinity where Henry Jackson (his former teacher) was unwilling to accept Cornford's challenge to his reading of the *Cratylus*.[10] Undeterred, Cornford tried again in 1899 and was successful. By 1902, he was assistant lecturer in Classics at Trinity. In 1904, he assumed a full lectureship. In the years before he published *Mythistoricus*, Cornford had achieved a degree of relative academic security and was carving an important place for himself in the hierarchy of Trinity and Cambridge.

The year before Cornford's triumphant return to Trinity, he met the other great influence on *Mythistoricus*, Jane Ellen Harrison (1850–1928), then a lecturer in Classics at Newnham College, Cambridge. Harrison became Cornford's close personal friend as well as a significant intellectual partner in this early stage of his career. It is from her that his interest in Thucydides probably first arose, and it was she who led him to an interest in the survival of mythical and tragic thought in Greek intellectual culture. It is therefore worth pausing for a moment to consider their relationship in greater depth. Cornford first encountered Harrison giving one of her famous lectures at the Archaeological Museum in Cambridge. This event must have left quite an impression on the young scholar as he promptly wrote her a personal letter on some point that had struck him powerfully. Harrison replied and asked him to come talk it over, and so began 'the series of innumerable conversations over the black brew of Indian tea' that came to mark the beginning of both a friendship and a remarkable scholarly collaboration. Modern scholars have labelled Harrison and Cornford, alongside Gilbert Murray (1866–1957) and A. B. Cook (1868–1952), the 'Cambridge ritualists' because of their common interest in the search for the roots of later forms of Greek thought (such as philosophy, religion, history) in early tragic and ritualistic practices. A certain amount scepticism has been levelled at the idea that these four formed some sort of unified scholarly movement (see, for example, Calder III 1991a), but the term serves a suitable purpose in denoting a close group of friends joined by a common interest in the application of the modern disciplines of sociology, psychology and anthropology to the study of ancient Greece with the overall aim of revolutionizing the study of the ancient world.

Biographers of Harrison have focused mainly on her personal, even possibly romantic, relationship with Cornford and the effect that their coming together had on her work (Peacock 1988: 151–78; Beard 2000: 156–7; Robinson 2002: 124–6, 208, 213–14; cf. Stewart 1959: 82). It is less often remarked that Harrison was a key figure in arousing Cornford's interest in Thucydides. In 1906, Harrison published *Primitive Athens as Described by Thucydides*. This book represents a defence of the German archaeologist Wilhelm Dörpfeld's (1853–1940) interpretation of the archaeology of Athens against the attacks of scholars such as Arthur Gardner (1862–1939), who Harrison had stood against in vain in the competition for the chair in archaeology at University College London in 1896 (Calder 1991b). The earliest indication we have for this book project is a letter sent by Harrison to Murray on 3 May 1905. She worked on it exclusively from May to September 1906. Harrison was convinced that Dörpfeld's interpretation of Thucydides' description of the ancient agora was correct and that this topic was of vital importance to scholarly understandings of the layout of 'primitive' Athens (Stewart 1959: 72–5). Crucially, Harrisons' main assistant on this project was Cornford, who helped throughout and revised the whole of the proofs (Harrison 1906: ix). A glimpse of Cornford's role in Harrison's work is provided in a footnote on the Kallirrhoë cavern in which the similarity to Plato's 'cavernous underground chamber' is noted (Harrison 1906: 129; *Republic* 7.514). Here we see Cornford's detailed textual knowledge combine with Harrison's archaeological expertise and skill in German language publications. Working on this book will have afforded Cornford the opportunity to become acquainted with Thucydides beyond the level of a student and, what is more, to read the text in the light of the latest archaeological discoveries. Nevertheless, we must acknowledge that the argument of *Primitive Athens* emphasizes what Thucydides himself can tell us about the archaic city, not what knowledge of archaic thought can tell us about Thucydides.

Harrison formed the central star around which the planetary bodies of Cornford, Murray and Cook orbited. In the case of Cornford, who was still relatively young when he made Harrison's acquaintance, she also provided a source of inspiration. It was she who encouraged Cornford to read Durkheim, Nietzsche, Bergson and Freud. Moreover, it was almost certainly Harrison who introduced Cornford to the idea that Greek thought evolved, one may even say 'progressed', from a dim and distant ritual past into religion, philosophy and eventually science.[11] Crucially she also inculcated in Cornford the idea that these earlier forms of Greek thought still existed in later texts, waiting for the scholar, like an archaeologist, to strip away layers of interpretation to reveal them to the world (Ackerman 1991: 4, 10–11). The implication of this insight is that one could not simply assume that Greek thought developed along a simple 'evolutionary' path from Homer, through the early dramatists, to the supposed 'rationalism' of Thucydides, Euripides and Aristotle. Nor could one simply import modern notions of history, causality and economics onto Thucydides. Rather, one must understand, through a close contextual analysis, his position in Greek thought as it progressed through time, making due allowance for earlier forms of thought that had become ossified in the *History* but were nonetheless waiting to be excavated. Cornford develops this point in a very important passage early in *Mythistoricus*. In it, he quotes a passage from *Greek Thinkers* by Theodor Gomperz (1832–1912), professor at the University of Vienna, where it is argued that there is a glaring 'contrast' between Herodotus and Thucydides (Cornford 1907: 68–70). Gomperz continues that Thucydides, unlike Herodotus, rejects natural forces in history and instead focuses on the caprices and passions of individual men and political factors in historical phenomena. The quotation concludes, 'It was [Thucydides'] constant endeavour to describe the course of human affairs as though it was a process of nature informed by the light of inexorable causality' (Gomperz 1896: 1.503). For Cornford, Gomperz here falls into a fallacy by asserting that Thucydides attempted to fill the void left by supernaturalism with the modern science of the fifth century BC. Cornford maintains that it was Herodotus, rather than Thucydides, who often attempts to rationalize or explain away myths and miraculous occurrences. Thucydides, on the contrary, attempts to remove the fantastic from his account of the Peloponnesian War without having the necessary modern methodologies of economics, politics and psychology to explain properly the causes and course of that conflict. As Thucydides removes the fantastical from his narrative, for Cornford, he is left with the older tragic interpretation of events, which had survived, hidden perhaps, in his thought from earlier ages. Here we see Cornford in full flow, examining in minute detail the 'evolution' of Greek thought from Herodotus to Thucydides while disabusing scholarship of its previous dearly held beliefs.[12] In short, Thucydides' place in the history of thought is far more complicated than the simplistic assertion that his thought was characterized by rationalism and Herodotus' by his religious and supernatural beliefs.

Richard Claverhouse Jebb (1841–1905) first proposed the idea that Thucydides was heavily influenced by tragedy in an essay on the speeches in the *History*. There, Jebb points to the need for a reassessment of Thucydides' literary art and its ability to convey complicated political thought. His essay begins by explaining that most early prose writers (except Ion of Chios) probably did not offer elaborate recreated speeches. Herodotus was the first. Thucydides then expanded upon the notions of his predecessor. However, Thucydides was the first to care about what an historical person would actually have said in a given historical situation. Jebb is using the speeches to analyse and assess Thucydides' success as a literary artist. He claims that Thucydides is writing tragedy and that episodes like the Melian dialogue 'foreshadow' future catastrophes (Jebb 1907: 399) and that the speeches are like tragedy in that they focus on the typical rather than on the individual (Jebb 1907: 402).[13] We shall return to Jebb later in this chapter when we explore Cornford's presentation of Thucydides as a tragic writer. Here, however, I wish to emphasize that Jebb was the first to suggest that Thucydides' literary style and language were not up to the task of describing the great thoughts and reflections of his mind:

> The originality and the striking interest of the historian's style consists, in fact, in this, that we see a vigorous mind in the very act of struggling to mould a language of magnificent but immature capabilities. Sometimes the direction of the thought changes in the moment that it is being uttered.
>
> Jebb 1907: 424

There is an echo here of Cornford's claim that Thucydides was a rationalistic writer constrained by the language and thought of his day. Jebb posed a challenge, in other words, to the assumption that Thucydides stood as the font from which modern historical science had sprung forth. Frustratingly, Cornford does not cite Jebb or discuss his work explicitly, although he must have been familiar with the essay. We can draw, nevertheless, important parallels between the approach of Jebb and Cornford's thoughts on the place of Thucydides in the history of Greek thought.

A brief examination of Cornford's treatment of the relationship between Herodotus and Thucydides points to the ways in which these various intellectual influences led him to write an entirely novel account of the Athenian historian's place in the intellectual history of Greece. Towards the end of *Mythistoricus*, Cornford offers an important discussion of the distance between Thucydides' historical project and that of Herodotus. From the earliest days of his reception, Herodotus gained a reception of credulity, even dishonesty, in his reporting of people and events. Over time, readers began to look more favourably on his portrayal of the extra Greek world and his interest in foreign peoples and countries. Nevertheless, Herodotus' reputation remained that of a credulous witness compared to the more scepitcal Thucydides, who was seen as accurate and truthful, even if his narrative was more narrowly focused on political history and the events of the war (Morley 2016b). In the nineteenth century, Herodotus' reputation as an historian improved somewhat, and he was even spoken of approvingly in disciplines such as the history of religions and anthropology. At the same time, Thucydides came to be viewed as the first 'scientific' or modern historian (Morley 2012, 2013) – an intellectual forebear for modern scholars to look back upon and to venerate. As we have seen, Cornford was attempting to take Thucydides down from this particular pedestal. As part of this endeavour, he emphasized how Herodotus, drawing on 'Ionian' philosophy, was frequently sceptical about the religious and mythical stories he relayed. Thucydides, on the other hand, often showed a noticeable reverence for traditional moral and ethical values.[14]

Cornford draws attention to the different archaic worlds that produced both writers. He presents Herodotus not as the first historian but as the last of the Homeridae, a tradition of Ionian 'festal recitation' that turned the story of the Persian Wars into an 'amusing and instructive tale of the quarrel of East and West' (1907: 239–40). For Cornford, Herodotus is a product of Ionia, sceptical and entertaining. Thucydides, by contrast, is a product of an Athenian aversion to this Ionian writing and its slapdash attitude to the truth. However, we should not view Cornford as necessarily attempting to place Thucydides above Herodotus. He notes that Thucydides could not understand that by rationalizing the stories he knew (Cornford here offers the example of the Spartan king and traitor Pausanias), the 'accretion of theological belief is removed', leaving behind it 'a mythical construction which contains and carries with it conceptions still more primitive' (1907: 242). Rather than showing Herodotus and Thucydides as the start of a historical tradition that culminates in nineteenth-century historiography, Cornford was trying to emphasize the archaic underpinnings of Thucydides' thought and its distance from Herodotus' more rationalistic and sceptical project that was intended to record and to entertain. In a letter to Murray, Cornford wrote that, 'I know you won't like what I have said about old Herodotus, but I must make out that Thucydides is really primitive, and Herodotus has to pay for it' (BL: MSS Add. 58427, (9)–(10).[15] Thucydides therefore stood not at the beginning of the tradition that led to scientific historiography in the nineteenth century, but rather at a crucial moment of change when the very ideas of rationalism, scepticism and tragedy were being debated and repurposed in ancient Athens.

From *Historicus* to *Mythistoricus*

With this background in place, let us now turn to the details of Cornford's engagement with Thucydides' historical project in *Mythistoricus*. This engagement is in two unequal parts, the first labelled *Thucydides Historicus* and the second *Thucydides Mythicus*. In the former, Cornford proposes that Thucydides was entirely ignorant of the 'true' economic and political causes of the war, which lay in a shift in Athenian society and politics towards a naval and mercantile class that were looking to expand the empire and commercial opportunities abroad. Chambers (1991) has usefully condensed and recapitulated this section. He correctly observes that Cornford's aim in this section of the book is to emphasize that Thucydides did not understand the 'true' causes of the Peloponnesian War because he misunderstood the influence of a 'party of the Piraeus', a group of merchants and seamen, who forced Pericles to enforce the Megarian decrees and already cast longing gazes at the distant island of Sicily. This account, Cornford claims, is derived largely from his reading of Busolt's *Griechische Geschichte* and to a lesser extent from J. B. Bury's *History of Greece*. These chapters are integral to Cornford's overall argument because in order to convince his readers that Thucydides' thought is shaped by a mythic and tragic view of the world, he has to first establish that Thucydides could not have understood the world as a modern historian would, that is to say through the prism of the long-term economic causes of the war, before proceeding to argue that the Greek historian was in fact writing *mythistoria*.

Before I consider the implications of Thucydides' supposed lack of knowledge of the true causes of the Peloponnesian War, let us first consider in more depth what Cornford means by 'the party of the Piraeus'. Cornford opens his book by announcing that the motives Thucydides gives Athens and Sparta are simply not sufficient to account for the outbreak of such a large war. Moreover, the claims of certain modern scholars that the war began because of Periclean policy or because of racial animosity between Dorians and Ionians or from tensions between oligarchy and democracy are all equally erroneous.[16] Instead, Cornford draws attention to the internal history of Athens, where, he argues, after the middle of the fifth century full equality had been achieved in the democratic constitution while victory over the Persians led to the expansion of imperial and commercial power and the search for new markets for Athenian wares (1907: 10–14). At this time, he imagines, parties dominated Athenian politics, specifically the party of the city and that of the countryside. The leaders of the latter had little political influence because they were suspected of oligarchic sympathies and Laconophilia (Cornford 1907: 17). The former, however, included the merchant classes, the artisans, the metics, the sailors – in sum, everyone rich and poor who had some stake in Athens' future as a trading and imperial nation. Their centre of power lay not in the rich farmland of Attica but in the port city of Piraeus, which linked Athens to the sea and to the wider world and had since the time of Themistocles expanded in both population and wealth (1907: 19–21). This group, Cornford believed, 'extorted' from Pericles 'socialistic measures' such as the use of the allies' treasure to beautify Athens (1907: 24). Later, they would force upon Pericles the Megarian decrees (1907: 30–2) to ensure that Athenian ships heading west (or coming back from that direction) could cross at the Isthmus of Corinth rather than make the long and perilous journey around the Peloponnese. The party of the Piraeus needed to keep Megaera open, through either diplomacy or coercion, to maintain her ease of trade with the west and Sicily and to give an advantage over Athens' commercial rivalry with Corinth.[17] Furthermore, the subsequent Athenian operations in the western theatre, such as Phormio's defeat of the Peloponnesian fleet, hint at the true purpose of the war, namely to further the commercial interest of the party of the Piraeus (1907: 47).

It is important for Cornford that a number of ancient sources operating independently of Thucydides place much more emphasis on the Megarian decrees as the significant element among the causes of the Peloponnesian War than is found in the *History*.[18] In Cornford's account, Pericles and indeed

Archidamus, king of Sparta, are forced into the war by the influence of parties within their respective *poleis*. Both statesmen, having adopted a course of action against their better judgement, attempt to employ a military strategy that will limit the damage of an undesired war. Pericles speaks only of a naval war that will never be able to execute the knockout blow against Athens' terrestrial enemies, while Archidamus simply invades Attica for three months a year, causing damage, but not seriously harming Athens. The influence of contemporary events in this description of the outbreak of the war lies ill concealed in Cornford's account of the causes of the Peloponnesian War (Gerson 2004: 174–5). Horsley senses here a representation of Campbell-Bannerman, British Prime Minister (1906–08), who tried to achieve calm at a time of considerable turbulence in British politics (Horsley 2008). In 1907, Athens made a suitable stand-in for a Britain riven by commercial and imperial interests which had been divided into rival political parties, one keen for war in the Transvaal and the other made up of those liberals and 'little Englanders' who were sceptical of the imperial project and the resulting cost in treasure and blood (cf. Grundy 1911: 315–32, who agrees with Cornford that economic motives lay behind the outbreak of the Peloponnesian War). Cornford later emphasized the influence of the Boer Wars on his own thinking in a 1921 paper in which he noted that he 'may have overstressed the financial aspects of imperialism' under the influence of contemporary events (Cornford 1967: 2–3).

A question arises from this radical reinterpretation of Thucydides on the causes of the war: why did Thucydides miss the importance of the Megarian decrees? Why did he neglect the economic factors leading to the outbreak of hostilities? Cornford proposes a simple answer. Thucydides thought only in terms of escalating quarrels. In his chapter on Thucydides' 'Conception of History', perhaps the most important section of the book, Cornford argues that Thucydides had no notion of causation akin to that employed by modern historians; rather, he saw the Peloponnesian War as rooted in 'grievances' and 'quarrels'. Cornford (1907: 64–5) notes that Thucydides is 'writing from the Athenian side' and consequently knows much less about Corinth and Sparta, which he treats as homogenous wholes. 'Thus, he tells us of the "fear of *the Lacedaemonians*", and "the intense hatred of *the Corinthians*" [Cornford's Italics]; but Archidamus and Brasidas are the only two individuals on the Peloponnesian side whose motives are even dimly apprehended' (1907: 64–5). When it comes to Athens, however, Thucydides is able to speak of the character of the Athenian *demos* – it was there for him to see at meetings of the *ekklesia* – and the motives of the leading men such as Pericles, Cleon, Alcibiades, Nicias and so on. The influence of these politicians on the *demos* is explored further through speeches: 'The disinterested ideal of Athens' glory is impersonated in Pericles; her restless covetousness (*pleonexia*, πλεονεξία) in Cleon; her ambition of conquest in Alcibiades' (1907: 64–5). For Cornford, it is the exclusive concentration of the ancient historians, including Thucydides, on the motives and characters of men and states that marks the divergence between their histories and the modern discipline of historical science. Thucydides had no vision of the complex influence of environment and economics on human events, nor did he have any notion of those historical laws that dictate the actions of men. Thucydides saw the true cause of the Peloponnesian War as an escalating series of grievances driven by the psychological states of the *poleis* embodied in their statesmen.

The distance between ancient and modern notions of historical causation are further worked out through an analysis of the meanings of the Greek terms *prophasis* (πρόφασις) and *aitia* (αἰτία), terms which Cornford believed Thucydides used 'interchangeably' (1907: 59). Hornblower, following the dominant tradition in Thucydidean studies in the twentieth century, contrasts these two words. In his commentary on 1.23.6 he argues that '*althestaten prophasin*' (ἀληθεστάτην πρόφασιν) refers to the truest cause of the Peloponnesian War, that is, the Spartan fear of the growth of Athenian power, while *aitia* is used to describe the more immediate 'reasons' for conflict, namely Corcyra and Epidamnus (Hornblower 1991: 65). Cornford, however, argues that both phrases merely refer to the complaints and grievances that drove each party towards war. Indeed, he specifically approves Thomas Hobbes' translation of *prophasis* at 1.23.6 as 'the truest *Quarrell*, though least in speech' (Hobbes 1989: 14–15). The implication of this argument is that Thucydides thought only in terms familiar from Homer and Herodotus of wars caused by grievances between men and states. In other words, he was completely ignorant of the more 'hidden' political and economic pathologies that modern historians search for in their accounts of the causes of conflicts and historical events (1907: 66). This is an innovative and controversial stance to adopt in the early twentieth century. Ultimately, Cornford claims that Thucydides (and presumably all ancient historians) did not and could not possess the conceptual categories and tools to understand history scientifically, in the modern sense of that term.

The true character of Thucydides' vision of human nature is worked out in the second part of Cornford's book, titled *Thucydides Mythicus*. Here Cornford introduces the central tenet of his argument, that Thucydides' claim to have removed *to muthodes* (μυθῶδης) from his *History* obscures the important ways in which mythical, tragic and even religious thought fundamentally underpinned the Greek historian's account of events. This argument is worked out through a novel comparison of Thucydides' literary art with that of the fifth-century Athenian dramatists, especially Aeschylus. There are two connected elements. First, Cornford presents Thucydides as depicting fortune, hope, embodied in individual actors such as Pericles and Cleon, as external agents, which take the form of psychological states that overcome the minds of the Athenians, thereby, defining and constraining their actions. Second, Cornford sees Athens as inexorably locked into a tragic pattern of events that begins with *hubris* (ὕβρις), proceeds through persuasion (*peitho*, πείθω) and blindness (*ate*, ἄτη), before culminating in *nemesis* (νέμεσις) in the form of the destruction of the Athenian fleet in the bay of Syracuse. In other words, Cornford sees Thucydides as composing a tragedy in books two through to seven in which Athens is the main protagonist, the tragic hero, which is directly comparable to Aeschylus' portrayal of Xerxes and the invasion of Greece during the Persian Wars (1907: 188–200).

Cornford begins his exploration of *Thucydides Mythicus*[19] with an analysis of fortune (*tuche*, τύχη) in the Pylos episode, when a storm trapped an Athenian fleet in a bay in Spartan territory. The Athenians fortified their position thereby gaining a significant advantage over their enemies and eventually capturing around 120 Spartan warriors (4.38). This was perhaps Athens' most significant victory in the entire war and Cornford is at pains to point out that fortune (*tuche*) appears to accompany them every step of the way. In Cornford's estimation, Thucydides contrasts human foresight (*gnome*, γνώμη) with *tuche* in his depiction of Pylos. Certain humans can use their knowledge to plan future actions, but fortune possesses an 'agency' of its own, which either aids or hinders them. It was therefore luck that the Athenian fleet was forced into Pylos harbour, that arms and reinforcements arrived at the right time, and that during the battle on the island in the harbour a Spartan soldier kicked over a hearth leading to a forest fire that denied his comrades cover (1907: 82–109). The element of fortune or chance was not simply a literary device. Rather, Thucydides, in Cornford's argument, remained in the grip of older forms of Greek thinking, which viewed *tuche* as a force in the universe that could strike down men and states at will and change the course of historical events.

Named actors in the text similarly exert force over the Athenians and compel them into following a tragic pattern of action. Thucydides' actors are not simply individuals but rather they are dramatic types: Cleon is the 'most violent of the citizens' and Pericles is the 'most powerful man in speech and action' (Chambers 1991a: 69). These characters can themselves provide the conduit through which the tragic passions enter into the collective Athenian mind. So, for example, Alcibiades introduces the forces of *elpis* (ἐλπίς, hope) and *eros* (ἔρος, desire) when he convinces the Athenian *demos* to invade Sicily (1907: 200–19). Alcibiades is also a 'mythic' character who personifies *apate* (ἀπάτη, deceit), who, through false logic and empty promises, leads Athens to the path of *nemesis* (1907: 198–200). Because his characters are tragic archetypes, Cornford argues that Thucydides' 'observations on human nature are less noble than those of an ordinary novelist of to-day' (1907: 79). It is less noble in the sense that Thucydides fails to portray the complicated interplay of many emotions on the protagonist's mind as modern novelists often do. Nevertheless, the novelty of Cornford's schema lies in the way it presents Thucydides as following closely a narrative pattern derived from Greek drama, particularly from Aeschylus, that imports specific psychological states and examines how they impact upon Athens as the 'tragedy' plays out. He does not simply claim that Thucydides' prose has the force of drama in the effect it has on the reader. To make this distinction clear, compare the following definition of the dramatic in Thucydides offered by Jebb:

> The epithet 'dramatic' is sometimes applied to narrative when no more is apparently meant than that it is vivid or graphic. In the proper sense, however, a narrative is dramatic only when it elicits the inherent eloquence of facts. Thucydides is dramatic, for instance, when he places the Melian dialogue immediately before the Sicilian expedition. The simple juxtaposition of insolence and ruin is more effective than comment. The bare recital, thus ordered, makes the same kind of impression which the actions themselves would have made if one had immediately succeeded the other before our eyes. It might not be difficult, with a little adroitness, to represent Thucydides as a conscious dramatic artist throughout his work; and an ingenious writer has actually shown how his History may be conceived as a tragedy cast into five acts.
>
> Jebb 1907: 436

In comparison to Cornford's interpretation, Jebb's definition here is overly formulaic. He casts the *History* as proceeding through dramatic acts, which are elaborated upon in a footnote reference to Hermann Ulrici's *Charakteristik de antiken Historiographie* (1833). The first act comprises the plague, followed by the death of Pericles, the fall of Platea and the defeat of Mytilene. The second consists of the stasis in Corcyra down to the blockade at Sphacteria. The third is the surrender of the Spartans on the island, the peace of Nikias and Alcibiades' later arguments in favour of the Sicilian expedition. The fourth act is the crisis and the defeat of Athens in Sicily. The fifth act is the fall. Delayed initially by the recall of Alcibiades, the final ruin of Athens follows the Battle of Aegospotomai in 405 BC. There is no sense here, despite Jebb's protestations, that this analysis sees tragedy as anything more than a literary style that Thucydides is using to great effect in his work. For Cornford, tragedy was a mode of thinking; one might almost say an intellectual system that conditioned Thucydides' attitude to the world and therefore his depiction of Athens' decline.

Let us continue with the example of Pylos. Ultimately, the significance of this episode, Cornford concludes, is not simply as an act in a play but for what it tells us about the character of Athens in her own tragedy (1907: 167). The actions of the democracy at this time showed that she is adventurous, restless, quick and ambitious. If one scheme fails, then she immediately conceives of new ambitions with well-founded hope (*elpis*). But hope also exposes Athens as possessed of a dangerous temperament, liable to get carried away in the flush of success. The Pylos episode, in Cornford's reading, serves to introduce the modern reader to the notion that *elpis* as a concept should be read not through a modern Christian lens, but as a dangerous passion, that can lead men and states into a dangerous future: 'elpis is the passion which deludes man to count on the future as if he could perfectly control it; and thus she is a phase of infatuate pride, a temptress who besets prosperity' (1907: 168). Here we arrive at the heart of Cornford's argument. Thucydides structured his *History* in a tragic way not for the sake of literary art or presentation, important as that undoubtedly was, but, unconsciously, as a meditation on the interplay between the character of a hero (in this case Athens) and the nature of the dramatic passions that influence her decisions and distort her mind.

The politics and ethics of *Mythistoria*

Cornford's presentation of Thucydides' tragic historiography represents a major break with previous scholarship and a significant reinterpretation of the Athenian historian's place in intellectual history. It also represents a significant milestone in the development of the idea that it was possible to use Thucydides to critique modern political and social problems. This section will focus on how Cornford imagined mythistoria might relate to both ancient and modern political concerns. Cornford's *Mythistoricus* posed the following questions: if a writer like Thucydides could be constrained by the language and thought of his own day, might the same not be true for contemporary Britons? Moreover, if one's thought is so constrained, what implications does this have for one's ability to make decisions and alter the course of events? These are provocative questions to which Cornford offered no easy answers. In the years before Cornford published his monograph, these questions had already been raised. The American scholar Paul Shorey had already wondered in 1893 whether it was possible to gain any contemporary benefit from Thucydides' political and ethical thought. He offered a rather equivocal answer, which I will pause here to dissect in order to throw light on the novelty of Cornford's thought by way of contrast.

Shorey was a professor of Classics at Bryn Mawr College in Philadelphia and later at the University of Chicago. His most important contribution to Thucydidean scholarship was his 1893 paper *On the Implicit Ethics and Psychology of Thucydides*, which argues that the chief interest in the *History* is not literary art but 'in the fact that it is the embodiment of a subtle and consistent, if one-sided, philosophy of life; that it is, to adapt a phrase of Carlyle, a portion of human history penetrated and informed by the spirit of the man Thucydides' (Shorey 1893: 66). Shorey then goes on to suggest that for Thucydides human nature is defined by a 'primitive core' of 'elementary appetites' around which are wrapped ethical, social and religious pretences. This primitive core of human nature is unchanging but the pretences in which it is wrapped may develop over time. Shorey is unsure whether it is possible to find any ethical thought in Thucydides more profound than the assertion that human nature, at its basest, is given over to fear, greed, honour and so on. Instead, Shorey claims, 'We want a systematic ethical terminology based on a psychological analysis of the chief springs and motives of human action' (Shorey 1893: 69). Thucydides certainly comes close to offering such an analysis, for example in Diodotus' utterances at 3.45 in the Mytilenean debate, but may ultimately have failed because it was unclear whether his Greek was up to the job and whether the sophism of his day really had anything to offer political theory. Therefore, we find Shorey agreeing with Jebb's proposition that in Thucydides we find a great mind attempting to mould a magnificent but immature language to new political realities and, at the same time, attacking Thucydides' obscurity and his tendency towards the abstract and general. It is the archaic nature of Thucydides' Greek, combined with the new intellectualism of his day, which make it so difficult to understand his ethical thought. Shorey finishes his paper with the following thought:

> In conclusion, it would be an interesting if elusive inquiry, to ask how much of his disputations, analytic, antithetic, cynical manner was due to the fashion of the new theoretical dialectic, how much to the disintegration of popular morality under the stress of the war, how much is the real expression of the mind and heart of Thucydides.
>
> Shorey 1893: 84

Cornford, I believe, would reply to Shorey that the true nature of Thucydides' thought can only be recovered through the analysis of the text as a literary artefact. His true aim in outlining the divergence between Thucydidean and modern historiography is not to criticize the ancient historian but to strip away accumulated layers of modern interpretation in order to understand his true views of human nature, the causes of events, and of man's place in the universe. Shorey's historicist critique denies that Thucydides can be relevant to the modern world. Cornford leaves the door ajar. It also emphasized how, in Thucydides' political thought, it was not the external 'laws' of economics and topography that constrained and shaped the destiny of man. Rather, in Cornford's estimation of Thucydides, each man, each *polis*, was susceptible to the external 'tragic' forces, to the foibles and the weaknesses that afflicted them as they wove their course through life with 'inexorable causality'. Here we hit upon the key aspect of Cornford's reading of Thucydides' political thought. Men are not necessarily free to choose their own paths, or even avoid mistakes, but are constrained by their natures, and preconceived patterns of knowledge, to pursue certain courses and to fall into certain patterns of grievance. This constraint of action potentially exists, *mutatis mutandis*, in the modern world as much as the ancient.

The task facing the scholar is to strip away the layers of accumulated interpretation so one might thereby approach the true nature of Thucydides' ethical and political thought. Cornford communicated this Thucydidean thought in his usual succinct and elegant prose:

> Man, isolated from, and opposed to, Nature, moves along a narrow path, unrelated to what lies beyond, and lighted only by a few dim rays of human 'foresight' (gnome), or by the false, wandering fires of Hope. He bears within him, self-contained, his destiny in his own character; and this, with the purposes which arise out of it, shapes his course. That is all, in Thucydides' view, that we can say; except that, now and again, out of the surrounding darkness come the blinding strokes of Fortune, unaccountable and unforeseen.
>
> Cornford 1907: 69–70

This is Cornford's interpretation of Thucydides' political philosophy in a nutshell. It is uncomplicated and perhaps, even, frightening. Note that he refers to man, and not specifically to ancient man. According to Cornford, Thucydides' ethical and political view of the world is that man is not master of his own destiny. We must not let the simplicity of this argument blind us to its profundity. What Cornford achieved in passages like this was to strip away from Thucydides the need to define historical 'laws' or mechanisms that could be derived from the text and applied to the present day. In its place, he offered a Thucydides who was a keen observer of human nature, who probed the relationship between man, the state, action, choice and external events but who was also alive to the limit of foreknowledge and the vagaries of fortune.

Cornford was presenting this interpretation of the character of man and cities as trapped in a tragic pattern of action in the context of his radical proposals for university education and his opposition to the Boer Wars. In the years before he published *Mythistoricus*, Cornford was dissatisfied with the way Classics was organized and taught in the university and he wasted no time in advocating change. In November 1903, he gave a paper to the Cambridge Classical Society criticising the organization of lecture courses by the individual colleges, which could mean that in one term there may be half a dozen courses available on Pindar and none on Thucydides, for example (Johnson 2008; Lubenow 2010: 24-5). Moreover, Cornford advocated shifting the focus of the Classics away from 'pure scholarship', he might have said 'pure philology', towards a more humane type of discipline that would explore the artistic merit and intellectual achievements of the Greeks. He was advocating nothing less than a fundamental reorganization of the classical tripos and a reconsideration of the educational value it bestowed on the undergraduates.[20] *Mythistoricus* represents an extension of this earlier programme, even a proof, of the type of scholarship that this more humane approach to the Classics could produce: it demonstrated that Thucydides' political and ethical principles could be read and interpreted usefully by careful students.

While few doubt the radicalism of Cornford's university politics, his attitudes to Britain's, and the world's, problems remain the subject of some controversy. In *The Times* obituary for Cornford, written by Murray in 1943, it is emphasized that Cornford was not an academic who sequestered himself in the ivory tower but rather someone who cared deeply for the world around himself, even if he resolutely refused to allow the intrusion of his political beliefs into his scholarship. This view is echoed by Guthrie (1967: xviii), who remembers that Cornford 'did not consider his political views relevant to his search for the truth about the Greeks', before labelling him a fabian socialist. However, Gal Gerson (1998: 346) points out that in the 1930s Cornford declared himself a liberal in opposition to Marxism, which he feared might produce a rupture in British society between an uneducated rabble and scholastic academics. Such a gap could only grow larger over time and might, eventually, lead to the breakdown of society. The solution Cornford found to this problem, Gerson suggests, was the opening up of Classics to the lower orders of society and, at the same time, the reorientation of the subject in a more humane direction, thereby integrating his views of university politics with his concern for society at large.

More importantly for the subject of this book, however, Cornford explicitly suggested that similar forces were at work in Britain as in Thucydides' characterization of Athens. *Mythistoricus*, therefore, could be seen to represent an early iteration of Cornford's liberal anxieties over empire and democracy. Cornford believed that just as tragedy unconsciously conditioned Thucydides' view of the world, so might modern ideas, such as evolution, define and shape contemporary British thought in barely perceptible ways. Murray (1907: 407) notes in his review of *Mythistoricus* that 'Athenian thought at that time tended to fall into this tragic mould, as thought now falls into the mould of Evolution.' Following this line of thought, evolutionary science was not necessarily a system of thought that arrived at an independent truth. Instead, it was one way of looking at the world determined by late Victorian society, language and politics. Gerson (1998: 347) notes that for Cornford, 'concepts and arguments were preconceived, not independently arrived at or objectively valid'. Gerson later argues that this thought posed a fundamental challenge to Cornford's liberalism (2004: 174–5). If all thought was formulated through a prior vocabulary, then it leaves little space for liberal beliefs such as the theology-free approach to nature, the mutual autonomy of the sciences and the role of the individual thinker. However, I believe this was entirely the point. Cornford was challenging his own and others' liberal beliefs through his classical scholarship. By examining the limits of liberal thought in the preconceived vocabulary that lurks in all minds, Cornford could challenge and, hopefully, strengthen his own dearly held beliefs.

If we follow this line of thought yet further, we see that *Mythistoricus* was not only a challenge to the *communis opinio* on Thucydides but also a subtle critique of British debates surrounding the Boer Wars. In 1907, Britain was still reeling from her experience of imperial warfare in South Africa. Cornford later admitted that he had written on Thucydides 'under the effect of the Boer war and seeing some resemblance between Balfour and Pericles, & Cleon & Chamberlain' (quoted in Gerson 2004: 175). Thucydides, as presented by Cornford, tells the story of how a violent imperial state such as Athens can easily succumb first to blindness and then to *hubris* as success on the battlefield, actually occasioned by chance, leads to human overconfidence. Such a rise necessitates a fall. Athens met her day of nemesis when the devoutly religious Athenian commander Nicias postponed the evacuation of the Athenian military from Sicily, condemning the soldiers and sailors to a bitter defeat and almost certain death. There is clearly an element of analogy here. The main British politicians in the Boer crisis would seem to map onto Athenian counterparts in the Peloponnesian War. Thucydides can certainly be read in this way, as a text warning of the dangers of unfettered imperialism. But there is also the broader question of political choice. In presenting Thucydides' thought as fundamentally conditioned by the mythical and tragic worldviews, Cornford is asking whether any Athenian politician could have averted the impending crisis, or was Athens locked into an historical path from which there was no escape? By analogy, the same question could then be asked of Britain after giving due allowance for the different ways in which the intellectual forces current in the modern world constrain British thought. Were the more modern 'laws' of economics, anthropology and biology leading Britons unconsciously down the road of aggressive imperialism, cultural corruption and political decline? The question of contemporary relevance is never explicitly raised by Cornford in *Mythistoricus*, but it is ever present. In a letter to Murray thanking him for his positive review of *Mythistoricus* Cornford admits that:

> Your point about a people pursuing a policy without knowing it is one which I have thought about quite often, (with little result – as you point out!). I suppose I imagined, when I was writing that stuff, to the view that in such case the real moving force is the quite conscious will of a few individuals, who somehow manage to carry the rest with them.
> 18 June 1907; Cornford Trinity College Archive C1/167–C1/185

Here we see the twofold political importance of the *Mythistoricus*. First, it invites readers to draw historical analogies between Thucydides' depiction of the Athenian Empire and the British experience of imperial conflict at the turn of the twentieth century. Certainly, Cornford nowhere invites his readers to draw these parallels in the book itself, but his later pronouncements demonstrate that they were there operating in his mind and that astute readers like Murray picked up on these contemporary resonances. However, on a deeper level, Cornford invited his readers to meditate on the role of language, society and beliefs in shaping our worldview and even our actions. The Athenians were carried along by their politicians in a series of events that Thucydides came to see as a tragedy. It is not clear whether those politicians could ever stop or alter the process of events. Neither is it clear that modern people can also change their own paths. Moreover, and perhaps more disturbingly, could forces beyond their comprehension shape modern peoples' decisions and destinies?

Cornford's effort to archaicize Thucydides' thought, therefore, does not mean that he was not also alive to the contemporary relevance of the *History*. Yet *Mythistoricus* is a book that is remarkably devoid of explicit contemporary parallels. Cornford does not tell his readers directly why his vision of Thucydides matters and what it means for contemporary philosophy and politics. The value lay in a challenge Cornford was implicitly making to his readers. If Thucydides' thought, so this argument runs, is constrained by the mythical and tragic mode of thinking in Greece, so too might modern visions of the world be constrained by unwritten and unacknowledged modes of thinking. Cornford offers an inkling of his thought in this direction in his 1921 essay *The Unconscious Element in Literature and Philosophy*:

> Now this is not to say that Thucydides' philosophy of life is not, within its limits, a true philosophy – as true as any alternative our own minds may contribute. It may even be truer. Fourteen years ago, writing under the impression of the South African war, I may have overstressed the financial aspect of imperialism. Since 1914 Thucydides' moral interpretation of history has seemed more profound. But that does not touch the main thesis, namely that there are alternative interpretations; that each is limited and tends to obscure the truth contained in the others; and that the criticism of an ancient historian should begin with the study of his a priori forms of thought, fashioned in a time when economic science, for instance, was not invented.
>
> Cornford 1967: 2–3

Cornford here emphasizes how Thucydides embarked upon a rationalistic project that intended to strip away the fabulous and the religious from Greek events. Without knowledge of modern social sciences, he had been left only with a mythical and tragic substratum. Thucydides was 'unaware that what remained was mythical in origin, and not a fresh statement of the facts of life drawn from direct and unbiased observation' (1907: 242).[21] This attempt, however, should not be seen as simply a failure. Thucydides had undoubtedly produced a great work of literary art. More than that, the *History* stood as a monument to Thucydides' own philosophy of life. This philosophy focused not on the 'systems' of the democracy, the *polis*, or interstate relations, but on the passions of man and their relationship to historical action and causation. The passions that Cornford believed he had found in Thucydides were preserved forms of early mythical thinking but their archaic nature did not mean that they were irrelevant, or that they did not have important messages to teach the modern world. Thucydides was a moral writer who cared about the lot of man more so than the flippant and sceptical Herodotus. He described how blindness and *hubris* entered into the minds of men and the souls of states and how this ultimately led to *nemesis* and destruction. In pursuing this project, Cornford's Thucydides had created a political philosophy that showed how human action was shaped and even constrained by psychological factors. It was a frightening vision that suggested, perhaps, that even modern nations themselves were subject to moods, passions and psychological states that governed the actions of great men and nations alike and were beyond easy comprehension.

Conclusion: Reception and influence

I have argued above that Cornford's *Mythistoricus* is the first work in what I am terming the Thucydidean turn not only because of its fundamental reassessment of where Thucydides sits in the history of historical and political thought, but also because it tried to shift analysis of his ethical thought away from the study of systems (that is, whether Thucydides supported democracy, Pericles, empire and so on) to offer a new interpretation of his moral outlook as rooted in the traditions of Greek tragedy and thought. It is undeniable that Cornford had produced a remarkable, eloquent and challenging reappraisal of Thucydides' literary art. It was, inevitably, also a controversial book. We shall see throughout the remainder of this monograph how Abbott, Zimmern, Toynbee and Powell all read, interpreted and reacted in very different ways to Cornford's ideas about Thucydides. To conclude this chapter, however, I will emphasize another way in which Cornford proved important in subsequent scholarship, namely, the way he opened a debate over whether Thucydides should be viewed as a scientific or as a tragic writer.

Mythistoricus' contemporary reviewers were divided over the scholarly merit of Cornford's arguments. Anonymous reviewers in *Hermathena* and the *Journal of Hellenic Studies* found Cornford's arguments unconvincing (anon. 1907a, 1907b; see also Postgate 1907; Perrin 1908),[22] while Murray reviewed the work favourably (Murray 1907). Chambers notes that a number of reviewers pointed to the distance between Cornford's views and those of Gomperz, suggesting that the reinterpretation of Thucydides in the history (or evolution) of Greek thought was already thought of as a bone of contention among scholars (1991: 70). Cornford's influence was also felt quickly in wider Classical Studies. His claims about the true causes of the war could hardly be ignored and so started a vigorous debate about the economic motives for the Peloponnesian War (cf. Dickins 1911; Grundy 1911; Grundy and Dickens 1913). This debate focused less on Thucydides' political thought and more on the causes of the Peloponnesian War as historical problem. Cornford's literary analysis of Thucydides gained more traction, although many were hesitant to accept all the nuances of the *mythistoricus* interpretation. Shorey notes the implications of Cornford's arguments in a critical review.

> That Thucydides's sense of the moral significance and the dramatic contrasts of history was quickened by reminiscences of Aeschylean tragedy, is probable enough. But sober criticism will know how to make a light and tactful use of such suggestions without converting them into a rigid and systematic method of exegesis.
>
> Shorey 1907: 205

In other words, Shorey accepted the literary and intellectual connection between Thucydides and Aeschylus but was hesitant to view tragedy as a 'system' that defined Thucydidean thought. J. B. Bury, Regius Professor of Modern History at Cambridge, published a series of lectures on the Greek historians given in 1908 in Harvard and released the following year. In his lecture on Thucydides, he dismissed Cornford's arguments about the confusion between *aitia* and *prophasis* but was nonetheless prepared to concede that there was a clear dramatic literary influence on Thucydides.

> The truth is, I think, that the style of Thucydides was influenced by the Attic drama, no less than by the rhetoric of Gorgias, and it is one of the merits of Mr. Cornford's monograph to have illustrated this influence. But that the tragic phrases and reminiscences, and the occasional use of tragic irony, cannot be held to have more than a stylistic significance, and that Thucydides did not intend to cast the war into the typical scheme of a tragic development, will be apparent if we consider his own clear statements.
>
> Bury 1909: 124

Cornford's harshest pre-Great War critic, however, was Sir Walter Lamb, who published a monograph on Thucydides' literary art, *Clio Enthroned*, in 1914. Lamb had lectured on the Classics, but in 1914 became Secretary to the Royal Academy. His book is a 314-page polemical argument against Cornford's views, which he found not only too dangerous but also too useful to ignore. 'An alarm has been raised, and with some reason, that the enthusiasms of anthropology are likely or even eager to obscure the front of the classical temple with the distresses and nostrums of primitive savagery' (Lamb 1914: xi). For Lamb, Thucydides was a great thinker who thoroughly understood the new science of politics current in the fifth century BC and offered convincing psychological portrayals of his characters that did not default to tragic archetypes as Cornford had maintained. In other words, Thucydides was really the first scientific historian and his 'system' of political analysis did not depend upon the literary model of tragedy but instead the close empirical observation of the psychology of the *History*'s actors.

It is not until after the Great War, however, that the fullest criticism of Cornford's thesis emerged in the shape of Charles Cochrane's 1929 monograph, *Thucydides and the Science of History*. Cochrane was then a young teacher of Classics at the University of Toronto who, in later life, would become an eminent Canadian philosopher (Innis 1946: Beer in Cochrane 2017). In his book, Cochrane argues that Thucydides was indeed a scientist because his historical and political thought was based upon a system of close observation, which he had learnt from the Hippocratic corpus. Just as the Hippocratics used observation to diagnose and understand disease, so too did Thucydides seek to understand the political malaise that was affecting the Greek world. Cochrane opens his book with a very short introduction (1929: 1–3) where he draws a sharp division between his arguments and all previous interpretations of Thucydides. He notes that Cornford stood against the remainder of English-speaking critics in his insistence on the role of the mythic in Thucydides. Yet, Cochrane notes that all those critics, including Cornford and Bury, argue that Thucydides is deficient in 'scientific categories', in other words that his Greek language and his thought simply cannot convey modern scientific principles, thereby making the distance between Thucydides and nineteenth-century historiography greater than the distance between Thucydides and Herodotus. Cochrane sets his work against the rest of Thucydidean scholarship because he believes that Thucydides was in fact a scientist whose language and methodology perfectly convey scientific history. In the first chapter, Cochrane explains that Thucydides' scientific principles derived, ultimately, from Democritus and the early atomist philosophers of Ionia, who in turn influenced the early medical writers.

It may be doubted whether there is such a strong link between the atomists and Hippocrates as that claimed by Cochrane (Shorey 1930: 96). Certain scholars have also wondered to what extent Thucydides was influenced by Hippocrates, particularly in obviously medical passages such as the plague narrative (Page 1953; Holladay and Poole 1979). Against these arguments, a convincing study by Rosalind Thomas points out that Hippocrates and Thucydides use much of the same vocabulary when describing disease (Thomas 2006: 95–6, 2017; cf. Alford 1998). Thomas even suggests that Thucydides may have been attempting to produce his own medical theory in rival to those of contemporary doctors (Thomas 2006: 103). Cochrane, I believe, would have been interested in such debates but would have felt that they missed his essential point: the Hippocratics were philosophical materialists. They looked for the material cause of disease in the environment and then explored its material effect on the body. Thucydides learned from these writers the importance of observation and the necessity of understanding the material reality of life itself, not simply a literary 'scientific' paradigm to emulate.[23] Cochrane's focus on materialism explains his need to link atomist thought to medical writing. If one accepts Cochrane's arguments, then it represents a devastating attack on Cornford's tragic and mythical position.

However, already in the 1920s and 1930s various reviewers felt that Cochrane had gone too far in his depiction of Thucydides as a scientist (Grant 1929; Gomme 1930; Shorey 1930) and relatively few scholars today believe that Thucydides was as cold and objective an observer of events as Cochrane paints him. There are, of course, individual voices such as Sears (1977) and Palmer (1992: 2–3) who emphasize the 'scientific' side of Thucydides' thought, but many more would agree with Balot (2001: 137), who cites Cochrane when he attacks the 'old' view of Thucydides' historical objectivity, which he maintains is untenable following the work of Connor (1984) and others. Cochrane is still routinely cited today but often simply as the summation of this old objective view, which is summarily dismissed with little or no further comment (for example Orwin 1994: 33; Crane 1996: 27; Thomas 2006: 92–3; Zumbrunnen 2010: 72). However, de Ste Croix argued as early as the 1970s that the criticism of Cochrane had gone too far (1972: 29–33). Recently, Arieti (2005) has emphasized the nuances of Cochrane's arguments in a history of ancient philosophy. He argues that for Cochrane there is a hierarchy of the sciences. The physical sciences are the most exact, followed by the biological. History is the least exact of the sciences, but it is still useful. It allows Thucydides, through empirical observation, to study the actions of man in society. He can, therefore, present the growth, development, retrogression and destruction of various kinds of political orders, whether they be treaties, alliances or even cities themselves. 'The job of the historian is to trace this movement, this process, in groups of men' (Arieti 2005: 143).

Other scholars, however, were more receptive to the import of Cornford's arguments. In 1913, a young Scottish scholar, J. A. K. Thomson, published a collection of essays titled *The Greek Tradition*, which included an essay on Thucydides. Thomson was a promising young academic who was being mentored in his professional development by Murray (McManus 2007). His essay represented an attempt to understand Thucydides as a man and as a thinker. He paints a picture of the historian as deeply affected by the plague and the war, but who also managed to transcend the urge for simple explanations or to blame his opponents. Thomson claims that the impartiality of the *History* is a proof not merely of Thucydides' high conscience as a historian but also of his extraordinary magnanimity as a human being (1913: 47). Thomson appears to have been deeply influenced by Cornford's emphasis on the role of the dramatic in Thucydides. He maintains that all Greek writers are dramatists because their psychology is creative and not analytic: 'There is hardly any attempt at the exact description of emotional states' (Thomson 1913: 20–2). This is because Greek writers hardly ever attempt to describe the psychology of individuals – in a world in which every man lived in, of and for the *polis*, their psychology is understandably collective. For that reason, their characters can appear shallow. Such conventions do not satisfy Thucydides, but he uses it far as he can, perhaps for want of a more precise terminology for depicting individual and collective psychology. Clearly, in a psychology of this sort, the qualities which compose what we call a 'personality' will have little significance. A man becomes the embodiment of a single 'ruling passion'. Aristides becomes the Just Man, Pericles the Magnanimous Man, Cleon the Violent Man (1913: 23). This is all too simple, naïve and romantic (even exasperating) to an age that reads Dostoevsky and Henry James precisely because it takes no account of mixed motives or the messiness of human psychology.

The focus on Thucydides and tragedy, however, continued throughout the twentieth century until today. Over time, scholars have moved beyond Cornford's claim that Thucydides was primarily inspired by Aeschylus to consider his borrowings from a host of other ancient texts. Indeed, as early as 1938 J. H. Finley argues that Thucydides was deeply influenced by Euripides and that both writers shared certain opinions in common (Finley 1942, 1967). Lowell Edmunds (1975a, 1975b) and Nicole Loraux (1986) both argue that Thucydides' thought was deeply influenced by the archaic poet Hesiod, while Colin MacLeod (1983) compellingly maintains that Thucydides' account of the Sicilian expedition accords to a 'tragic' pattern of storytelling or narrative that ultimately derives from Homer. Peter Euben (1990), in a wide-ranging study, contends that Greek tragedy generally provides the context for Greek political thought. It is, therefore, impossible to properly understand Thucydides and Plato without considering their works in light of the surviving tragedies written by Aeschylus, Sophocles and Euripides. These scholars have all pushed their own arguments far beyond those of Cornford. At the same time, the continuing return to the influence of poetry and tragedy on Thucydides points to the importance of the questions that Cornford himself first raised and, it must be remembered, their significance even today.

3

Thucydides, Realism and Political Psychology

Of all the figures explored in this book, Alfred Eckhard Zimmern (1879–1957) is the most prominent in the early history of the discipline of International Relations. In 1919, Zimmern won the first chair ever established in International Relations at the University of Aberystwyth before teaching that subject at Cornell and later winning a second chair established at Oxford in 1930 (Markwell 1986, 2004). In his day, Zimmern was an eminent supporter of the League of Nations and the British Commonwealth and a prominent liberal public intellectual. However, his educational roots lay in the Greek and Roman Classics. Before the war, Zimmern was a fellow in ancient history at New College, Oxford and was famous among the reading public as the author of *The Greek Commonwealth* (1911), a liberal and idealist description of the rise of the Greek polis and the golden age of Athenian culture, democracy and empire under Pericles. This chapter is an interrogation of Zimmern's changing view of Thucydides as his career developed from Classics to International Relations. It argues that before the Great War, Zimmern found Thucydides an unsympathetic figure, who was, nevertheless, essential to his historical study of fifth-century Athens. The Boer Wars deeply affected his thought at this stage in his career. Zimmern's aversion to Thucydides was rooted in his dislike of the Athenian historian's empirical realism and his supposed support for the military excesses of the Athenian Empire. After the Great War, however, Zimmern's career and thoughts came to focus on contemporary events. It is then that he came to embrace Thucydides' realism as the foundation of his methodology of 'political psychology', that is to say an approach to politics that focused on the different mentalities and motivations of states, which Zimmern implored his readers to learn and even emulate as a useful tool to analyse a Europe shattered by war. Zimmern was the first to label Thucydides as a psychologist.

Despite their complexity and resonances with contemporary scholarship, Zimmern's readings of Thucydides are rarely cited today.[1] If his work is studied by contemporary scholars at all, it is for his contribution to the early history of the discipline of International Relations or for his idealist and liberal interpretations of the British Commonwealth. This scholarly lacuna represents a missed opportunity because Zimmern was one of the first commentators to ask why and in what ways Thucydides' thought might prove useful to the contemporary world. There has been a growing number of engagements with Zimmern's International Relations thought in recent years (see, for example, Markwell 1998; Osiander 1998; Morefield 2005; Low 2007; Morefield 2014; Baji 2016). For a long time Zimmern's work was neglected due to his characterization as an 'idealist' thinker by early historians of International Relations,[2] marking him as part of a group that dominated interwar British thought and included S. H. Bailey, Philip Noel-Baker and David Mitrany. These thinkers were all deeply affected by the carnage of the Great War and put their faith in the League of Nations as an institution that could ensure world peace. They were, of course, proved dramatically wrong by the rise of Nazism and the outbreak of the Second World War, discrediting idealism for a generation.

The term 'idealism' first appeared in an attack on their writings by the British historian and diplomat E. H. Carr in *The Twenty Years' Crisis* (Carr 1939), although it was not a label that Zimmern ever applied to himself. Carr argued that Zimmern was naive in his belief that states could impose their internal morality on the bear pit of international politics. Rather, states were driven solely by their own national interest and all other concerns were secondary. It is certainly true that Zimmern believed that the best hope for peace was through the imposition of external political orders on states through the establishment of supranational institutions. He hoped that the legal apparatus provided by the League of Nations and the communal purpose of the British Commonwealth could ensure peace into the future. Zimmern's most treasured belief was the assertion that education offered the surest path to global security (Rich 1995). In pursuit of that end, Zimmern was a major contributor to the foundation of UNESCO after the Second World War (Toye and Toye 2010; Laqua 2011). However, in the 1930s Zimmern was aware of the challenges posed by the rise of fascism and Nazism and was becoming increasingly pessimistic in his views that peace could be sustained. Recent scholarship presents Zimmern as a pivotal, if flawed, figure in the early history of International Relations, or, alternatively, as an elusive thinker with a multidimensional career (Rich 2002). Osiander (1998) has argued that Zimmern was in fact prescient of many of the tenets that came to be seen as a 'realist' after the Second World War but felt they were anachronistic and dangerous in an age of industrialization and mechanized warfare. That is to say, remove the morality from the study of international politics and one may end up provoking rather than avoiding conflict. One might imagine that the outbreak of the Second World War vindicated this view.

I will argue in what follows that Zimmern saw Thucydides as first and foremost a realist. However, his moral and ethical responses to Thucydides' realistic depiction of politics changed in the years from 1905 to 1929. His thought developed as his knowledge of international affairs deepened and, in particular, political events changed. This development is best assessed through the publication of three essays. First, there is the 1905 piece, *Thucydides the Imperialist*, in which Zimmern expresses animosity, even disgust, to Thucydides' cold and realistic portrayal of the Athenian Empire. Zimmern's reading was deeply affected by his liberal reaction to the Boer War. Second, there is the 1921 essay, *Greek Political Thought*. Here Zimmern presents Thucydides' realism as underpinning a vision of political psychology that modern students of politics would do well to emulate. Here we can see that Zimmern's reading was deeply affected by the devastation of the Great War. Finally, we come to the 1929 essay, *The Scholar in Public Affairs*, in which Zimmern uses Thucydides to consider how the modern scholar should influence politics through his work. These three essays represent Zimmern's major contribution to the Thucydidean turn. They are a chronicle of his evolving reception of Thucydides' literary realism and the ways in which it could be used to underpin the new sciences of International Relations and Political Psychology.

Before the Great War

Before I turn to the depiction of Thucydides in *Thucydides the Imperialist*, I will first explore Zimmern's liberal anxiety over empire. It is in the context of the Boer War and its polarizing effects in Oxford that Zimmern first comes to Thucydides. These issues are crystalized in his most famous work, *The Greek Commonwealth* (1911), which is a history of Athens that serves as an allegory for the history of Britain.[3] Zimmern was born in Surbiton in 1879 to German Jewish parents and was educated at Winchester College. He later went up to New College, Oxford to read Classics, where he won the Stanhope essay prize in 1902. After Oxford, Zimmern, who spoke fluent German, studied ancient history in Berlin under Wilamowitz and Eduard Meyer, maintaining a correspondence in later years with the former (Caldeb III: 1989). In 1903, Zimmern returned to New College where he became a lecturer and later fellow in ancient history. In 1909, he abandoned his life in Oxford to head to Greece where he studied at the

British School at Athens and wandered the countryside for two years. This time was put to good use as it informed his writing of *The Greek Commonwealth*, a monograph describing the political, economic and social forces that had led to the golden age of Periclean Athens, which included at its heart a translation of the funeral speech recreated by Thucydides. In the book Zimmern attempted to use the latest insights from psychology, sociology and archaeology to move beyond a dry account of the political machinations of ancient Greek politicians and city states to portray the reality of their society, including accounts of the lives of women, slaves and the poor – topics that continue to be of interest to contemporary scholarship. In pursuing this goal, some reviewers felt that he had excessively 'modernized' the Greeks by making them too much like late nineteenth-century Britons (Huth 1912; cf. Wills 2009: 45–7).[4]

In the first 80 per cent or so of *The Greek Commonwealth*, Zimmern attempted to describe the growth of the *polis* as an economic and social unit. Inevitably, much of his evidence, and therefore his narrative, focused on Athens. We learn from these pages that Greek politics was rooted in the family unit. The *polis* was just a recreation of familial social ties on a larger scale. Over time, Athens had become an increasingly complicated polity in her economic and social make-up, a process accelerated by politicians such as Solon. Solon wished to make the *polis* richer and more powerful while avoiding the evils of class strife and stasis. Poor Athenians began to abandon the land to take up manufacturing and trade. These Athenians formed the majority of the manpower for the fleet. The acquisition of the empire and the outbreak of the Peloponnesian War had awakened the *polis* to the possibilities of this new economic reality based on trade and tribute and allowed the spread of the war fever. There is a significant influence here from Graham Wallas' 1908 work *Human Nature in Politics*, which argued that the equilibrium of modern society had been disturbed by the rise of capitalist greed (Stapleton 2007: 277).[5] Interestingly, however, Zimmern does not choose to cite Cornford's study of the party of the Piraeus in his account of the rise of commercial interest at Athens, although he must have carefully read *Mythistoricus*.

Part of this tendency to modernize the Greeks was Zimmern's desire to bring the modern insights of the social sciences to bear on the ancient world. However, he also had political motives in mind. The most astute commentator on Zimmern today, Jeanne Morefield, points out that *The Greek Commonwealth* is really a book about British liberal anxiety over the possession of an empire (Morefield 2005, 2014).[6] Like Cornford, Zimmern was writing in the years following the Boer Wars and during increasing challenges to Britain's military and economic hegemony from the US and Germany. Zimmern was also a liberal who remained wedded to the idea of the empire as a force for good in the world. However, he was more forthright than Cornford in his comparisons between ancient and modern politics. Zimmern's Athens provided a suitable historical example of a liberal 'state' which had failed to realize her domestic values in her imperial policy. His study of the history of the *polis* allow him to think through the following questions:

> What ... made the British Empire any different from the German? If the British Empire was not motivated by a sense of cultural superiority, then what motivated it? If domination could not be justified in terms of race, then by what terms could it be justified? What was it that made the British both better able and ethically entitled to rule much of the world?
>
> Morefield 2014: 33

Athens was important to Zimmern as an imperial example because, he believed, she had for a time successfully established an equality of nations in her imperial system (Morefield 2005: 96–135). This equality, of course, had not survived the outbreak of the Peloponnesian War. In pursuing these questions, Zimmern was thinking deeply about the contemporary nature of the British Empire and its role in a changing world. He was working within a long tradition of British liberal thought that had worried over the tension between liberty at home and tyranny abroad within an imperial system (Mehta 1999; Armitage 2000; Bell 2007, 2016). It is beyond the scope of this chapter to judge whether Zimmern's intervention in these debates was successful (cf. Mazower 2007). Rather, I wish to emphasize that Thucydides as a historian of empire posed problems for Zimmern's idealist concept of empire, which could not be easily resolved. Namely, how could a liberal state, faced with the prospect of a conflict as terrible as the Peloponnesian War, arrest the political processes that would lead to increased greed and pride in imperial dealings and remove morality from political and military decisions?

This was a pressing concern for Zimmern, and other Oxford liberals, in the first decade of the twentieth century. The brutality of the Boer War had forced liberal thinkers to better define their own ideas of colonialism. Although many abandoned a commitment to imperial expansion, pro-imperial views remained strong in Oxford, and among the Liberal Party. These views focused on an a kind of imperialism that sought to prepare indigenous people for self-government (Morefield 2005: 106) and an equal community among the white settler colonies of Australia, New Zealand and Canada in which Britain would be *primus inter pares*. However, it was not just the nature of the empire that troubled Zimmern.

He worried over the ease with which the 'war spirit' had taken hold in Britain, leading to imperial jingoism and the acceptance of militarism. In 1901, J. A. Hobson had published the *Psychology of Jingoism*, exploring this change in political psychology. Hobson offered this work as 'an analysis of the modern war-spirit' (Krebs 2004: 26ff.). It was an attempt to understand the 'national arrogance of the imperialists' and business interests and how they had managed to lead the whole country, the whole empire, into a grinding and thankless war in the Transvaal. Zimmern believed that a similar war spirit had taken hold of classical Athens, which corrupted her earlier imperial and democratic ideals and led to moral corruption and political decline. Thucydides, he believed, chronicled the emergence of this war spirit.

Thucydides occupies a difficult place in *The Greek Commonwealth*. The inclusion of the translation of the funeral speech does not mean that Zimmern found Thucydides an author entirely germane to his liberal political views. Indeed, Morefield (2014: 53) argues that Zimmern's account of the earlier empire often bypasses Thucydides' evidence to draw instead on material from alternative sources, such as Diodorus Siculus. It is in the final chapter, where Zimmern considers the rise of a war party or spirit in Athens and the outbreak of the Peloponnesian War, that Thucydides can no longer be ignored (1911: 414–37). This chapter explains the death of idealism and the moral decline of Athens during the Peloponnesian War down to the siege of Melos and a brief allusion to the Sicilian Expedition, which concludes the entire book.[7] In Zimmern's argument, the 'forces' which led Greece on a path to war were, initially at least, sentimental rather than material. That is to say, they concerned matters of honour rather than disputes over power or trade (Zimmern 1911: 417), thereby contrasting with the vision of the causes of the war Cornford put forward in *Thucydides Historicus*. Pericles, the great statesman of Athens, was for peace but recognized the necessity of war. To mitigate its evils he suggested a strategy that would not defeat Sparta but exhaust her through the judicious use of sea power[8] to harass her coast and her allies (Zimmern 1911: 422). However, the arrival of the Peloponnesian army in Attica stirred new feelings and psychologies within the Athenian people. 'The old hope and reverence and self-discipline and joy had passed away as in a dream. In their place were anger and greed and suspicion, mean-eyed envy and weak despair, and all the devils of disillusionment' (Zimmern 1911: 425). This argument recalls Cornford's depiction of Thucydides to the extent that Athens is characterized through a series of distinct psychological states. Forces exist outside of Athens operating between the Greek city-states. These forces lead to a war, which, in turn, unleash hidden passions within the people. However, these passions do not follow the sequential pattern of tragedy. Rather, they all emerge at once. Zimmern writes that Athens 'awoke' to the 'clear-eyed realities of her power', that she was not a missionary of freedom against the Persians but a tyrant city with an empire. The psychologies of greed, suspicion and envy, which had lain dormant in the Athenian mind for a long time, became more acute over time. The death of Pericles accelerated this process (Zimmern 1911: 428).

In Zimmern's interpretation, the association between the growth of the war spirit and Pericles' death is problematic. The first sentence of this section of the chapter possesses a footnote to 2.65 and Plutarch's *Life of Pericles* 36–8. This is a strange argument, as Pericles was a significant instigator of the war and 2.65 arrives straight after a speech in which he begs the Athenians not to send to the Spartans to sue for peace following the devastation of Attica. Indeed, as Thucydides explains, Pericles had done little to restrain the 'war spirit'. Rather, he led the multitude due to his rank, ability and integrity (2.65.8). The difficulty was that following his death no Athenian politician emerged who possessed the ability and strategic insight to lead the *demos*. Rather, his successors were all grasping for supremacy through flattery of the *demos* (2.65.10). Zimmern uses the example of Athens' abandonment of Plataea as proof of the increase in the war spirit following Pericles' death. Plataea was Athens' oldest ally and lay only two days' march away. 'As [Plataea] was trustful, the Athenians, watching the sun set behind her mountain, could afford to neglect her' (Zimmern 1911: 429). Although one might well imagine that Pericles, had he lived, would not have acted differently. Zimmern continues to explore the issue of declining leadership and the war spirit through a discussion of Cleon, 'the very embodiment of the mad war-spirit which was driving Athens down the decline' (Zimmern 1911: 429). Cleon argued that all the male inhabitants of Mytilene should be executed after their failed revolt and advised the Athenians against making peace with the Spartans after the Battle of Pylos. We should recall at this stage that scholars today still argue that the political passions in Thucydides' *History* are antithetical to rationality (Mara 2008; Wohl 2017), or at least antithetical to how those political passions might be shaped by Thucydides' rationality (Strauss 1978; Orwin 1994), and, in particular, that the political passions disturb democratic decision-making (Ober 1998; Saxonhouse 1995; 2017). Zimmern would have been wholly in sympathy with these sentiments.

Immediately after Pericles' death, the *demos* still maintained common sense if not morality. Their eventual decision to reject Cleon's draconian treatment of the Mytilenians was based upon the potential to draw future reparations and tribute from the captured town (Zimmern 1911: 430). At the same time, however, the clear-headed desire for money, and the power that it could buy, was becoming more pronounced as demagogues such as Cleon tightened their grip on the affairs of the Athenians (Zimmern 1911: 433). This argument is reminiscent of Murray's letter to Cornford, in which he talks about how easy it is for one man to get a group of people to go along with him and Cornford's retort that when he was writing *Mythistoricus* he was thinking subconsciously of British politics during the Boer Wars (18 June 1907; Cornford Trinity College Archive C1/167–C1/185, see page 45). There is certainly a great deal of anxiety over Britain's imperial adventures in *The Greek Commonwealth*. When Zimmern was writing it, he was part of the Round Table association, a group of liberal intellectuals who were searching for ways to foster peaceful cooperation within the British Empire. In particular, they advocated free trade and imperial federation (cf. Kendle 1975). Yet despite this group's enthusiasm for empire, there was an awareness that the imperial project was difficult to justify on grounds other than cultural and racial superiority (Morefield 2014: 41). A liberal ancient Greece increasingly unified by external political, social and cultural forces allowed Zimmern to fantasize that the same processes may be underway in the British Empire, allowing Britain to move beyond imperial doctrines based upon culture and race to create an international commonwealth of equals, with Britain as *primus inter pares*. The final chapter of the *Greek Commonwealth* exploring the war spirit and the Peloponnesian War was Zimmern's attempt to understand how this process of unification or federation had unravelled in ancient Greece. In his view, the rise of demagogues such as Cleon was a symptom of that decline but not its cause. Rather, Zimmern was pessimistic about the human condition. Even the citizens of the most flourishing cultural state the world had ever known were greedy and avaricious. It only took the outbreak of war and the death of a statesman to reveal these passions. External factors dictated psychological states in Athens just as much as in modern Britain.

Although this account of decline offered in the final chapter is clearly drawn from Thucydides, in the *Greek Commonwealth* Zimmern does not offer his opinions on the personality and thought of the Greek historian. We have to turn to the essay *Thucydides the Imperialist* (1905)[9] to hear his views on this matter. In the essay, Zimmern depicts Thucydides as a wholehearted supporter of the Periclean vision of empire, a figure blinded to the human cost of the imperial project by the riches and glory of fifth-century Athens. Later, Athens' defeat in the Peloponnesian War breaks Thucydides' view of the world. For Zimmern, Thucydides was a figure drawn to the liberal ideals of Pericles, embodied mainly in the funeral speech, which presented Athens as a 'patriotic' polity geared towards the establishment of a hierarchical, yet civilized, order both at home and in the empire abroad. Thucydides described not only the epitome of this society, but also its progressive degradation under the influence of the Peloponnesian War. Following Wilamowitz, Zimmern saw in Thucydides a man broken by the unravelling of the international order imposed by the Athenian Empire under Pericles, which was then destroyed by Cleon and his successors. Thucydides only rediscovered his love for his *polis* at the end of his life, when he wrote the funeral speech (Morefield 2014: 54).

Thucydides the imperialist

Zimmern encapsulates these problems of Thucydides and Pericles, Thucydides and Empire, and Thucydides and ethics in his essay. He notes that while the glory of Athens, as presented in the funeral speech, might just justify Athens' control over her subject allies, it is only in Pericles' final speech that Thucydides allows him to speak about his ideals of imperialism. These, for Zimmern, are the same as those later expounded by Cleon. Athens, so free in her own ideals at home, acts as a tyrant *polis* to the rest of Greece. Her own unique and glorious self-development has imposed this harsh necessity upon her. 'If she abdicated her tyranny, she would abdicate her power: and if she abdicated her power, all the ideals of the Funeral Speech would go with it' (Zimmern 1928: 86). Thucydides even depicts these ideals as conferring a highly nebulous benefit on the allies. They may have to send 600 talents of tribute, alongside soldiers, sailors and ships, but that meant that they were associated with the glories of the Periclean Empire. Zimmern writes that the Periclean theory of empire claims that the 'mere connection with Athens, the mere fact of being a small fragment or appendage of the greatest and most glorious state in the world outweighs all vulgar and material considerations of profit and loss' (Zimmern 1928: 88–9). However, this is no utopia. Athens still needs ships and money to maintain her position in a violent and anarchic world. Athens, of course, offered her allies protection from a warring world and the return of Persia, but they were never grateful. For Zimmern, neither Thucydides nor Pericles offers this ideal with any cynicism; they truly believe this ideal of Athens and her relationship to her empire. 'The glory of helping Athens to assert her ideals against the Philistinism of Corinth and the drill sergeant morality of Sparta is recounted by Thucydides just as gravely and just as quietly as the contradictory theory in the Melian Dialogue'

(Zimmern 1928: 89). If Thucydides and Pericles are not cynical about this particular view of empire, Zimmern himself appears to have had his doubts. It was not the inherent contradiction between taxing allies to fund Athenian greatness so much as the fact that Athens was not a utopia. She had to live in the real world with states opposed to her who could not possibly understand the Periclean ideal. As the war goes on, Athenian ideals pulled them in one direction and her efforts to realize them in quite another. 'What shall it profit a nation if it gain the whole world and lose its own soul?' (Zimmern 1928: 91). Empire abroad corrupts at home.

Despite the vividness of Thucydides' depiction of the horrors of war and the moral and material degradation of the Athenian Empire, Zimmern felt that there was a certain humanity lacking in his work. This lack of humanity is emphasized in the closing pages of the essay where Thucydides is described as a 'practical student of affairs – the mine-owner, the statistician, the master of business detail. For Thucydides, as for Machiavelli, nothing is beneath the statesman's notice – nothing is too vulgar or too commonplace or too un-Utopian' (Zimmern 1928: 96–7). Thucydides wants us to study the war with practical considerations – money, men, ships – always in mind: 'he allowed his mind to become so much occupied with talents and triremes and tribute, that power and the material display of power seemed to him sometimes almost an ideal in themselves. He likes bigness in things, quite irrespective of their greatness' (Zimmern 1928: 98). *Dunamis* (δύναμις) is his word for conveying greatness and often simply means material greatness or the capacity to display material greatness. But this focus on power and money lacks an important element, the human value of ideals. 'Did Thucydides think that finance alone could have built the Parthenon?' (Zimmern 1928: 100). While Zimmern allows that Thucydides probes the material and psychological horrors of the war and the way that they permeated the fabric of Greek society, he never came to see the war itself as 'deplorable'.

> Thucydides never quite came to agree with Euripides, because he was not so tender-hearted, because he was rather a clear-sighted statesman than (let us say it boldly) a civilized man: because he was not the ideal historian who is both of these. He can see only too clearly, and explain only too poignantly, the effect of war upon states and societies: but he cannot see, or never lets us know that he sees, its effect upon individual men, women and children.
>
> Zimmern 1928: 102

Zimmern is here referencing Euripides as author of the *Trojan Women*, a play he believed demonstrated that the playwright fully understood the horrors of war.

Thucydides may tell us about Mycalessus, but only as an illustration of the dangers of employing mercenaries. Moreover, Thucydides does not tell us about the women and children sold into slavery as victims of Athens' imperial adventures or the bereaved families left behind by countless dead soldiers.[10] This makes Zimmern doubt Thucydides was a civilized man. Intriguingly, in the original typescript the word initially used in place of civilized was good (MS. Zimmern 136: 95). When this deficiency in Thucydides' thought is understood, then the reader will realize that the Athenian historian is ultimately merely a Periclean – both the patriot and the imperialist – while the higher insights of Euripides and Plato were beyond him. 'If he had joined those to what he has given us, I do not know where we should look for his equal' (Zimmern 1928: 102). In his first essay on Thucydides, therefore, Zimmern saw the Athenian historian as a Periclean and a supporter of empire, whose political insight, although considerable, was hampered by his inability to understand, or at least describe, the true human cost of conflict. Before 1914, therefore, Zimmern appears conflicted as to the contemporary relevance of ancient history. Athens becomes a negative example. She shows Britain what is possible in a liberal empire, but also provides an example of how such an institution can easily unravel. Thucydides' *History* underpins this narrative. Thucydides himself is a problematic figure for Zimmern. A man of great political insight but someone who does not share modern British liberal concerns. He may not even have been a moral man. As we shall see in the remainder of this chapter, this critical view was later to be tempered by a growing appreciation of Thucydides' depiction of human passion and political psychology over the following two decades following Zimmern's experience of the Great War.

Greek political thought and modernity

Let us now turn to how and in what ways Zimmern's reading of Thucydides became increasingly complicated and nuanced following 1918. The Great War had a profound effect on Zimmern. Although he had not fought on the front, he had seen many of his Oxford colleagues killed or maimed. Zimmern believed that the emergence of a worldwide capitalist system had led to a global selfishness that paved the way to war (Osiander 1998; Morefield 2005: 97). Therefore, statesmen needed to create international systems that could ensure an equality of nations and solve disputes through legal means. Immediately after the war Zimmern was heavily involved in the Paris peace process and was active in support of the League of Nations, an institution he helped to establish and form through his work on the Cecil Draft and whose educative arm, the League of Nations Society, he and Murray had supported from its inception (Morefield 2005: 174–87). At the same time, Zimmern's liberalism appears to have deepened. He declared at the beginning of the war that 'the enemies of liberalism, whether within or without the allied countries, are the enemies of the human race' (quoted in Morefield 2014: 35). As Stapleton memorably puts it, Zimmern's work on the League and his subsequent career in International Relations represents an attempt to turn chaos into cosmos (2007: 282). Yet before the political malaise that was afflicting the world could be properly treated, it first had to be identified and studied. In the wake of such a momentous and destructive conflict, ancient thought could appear parochial, unhelpful even. Yet in a 1921 essay titled simply *Political Thought*, Zimmern argued that Thucydides, Plato and Aristotle all had something to offer the contemporary world. Specifically, Thucydides offered a novel approach to understanding the political psychology of nations, which was crucial to any attempts to aid a shattered Europe and rebuild international political order from the ground up.

Zimmern's essay appeared in a volume edited by Sir R. W. Livingstone, a noted British Hellenist, called *The Legacy of Greece*. This volume featured essays by Gilbert Murray, Arnold Toynbee and a host of other contemporary luminaries. It intended to demonstrate to a Britain ravaged by war the utility of studying the Greek Classics. There were essays on the value of ancient literature, art and history. In his essay, Zimmern proposed that in order to extract usable knowledge from Thucydides, readers first need to identify what is local and what is universal in his thought. This is no easy task. It required Zimmern to abandon his earlier tendency to simply 'modernize' the Greeks and to instead focus on the differences between antiquity and modernity in order to separate what is timeless from what is local in Greek political thought. The universal that Zimmern identified in Thucydides was a 'realist' view of man as he really was. Thucydides, along with Plato and Aristotle, had taken man as their object and study and each, in their own way, had presented a different aspect of human nature. Thucydides was the great 'political psychologist' who described the differing political motivations of the various states of ancient Greece. The 'psychology' of the Corinthians, Athenians, Spartans and so on did not map exactly on to France, Britain and the US, but the methodology employed by Thucydides in describing the political and social pathologies that affected them was unmatched by any later writer and could provide a model for modern political scientists.

Zimmern was the logical choice to write the essay on Greek political thought because he was trained in the Classics, but by the early 1920s was beginning to make a name for himself in the new discipline of International Relations. During the war, he worked for the government in a number of capacities, including at the Foreign Office. He had also produced political propaganda. As part of his duties in the latter capacity, he had his translation of the funeral speech, which first appeared in *The Greek Commonwealth*, reprinted in pamphlet form to remind British servicemen of the liberal democracy they were fighting for. Zimmern also had *The Greek Commonwealth* reissued in 1914 to emphasize further the parallels between Britain and Athens.[11] However, at this time Zimmern's thoughts turned increasingly to contemporary political problems and in 1919 he published a collection of essays, *Nationality and Government*, in which he considers the relationship between nationalism, industry and a number of other institutions and organizations. His reputation as an eminent supporter of the League of Nations and the British Commonwealth was growing all the time, and he was becoming a prominent liberal public intellectual (Stapleton 2001).

Zimmern's essay is important because it is a very early attempt in the twentieth century to apply Thucydides' methodological thought directly to the modern world. We saw in the last chapter that Cornford had opened up a debate about the nature of Thucydides' political thought itself. Cornford had problematized the views of Shorey and Jebb that Thucydides' language was not up to first-rate political analysis. He had also attempted to understand Thucydides' political thought on its own terms and its relationship to his own reaction to the Boer War. Beyond Cornford, many other historians had characterized Thucydides' political thought by his attitude toward institutions, such as the democracy, or individuals such as Cleon. So, for example, we find that Grote had stoked up a controversy on the validity of Thucydides' view of the democracy and his treatment of Cleon (Stray 1997; Demetriou 1999; Kierstead 2014). Zimmern's essay represents the first attempt to interpret Thucydides' presentation of the political psychology of Greece as a methodology usable by students of modern political problems. For Zimmern, discussing Thucydides' view of democracy or Cleon in isolation was to focus on what was local. Instead, scholars needed to pay attention to the universal in Thucydides, his depiction of human nature and psychology.

In his short preface to the *Legacy of Greece*, Livingstone explains that, in spite of the many differences, no age but the modern has had a closer affinity to the classical Greek world. He is clear that history does not repeat itself, but also that, 'Again and again, as we study Greek thought and literature, behind the veil woven by time and distance, the face that meets us is our own, younger, with fewer lines and wrinkles on its features and with more definite and deliberate purpose in its eyes' (Livingstone 1921). For this reason, modern Britons are in a position to understand the ancient Greeks better than any previous age and also to see reflected in this history an image of their own civilization. This preface acts as a provocation. It challenges the writers of the following essays to think critically about the deep relationship between antiquity and modernity without resorting to a cyclical view of history to explain any parallels.

Murray modifies Livingstone's provocation in his essay, which opens the volume, *The Value of Greece to the Modern World*. Murray draws a distinction between the sciences of geometry, medicine and grammar, invented by Euclid, Hippocrates and Dionysius of Thrace respectively, and the 'genius' of Greek literature. Greek science had lasted over 2,000 years. Euclid, Hippocrates and Dionysius had only stopped being read as textbooks in the nineteenth century. They were undoubtedly works of genius but they were also obsolete. 'But when we read Homer or Aeschylus, if once we have the power to admire and understand their writing, we do not for the most part have any feeling of having got beyond them' (Murray 1921: 5). That is not to say that technical knowledge has not progressed. 'We have done so no doubt in all kinds of minor things, in general knowledge, in details of technique, in civilization and the like; but hardly any sensible person ever imagines that he has got beyond their essential quality, the quality that has made them great' (Murray 1921: 5). Murray, therefore, creates a distinction between technical elements of Greek thought that the Western World has exceeded and the more literary and artistic fields, where it may never be possible to reach the heights achieved by the ancient Greeks. Livingstone and Murray, therefore, laid out in different ways the central problem that the book sought to examine: in what ways might the varied aspects of Greek thought prove useful to post-Great War Britain?

Zimmern adopts a different tack to Livingstone and Murray when discussing the relationship between ancient political thought and modern political problems. He argues that while Greek art, literature and philosophy are among the world's abiding possessions, Greek political thinking is so much bound up with the world of the *polis* 'that its interest might appear to have passed away with the regime to which it owes its existence' (Zimmern 1921: 321). It is not immediately apparent what Thucydides, with his long and detailed account of an inter-tribal or inter-municipal war, or, for that matter Plato with his imaginary utopia or Aristotle with his 'municipal pathology', have to offer the modern world with its problems and conflicts of global proportions. But there is, of course, value in the thought of these three thinkers. The first duty, for Zimmern or anyone who seeks to understand this value, is to acknowledge the limitations of Thucydides, Plato and Aristotle's thought. 'These limitations can be summarized under two main heads. They arise, firstly, from a difference of scale, and secondly, from a difference of outlook, between ancient and modern political thought' (Zimmern 1921: 322).

The issue of scale is simply the difference in magnitude between politics in the ancient and modern worlds. Ancient Greece represented a collection of tiny sovereign states, the largest of which were barely the size of a small English county. This meant that the hierarchy of Greek political orders was correspondingly much smaller. In the modern nation state, there were a series of political orders above and below, which would have been completely alien to the ancient Greek. Take Britain, for an example. Athens was far smaller than Leeds, but to be mayor of the Yorkshire city was hardly to fulfil a position of great political responsibility in the British Empire. Above the mayor lay the county, Parliament and then the Crown. 'To a British Premier passing from a coal strike which reacts upon the trade of the entire world to an Imperial Conference engaged in tracing out an agreed line of policy on the Pacific Question, the problems of a Pericles, or even of an Alexander, would seem but child's play' (Zimmern 1921: 322–3). Indeed, the Greeks had no real conception of 'foreign relations' because they divided the world between themselves and the barbarians. 'No Greek writer ever dreamed of a system of international cooperation between the governments of the world as men then knew it. All of them thought in terms of competition and ever-recurrent warfare or, at best, of a precarious balance of power' (Zimmern 1921: 328). Despite the vast differences in material reality between the ancient and modern worlds, many 'Englishmen' employ 'stray reminiscences' of their classical education. They based confident predictions of the failure of modern democracy or the fate of the British Commonwealth 'on some *obiter dictum* of Thucydides or Plato', which only leads to a 'practical man's suspicion of a classical education' (Zimmern 1921: 325). Instead, Zimmern cautions readers to 'be careful to distinguish the universal from the local and ephemeral' in Greek political thought. 'The latter is indeed of great interest and value; but we shall tend to miss the really precious and permanent elements in their thought if we do not take pains to disentangle Thucydides the disillusioned Athenian patriot from Thucydides the scientific historian and psychologist' (Zimmern 1921: 325). It is imperative, therefore, to uncover Thucydides' broader programmatic, even philosophical, thought.

Zimmern's placing of the onus of separating what is useful and what is not in Thucydides onto the shoulders of his readers represents a unique strategy to justify the Greek historian's utility. Most commentators who point to the utility of Thucydides have told readers what lessons are found in the text through essays, commentaries and translations. So, for example, Thomas Hobbes points his readers to Thucydides' supposed monarchism (Hobbes 1989: 572–3; cf. 2.65.9), or today Graham Allison draws attention to the Thucydides trap (Allison 2017). For Hobbes and Allison, Thucydides offers these lessons for posterity, and it has taken their scholarship to uncover them. Zimmern, instead, suggests that Thucydides' *History* is a layered artefact. The reader, like the archaeologist, must learn how to 'excavate' down through that which is only of local or antiquarian concern through to the 'universal' thought below. Indeed, Zimmern takes seriously Thucydides' implied flattery that only intelligent readers will be able to understand properly the import of his *History*. His essay is an exhortation to post-Great War readers to take this claim seriously to think more critically about what is useful in Thucydides and not to draw simple analogies between the ancient and modern worlds. The carnage wrought by industrial warfare and the conflicts spread to all four corners of the globe had, no doubt, convinced Zimmern that easy parallels between antiquity and modernity were best avoided. Already in July 1917, Zimmern had proposed making 'war a crime in any circumstances' (Markwell 1986: 280).

The second difference between Greek and modern political thought that the reader needs to be aware of is that of outlook. Here Zimmern is referring to the way that political order is perceived. Modern man begins with the individual and then proceeds to the state and society, from 'the inner to the outer' (Zimmern 1921: 329). Ancient thinkers, conversely, thought in the opposite direction, beginning with the interests of the state before those of the individual. This leads Greek writers to fail to distinguish properly between 'Nationality and Government' and 'Conscience and Public duty'; that is to say, they cannot understand that the individual could have thoughts, feelings and desires distinct from those of the polity under which they lived. It was not until Jesus' instruction to '*Render unto Caesar the things which are Caesar's and unto God the things which are God's*' (Zimmern 1921: 330) that this distinction begins to be drawn. 'If this had been said in the presence of Thucydides, the keenest practical brain that applied itself to Greek political thinking, he simply world not have known what it meant. To him Caesar and God, or, to translate them into his own language, Athens and Athena, were not opposing but practically identical terms' (Zimmern 1921: 330). Zimmern is thinking here in a tradition that began in the wake of the French Revolution. Famously, Benjamin Constant (1988) had drawn a sharp distinction between the 'political' liberty of the ancients and the more various individual liberties of the moderns in a famous speech delivered in 1819. Zimmern references the noted nineteenth-century French historian Fustel de Coulange's argument that in fact ancient man had no conception of liberty at all (Zimmern 1921: 330). However, Zimmern is possibly being unfair to Thucydides here. In the funeral speech, which is evidently in the back of his mind while making these arguments, Pericles exhorts his fellow citizens to become lovers of Athens (*erastes*, ἐραστής). But the fact that he has to ask them to do this suggests that perhaps Athenian citizens did not believe that their interests, duties and liberties always coalesced exactly with their neighbours, with Athens and with Athena's. By the end of the *History*, Alcibiades even claims that because his city has turned her back on him then he owes her no loyalty (6.92). He need only serve his own interests. Thucydides does not endorse this view, of course, but it suggests that he was aware of the tensions between the individual, society and the state.

These are the two 'liabilities' that Zimmern identifies in Greek thought. They are hardly original. Scholars had been debating the difference between antiquity and modernity since the late seventeenth century and Zimmern's thoughts on the problem of 'outlook' are too brief and, perhaps, unfair to Thucydides and other Greek thinkers. However, the ground has now been prepared to consider what Zimmern thought of as especially valuable in ancient Greek political thought and Thucydides' greatest gift to the world: an analysis of 'political psychology'.

Thucydides and political psychology

Let us first note why Zimmern believed modern students should take an interest in ancient politics. First, for Zimmern, the Greeks invented politics. They took the problems of the body politic from charlatans and handed them to physicians (Zimmern 1921: 332). Although the Athenians opened up the political decision-making process to all citizens, this meant that many citizens had to learn how to discern the truth from political rhetoric. 'There is many a lesson in common honesty to be learnt by our politicians and public in the speeches of Thucydides' (Zimmern 1921: 336).[12] Second, the Greeks were realists rather than idealists in the sense that they based their notions on the world and human nature as it is. Furthermore, they are realists because they were psychologists who applied psychological methods to political problems.[13] In this respect Thucydides, Plato and Aristotle are sounder than the long line of thinkers who came after them.[14]

Zimmern explains that Thucydides could see the essential oneness of human nature, while accounting for the outlook of the different city-states and also exploring the effect of natural and human forces on events. No modern thinker had yet achieved such a synthesis of politics in the aftermath of the Great War. At the crescendo of the essay, Zimmern invites his readers to imagine Thucydides reborn to face the problems of post-Great War Europe. His first effort would have been to 'explain us to ourselves' (Zimmern 1921: 337) in the sense that he would force moderns to face the hard reality of their situation. He would not allow Europeans to sit idly in disillusionment, wallow in impatience of foreigners, or suspicion of Wilsonian idealism. Instead, he would ruthlessly hold up a depiction of the political psychology of Europe and the origins of the war moods that had led to the Great War. He would show the English their middle and upper classes shaken out of their complacency, faith in the Victorian world order shattered and their working classes brutalized, ignored and even starved by an uncaring free market. He would show a 'nerve racked' France emerging from her five-year nightmare. Her inability to articulate to her neighbours her need to return to life as usual, to the gentler arts and ways of living to become once again the 'Athens' of the modern world. Similarly, he would show the Germans, the Italians, the Belgians and the Americans their own peculiar psychological states unique to their own situations. Underpinning these national psychologies, Thucydides would explain the continuing role of Catholicism, Protestantism and Islam in modern life, the expanding role of socialism, the power of the banks and the moneymen, the place of the universities and institutions of government. In short, Thucydides would show European nation states their individual political psychologies and their relationship to their own histories and the transnational political orders that surrounded them.

> And then, and not till then, having shown us what we are, each of us in his niche and all of us together in our little corner in the vast Temple of mankind, having made us see our pettyisms and orthodoxies against a universal background of time and space, he would have broken silence and allowed himself to speak to us of remedies. Know yourself is the first, perhaps the only, message of the scientific historian to our bewildered age.
>
> Zimmern 1921: 340

We can see in this quotation that Zimmern is imploring his readers not just to read Thucydides but also to view the modern world through his realist eyes – realist here in the sense that Thucydides accurately describes these various political psychologies. This endeavour requires students of politics to account properly for the messy complexity of the world. Zimmern's subject is no longer Britain and her empire alone but all the major players of the Great War. Thucydides is now seen to provide insight into how a multipolar system functions, in which human nature may remain constant but local customs and culture alongside power, resources and esteem creates distinct psychologies among the various nation states of Europe. These different situations created different 'moods' among the Greek powers, which Thucydides helpfully characterizes and highlights for his readers through his use of speeches in the *History*, echoing a similar variety of 'moods' in post-war Europe. It is important to note that Zimmern is not claiming that Thucydides' thought is directly relevant as a source of comparisons. Instead, he is asking modern scholars and political scientists to learn from Thucydides' presentation of the psychology of his individual actors, in other words to learn from his historiographical technique, political methodology and system of thought.[15] This conception of the 'usefulness' of Thucydides represents an interesting take on the methodology statement at 1.22. There Thucydides had claimed that, given the human condition, events would likely recur in the same or a similar manner in the future. Zimmern argues that the social, economic and technological context has shifted, meaning that one cannot simply assume that the events Thucydides describes exactly mirror the contemporary world. Rather, it is the way Thucydides views political psychology, in other words his historical and political methodology, that holds value for contemporary readers.

As has already been discussed at length, the role of collective psychology is fundamental to Thucydides' view of history, a fact that was recognized, debated and hotly contested during the early twentieth century. However, Zimmern offers a much more complicated picture than that of his contemporaries. The debate over political psychology was opened by Cornford, who wrote in the summary of chapter 5 of *Mythistoricus*, provided in the table of contents, that '[t]he only natural causes of human events, considered by ancient historians, are *psychological* – the characters and immediate motives of men or of personified states; whereas moderns look to social and economic conditions, &c., and formulate abstract laws' (1907: xiv; quoted in Jaffe 2017a: 6–7). For Cornford, *ate, eros, peitho* and *phobos* (ἄτη, ἔρος, πείθω, φόβος) could be considered personifications that enveloped a man or *polis* to become psychological states, which in turn became first causes of actions and events. These 'tragic passions', therefore, were different from the psychological states described by modern psychoanalysts and novelists because they represented only a single emotion, rather than a complex interplay of feelings, psychological states and desires.

However, Cornford has raised a fundamental problem in Thucydidean scholarship: can Thucydides' view of psychology be married to an account of the social and economic conditions of the various *poleis*? Cornford answers in the negative. Thucydides' view of psychology is rooted in uniquely Greek ideas of the tragic and is, therefore, incompatible with modern ideas of economics and social change. Zimmern is important precisely because he is the first British commentator to suggest that Thucydides does not offer us a restricted view of human nature and political psychology, defined simply by fear, honour and greed. Rather, he argued that the local circumstance of each *polis* conditioned different political psychologies, just as modern European states reacted differently to the destruction of the Great War because of their individual histories and national mentalities. It took time and the experience of the Great War itself for Zimmern to develop his ideas about the complexity of political psychology in Thucydides.

Zimmern agreed with Cornford that psychological states were integral to causality in Thucydides, but he strongly disagreed that they should be separated from social and economic conditions. Instead, Zimmern probed deeply the relationship between social changes, economic developments and political institutions and the political psychology of the *polis* as presented by Thucydides. In other words, Zimmern's idea of psychology was rooted in his reaction to Thucydides' empirical realism: however, rather than suggesting there are universal psychological states as Cornford had done, he posits that the individual history of each polis shaped its outlook and response to the world. In pursuing this line of thought, Zimmern offered a vision of human nature and psychology in Thucydides that still appears fresh and exciting today. He came to believe after the Great War that Thucydides had successfully probed the link between culture, society, economics and political psychology. This reading is much broader than the 'Thucydidism' proposed by Stefan Meineke (2006), which posits a tradition of thought that stretches from Hobbes to contemporary realists that focused principally on fear, honour and profit as the primary drivers of all Thucydides' actors, perhaps even of all political history. For Zimmern, it is the individual historical trajectories of each *polis* that defines their psychology. In pursuing this line of thought, Zimmern echoes, perhaps even precedes, the interest of contemporary scholars such as Visvardi (2015: 44–93), who has examined 'collective psychology' in Thucydides, and Hunter (1986), who has drawn attention to 'mass psychology'. Most of all, however, Zimmern's conception of political psychology is in sympathy with Lebow's (2003) 'constructivist' Thucydides, an interpretation that emphasizes how Thucydides accounts for local variations in law, custom and outlook and how these variations affect the functioning of political order in the text.

Zimmern's portrayal of Thucydides in this essay is an attempt to understand the differing political psychology of the ancient and modern worlds. A good definition of the concept of political psychology is provided by G. B. Grundy, who we encountered in the previous chapter as the author of *Thucydides and the History of his Age* (1911) and a figure who Zimmern would have known as a colleague and fellow ancient historian in pre-war Oxford. In 1917, Grundy briefly turned away from the Classics to publish an essay titled *Political psychology: A science which has yet to be created*, in which he argued that national behaviour was driven by inherited qualities and peculiarities of human nature particular to individual nation states. In sum, each nation state exhibited a unique psychological make-up. Grundy further argued that politics had failed in the run-up to the Great War because each of the politicians leading individual nations had assumed that other nations possessed similar political psychologies, leading to misconceptions, miscommunications and eventually war. Grundy believed that this failure to understand the true nature of political psychology was rooted in a failure of education. In particular, he levels an accusing glare at Realpolitik, which he saw as a product of an excessive focus on the physical and biological sciences that had led politicians to believe in such false truths as 'Might is Right' or 'the End justifies the Means' (Grundy 1917: 163). What was truly needed to understand political psychology was a return to the humanities, which, through a focus on culture and history, could inculcate students with a sensitivity and sympathy to difference among the European nation states. As Grundy notes at the end of his essay, the search for a usable model of political psychology would, he hoped, diminish the frequency of wars in the future.

> Political psychology is, as has already been said, a science which has yet to be created. When it is established in something like a scientific form, not by the works of doctrinaire philosophers, but by compilation from the experience of those who are acquainted with the souls of their own and of other nations, there will be a good hope that those wars – and they are many – which are due to national and international ignorance may not in the future play the part which they have played in past history.
>
> Grundy 1917: 170

Zimmern, in his essay, argues that in fact political psychology is a discipline that has already been created by Thucydides. It is simply the case that modern scholars have forgotten. For Zimmern, Thucydidean psychology is bigger than the individual. It describes the mind of the nation, and compares that with the minds of other nations. Thucydides is then what we might term a political psychologist in that he is describing the comparative psychological pathologies of whole nations and societies. It is, therefore, unsurprising to note that Zimmern's first monograph on International Relations, *Europe in Convalescence*, published in 1922, was an attempt to understand the contemporary political outlook through a comparative study of the culture, society and political psychology of the European nations. In 'turning' to Thucydides as a political psychologist, Zimmern was, in part at least, searching for a methodology and intellectual genealogy for his new discipline of International Relations. In pursuing this goal, Zimmern's vision of Thucydides' political outlook appears markedly different from the views common in scholarship today. For example, the vast majority of realist scholars today define the national interest solely in terms of power. When examining human motivation in Thucydides, they point to the central position of fear, honour and profit in the pursuit of that power. The genius of Thucydides, in this view, is that he stripped away all culture and moral pretence to reveal the essential truth about the human quest for power and advantage (Crane 1998; de Ste. Croix 1972; Kagan 1969; Meiggs 1972). Straussian scholars, on the other hand, have drawn attention to the tension between justice, interest and necessity in Thucydides, thereby opening a door to the inclusion of moral concerns in discussions of power politics (Orwin 1994; Jaffe 2017a). Paul Rahe (1995) represents, perhaps, a similar reading to Zimmern's post-Great War Thucydides because of his acknowledgement that the Greek historian is both a hard-nosed analyst of power politics and, at the same time, a critic of an amoral vision of politics. For Rahe, Thucydides demonstrates how Athens becomes distracted from her true interests by desire (*eros*) over the course of the war. As desire grows among the people, fomented by Cleon and Alcibiades, they abandon faith in foresight and reasoned argument to give themselves over to ever-wilder schemes in pursuit of power and profit, leading eventually to the Sicilian expedition and the destruction of the Athenian fleet. In Rahe's vision of Thucydides, we can recognize an attempt to reproduce the 'political psychology' of Athens and its role in her foreign policy decisions. Rahe's model suggests that states begin as rational actors until certain blinding passions take hold. For Zimmern, each *polis*/state possesses a unique political psychology conditioned by history, culture and power and it is the genius of Thucydides to explain how these different psychologies interact and collide. In making these arguments, Zimmern's views are perhaps closest to those proffered by Fisher and Hoekstra, who explain how the theme of national character is woven throughout the entire work and 'influenced how their members interpreted and pursued their interests' (2017: 378).

A final point needs to be emphasized. The value Zimmern finds in Thucydidean (and Platonic) political psychology lies in its value as a tool to help modern students of politics create the most 'Utopian' international order possible, with an emphasis on the word 'possible'. Zimmern makes this point explicit in the final paragraph of the essay (1921: 352). Here we come closest to the realist characterization of Zimmern as an idealist. However, we must be careful. Zimmern believed that while readers of the ancient classics should aim to 'amend' the world around them, their first duty is to learn from Thucydides and Plato to look at man as he really is by eschewing falsehoods and to follow that truth in 'thought and actions' (Zimmern 1921: 352). Revolutions begin from the inner self and proceed outwards.

> It is often when the external world seems most sick and sorrowful, when selfishness and irresponsibility sit enthroned in the world's seats of government, that the power of truth is most active in the silent region of the soul, strengthening it in order that it may issue forth once again to impress man's unconquerable purpose of order, justice and freedom upon the recalcitrant material which forms the stuff of men's common problems on this small globe of ours.
>
> Zimmern 1921: 352

Zimmern reminds us that the distance between realism, political psychology and idealism is not far. Thucydides needed to be a hard-nosed realist to understand human psychology. It is an endeavour that is essential for modern readers in their quest to improve international politics in an anarchic and amoral world.

Thucydides: Man and scholar

Thus far, in this chapter, I have followed the evolution of Thucydides as a realist and political psychologist in Zimmern's thought. I will conclude with an examination of Zimmern's presentation of Thucydides as an intellectual and 'public' scholar.[16] Here, as with Zimmern's view of political psychology, a clear development can be discerned. I argued above that before the war, Zimmern did not warm to Thucydides. He found that the *History* lacked a concern for humanity or morality. After the war, however, Zimmern began to see Thucydides as a great 'public scholar' who, far from retreating to an ivory tower, had revealed the complexity of the world through the scientific and realist observation of man as he really was. In his capacity as a scholar of International Relations, Zimmern began to draw attention to the way Thucydides had used his literary and historical realism as the basis to paint a rich psychological portrait of the Greek world that was useful to policy-makers and students of politics. In his 1929 essay on *The Scholar in Public Affairs*, Zimmern holds the contemporary American historian and delegate to the Versailles peace conference George Louis Beer as the ideal scholar in public affairs. Thucydides features prominently in the essay as the first scholar of international affairs and a worthy comparison to Beer. Zimmern notes that for much of Western history, humanities scholars had retreated from the world. Plato and Aristotle forsook practical politics to retreat to the Academy, and medieval scholars sequestered themselves in the ivory towers of the great universities. In the post-war world, however, the humanities could no longer retreat from the world. 'Literature, philosophy, history, economics, and, above all, politics cannot be studied sincerely and truthfully from behind the Common Room curtain or in a secure and padded little world whither the heartbeat of reality can rarely penetrate' (Zimmern 1929: 3–4). The danger, of course, is that as the humanities become increasingly engaged in the world their independence will be compromised by the need for money and funding. However, Beer is the greatest example of a scholar in public affairs because he managed to be both a man of the world and free from the temptation to subordinate the truth to propaganda and the interests of business and government.[17]

Thucydides emerges in the 1929 essay as an ancient counterpart to Beer. Zimmern uses him to emphasize the achievements of the latter. In the essay, he argues that there is an absolute distinction between scholars of policy and policy practitioners and that Thucydides, despite his role as an Athenian general, remained firmly in the former camp. 'When Thucydides commanded at Amphipolis he was the Thucydides, the same observant, reflective and disinterested mind, that later wrote the history, including the record of his own misadventure' (Zimmern 1929: 6). For Zimmern, the fundamental distinction between a statesman and a scholar rested on the assertion that the former is focused on the 'background' to public affairs while the latter focuses on the 'foreground'. Thucydides, therefore, focuses on the background to Greek affairs. He, 'alone' among the Greeks of his generation, came to his work with a scientific understanding of the 'early history' of his country 'so that, perhaps for the first time in the history of the human mind, he could place the events through which he was living in the setting of time and space' (Zimmern 1929: 7). The scholar, of course, is always tempted to recommend such and such a policy or course of action, but this desire is always of secondary importance because the scholar is in the best position to grasp how little the actions of statesmen could arrest the march of the impersonal forces on events.

Zimmern further argues that it is better for the scholar of international politics to be trained in history than philosophy because the 'scholar in public affairs is a Realist; he has his feet on the rock of fact, of world facts' (Zimmern 1929: 8). Philosophers set up their utopias 'in an uncharted wilderness that will never be marked on the plain man's map' (Zimmern 1929: 9). Historians, conversely, must start with the familiar landmarks of affairs: Europe and America, capitalism and socialism, nationalism and internationalism. In short, the historian has to understand the interplay of various political orders, as they exist in the world. This distinction is perhaps a recollection of Nietzsche's claim that Thucydides is a cure to Plato's idealism, noted in Chapter 1. From this foundation, the scholar of International Relations can then proceed from local realities to universal observations. Thucydides, for Zimmern, is the first scholar to achieve this feat:

> Thucydides, the first and greatest scholar in public affairs, and the master of realists, began indeed as a historian but he ended as a psychologist. He began with his contemporaries, but he far outran them. And the same, in a lesser degree, will always hold good of all true scholars who adventure into public affairs resolved to continue learning and thinking and not to prostitute their equipment to purely ephemeral ends.
>
> Zimmern 1929: 9

Here we see Zimmern cast Thucydides the thinker, the intellectual, as the 'first' scholar in international affairs combined with a claim that his methodology developed from that of a historian to that of a psychologist. Thucydides is clearly an important intellectual forebear for Zimmern's new discipline, but there is a recognition here that he is an ambiguous figure who is hard to pin down. Thucydides the political psychologist suggests that human nature is knowable and may conform to predictable, or at least understandable, patterns. In the paragraph following this quotation, Zimmern explains that the mistake of the idealists is to suppose that the study of human nature is performed in a vacuum, set apart from time and circumstance (Zimmern 1929: 9–10). In fact, one must begin with the minute studies of the historian or the modern social scientist to understand the social and material society of man. Only after the facts of life have been ascertained can a true understanding of human nature be attempted, just as Thucydides had begun with history before moving on to human nature.

Out of a thorough knowledge of local reality, a more universalizing account of the human experience, approaching philosophy, can be attempted. Thucydides is the first thinker to recognize both the local reality of history and its potential universal applications.

Conclusion: A new Thucydidean paradigm?

It is to be regretted that Zimmern's post-war vision of Thucydides as a political psychologist has been largely lost to scholarship. It is not mentioned by Low (2007), who treats Zimmern as a liminal figure between Classics and International Relations and as a dyed-in-the-wool idealist. Nor is Zimmern's vision of political psychology mentioned by political scientists interested in Thucydides' view of psychology, such as Orwin (1994), Crane (1998) or Jaffe (2017a). Classicists and political scientists are not alone in their neglect of Zimmern's paper. While *Greek Political Thought* is cited by Morefield (2005: 75), it is passed over by many other intellectual historians interested in Zimmern's work (for example Markwell 1998; Osiander 1998; Sluga 2006; Baji 2016). The reasons for this neglect are not hard to find. Zimmern is a forgotten figure in Classics and a figure of only marginal importance in current debates in the history of Political Science and International Relations. A paper written in an obscure collected volume of essays, written primarily to justify the role of the Greek Classics in the post-Great War world, is unlikely to be hit upon in searches of library catalogues or, indeed, elicit much excitement. If Zimmern's reception of Thucydides has had an impact on later thought, it has been through his translation of the funeral speech, which formed a self-contained chapter in *The Greek Commonwealth*. This translation proved important after the Great War as a source of quotations for war memorials (Morley 2018b). Elizabeth Sawyer has further explained that in 1943 R. W. Livingstone produced a translation of Thucydides substantially based on the Crawley edition but which used Zimmern's translation of the funeral speech (2013: 129–33). Livingstone's edition became popular in America where it was read by Louis J. Halle in the 1950s, Kenneth Waltz in the 1960s and even continues to be cited in Congress today.

The lack of scholarly engagement with Zimmern's idea of Thucydides as a political psychologist is, I believe, a missed opportunity because he reminds us that Thucydides' psychological programme goes far beyond the study of fear, honour and self-interest. One could argue that there has been an excessive focus on the study of fear, in particular, in the text since the Second World War. De

Romilly (1956) and Luginbill (1999) both recognize it as one of the cardinal passions for Thucydides. So too do Desmond (2006) and Peterson and Liaris (2007), writing from an International Relations perspective. Most prominently, of course, Thucydides' presentation of fear is a key feature of Allison's presentation of the Thucydides trap. There is a tendency to reduce all motivations, all politics even, in Thucydides to the role of fear in causing actions and events. And yet Zimmern reminds us in his 1921 paper that even if the Spartans were motivated by fear to start the Peloponnesian War, other psychological states were at play in Athens, Corinth, Argos and a host of other significant states. It is only through a holistic view of every actor's psychological state that the scholar can begin to comprehend the multifaceted and complicated role of mentality in interstate politics. Zimmern's turn serves as a reminder that we must always be open to the complexity of Thucydides' thought.

4

Thucydides, Realism and the Great War

Walter Lamb, who I first introduced in Chapter 2 attacking the views of Cornford, opens his review of G. F. Abbott's 1925 monograph, *Thucydides: A Study in Historical Reality*, in the following way:

> Mr. Abbott's avowed purpose in producing this essay on Thucydides is to interest and, perhaps, instruct the student of modern politics by providing a clear and lively survey of that ancient master's account of a great war. If we wish him every success in his endeavour, we do so with no abounding confidence, though Prime Ministers do occasionally show us that they are able to keep a respectful and intelligent eye on the glories of Hellenic culture.
>
> Lamb 1926: 199

George Frederick Abbott's (1874–1947) monograph marks a significant milestone in the Thucydidean turn. As Lamb notes, Abbott's was the first monograph-length attempt in English to explain Thucydides to students and practitioners of politics. In other words, Abbott was the first to attempt to emphasize the contemporary relevance of the text, and its accompanying scholarship, to a non-classical audience. As Lamb argues, this endeavour is ambitious not because of politicians' general ignorance of classical Greece, but because of the difficulties inherent in justifying the relevance of a 2,500-year-old text to the contemporary political moment. Accordingly, Abbott positions his Thucydides not as a historical product of the glorious age of Hellenic culture but rather as a political analyst for all times, whose realistic and scientific discussion of events still had much to offer. 'In reading [Thucydides'] book,' Abbott writes, 'one feels that one is reading a book written by a man of the world for men of the world' (1925: 63).

To achieve this aim, Abbott presents Thucydides as a scientist and a realist. The former term need not surprise us. We have already seen how Cornford's powerful challenge to the long-held belief that Thucydides was purely a sober and factual historian led many scholars to reaffirm the contrary opinion that the

Athenian historian, in fact, possessed a scientific attitude to history and politics (Pires 2006). Cochrane's (1929) monograph is the quintessential example. Abbott, by contrast, offers no real insight into the scientific nature of Thucydides' thought, using it primarily as a ploy to justify the Athenian historian's contemporary utility to the student or practitioner of politics. Abbott simply took Thucydides' accuracy and even-handedness in good faith.[1] Of much more interest, for our purposes, is Abbott's claim that Thucydides is a realist. Abbott, as we will see, represents a liminal figure between empirical, psychological and theoretical forms of Thucydidean realism. In the introduction, I noted that Morley (2018a) has compellingly argued that there are three iterations of realism in the reception of Thucydides.[2] First, empirical 'realism' denotes Thucydides' cold hard recording of facts. Second, there is realism as a sensibility. This iteration is similar to the realism that Zimmern found in Thucydides. It refers to his unflinching depiction of human nature and psychology. The third iteration is a theoretical or doctrinal realism that proposes useful lessons derived from Thucydides' portrayal of the past.[3] This realism is familiar today among International Relations critiques of the *History*. It is during the Great War and its immediate aftermath that theoretical or doctrinal realism first emerges in British readings of Thucydides. Abbott's Thucydides is both an empirical realist, offering a clear-eyed depiction of human nature, and a doctrinal realist who presents a theory of greed and honour as the primary drivers of political events. For Abbott, Thucydides presents human nature as essentially the same in the ancient and modern worlds and history as moving in a linear pattern. What has happened in the past, he believed, is likely to happen again in the future (1.22). According to Abbott, this vision of politics excluded moral concerns, although Abbott allows that Thucydides himself was a man deeply concerned with the morality of actions.

Abbott's position in the history of Thucydidean reception is complicated. He can hardly be said to have 'started' realist readings of the text, which continue to be hegemonic in the field of International Relations today.[4] His work was little read after the Second World War, when Morgenthau, Waltz and others were reshaping the field and its approach to Thucydides. Nor can his work be said to mirror the presentation of Thucydides contained in current International Relations scholarship. Abbott is at pains to link Thucydides' status as a political historian and thinker as much to his literary art as to his unflinching portrayal of human nature. In addition, where modern neo-realism focuses on the anarchical nature of international politics, Abbott draws more attention to the relationship between human nature and the pursuit of power. Abbott's monograph is, in my interpretation, best understood as an important intervention into the post-Great War debate over Thucydides' *History*. His Thucydides is born of a growing desire to find new uses for the text and to explain politics to a generation traumatized by the Great War. Abbott's great innovation is to take Thucydides and to simplify him considerably. He does not emphasize the complexity of the 'tragic' political psychology advanced by Cornford, nor does he explore the number of different psychologies identified by Zimmern. Instead, he claims that Thucydides' view of humanity is simply recoverable from the speeches, which can then be used by intelligent students of modern politics to help them make sense of the world. His simplification represents a rhetorical gambit used to justify the relevance of Thucydides. At stake in this reading of the *History* is a trade-off between recognizing the complexity of the text and identifying the utility of Thucydides' thoughts for modern readers more concerned with modern, than ancient, politics.

Abbott's reading, although published in 1925, is evidently a product of shifting attitudes to Thucydides occasioned, or rather catalysed, by the Great War. The war had a profound effect on how critics read Thucydides, and I shall argue in the next section of this chapter that many came to embrace his empirical realism as key to his political vision. One hundred years earlier, in the aftermath of the French Revolution, scholars like Volney had argued that ancient historians, such as Thucydides, had little to teach the modern world because they described only wars and violent republic upheavals, not the kind of thought suitable to modern liberal nation states (see, for example, Volney 1800: 174–5). Throughout much of the remainder of the nineteenth century, Thucydides had been primarily considered as a scientific historian, the founder of a rigorous historiographical project that focused on criticism of the sources and the establishment of the truth. As Hans Muhlack (2011) reminds us, this view of Thucydides was rooted in a German reaction to the French Revolution that emphasized the distinction between historical periods. This movement was a political project that aimed to sequester modernity from the violence of the past (Süßmann 2012). When nineteenth-century British scholars did consider Thucydides' realism, they tended to dismiss it as unsuitable for the golden age of Greece. As early as 1874, J. P. Mahaffy, who held a chair in ancient history at Trinity College Dublin, had censured Thucydides' *History* for being clear, hard and unpleasing. Thucydides presents the Greeks of Pericles' day as 'possessing a great political insight' – greater, indeed, than their forefathers. However, this insight was based more upon the use of naked power that the cultural and intellectual supremacy for which Athens would later become renowned. Mahaffy writes in his treatment of

Thucydides that 'the notion of an empire of intellect and taste, without political supremacy had not yet even dawned upon the Athenians of the older generation. Consequently politics corroded the social life, as well as the literature, of Periclean Greece' (1874: 163). Murray offers a different criticism of Thucydides in his 1897 work, *A History of Greek Literature*, where he argued that Thucydides was in fact a Periclean (1897: 200–1), but he also claims that '[o]ne would not be surprised, however, to learn that Thucydides's speculative ethics found a difficulty in the conception of a strictly "unselfish" action' (Murray 1897: 199). Before the Great War, Alfred Zimmern (1911), as I argued in the previous chapter, wondered whether Thucydides was even aware of the moral implications of the Periclean Empire. The Great War inaugurated a change in British attitudes to Thucydides. Faced with the horrors of trench warfare and the shock of losing the Victorian global order, readers and commentators became more receptive to interpretations that stressed Thucydides' hard-boiled political realism. Perhaps, Abbott invites his readers to wonder, are we so different from Thucydides' Greeks?

One consequence of Abbott's realist portrayal of Thucydides is to focus on the value of the Peloponnesian War as a historical analogy to a world torn apart by the Great War. I argued in the second chapter that Cornford was reluctant to draw such parallels in *Mythistoricus*, but in Chapter 3 that Zimmern's experience of the Boer Wars and particularly the Great War led him to seek the methodology of political psychology in the *History* and apply it to the contemporary world. Abbott's use of Thucydides is different to the extent that he focuses on what he believes the Greek historian thought about democracy, empire and the causes of war in general. Methodology is important, but so too are Thucydides' reconstructed political views: Abbott draws attention to his antipathy to democracy (1925: 137,147; cf. Ober 1998), antipathy for the Athenian Empire (1925: 141–2; cf. Taylor 2010; Foster 2010) and concern about the balance of power (1925: 4). Here, Abbott again emerges as a liminal figure in the reception of Thucydides. Until the nineteenth century, it was common for British historians such as William Mitford to treat Thucydides as an anti-democratic authority. This tendency was tempered to a certain extent by George Grote and John Stuart Mill (Potter 2012), but re-emerges in the post-Second World War world period, when scholars adopt an increasingly sceptical position over the ability of democracy to provide the requisite level of competency and constancy in the leadership of an interstate hegemony and the pursuit of a great war (for example, Fliess 1959: 618; Halle 1955; Kagan 1969, 1974, 1981, 1987; Mara 2008; cf. Jaffe 2017b). Abbott's scholarship on Thucydides represents a bridge between nineteenth-century British and later twentieth-century International Relations critiques of democracy in Thucydides.

Abbott, Thucydides and the Great War

Before I consider Abbott's arguments in more detail, I would first like to draw attention to the ways in which the Great War had a significant effect on the reception of Thucydides in Britain. My analysis will emphasize how the experience of war, both at home and abroad, invited a diverse group of readers to draw direct parallels between ancient and modern conflicts. Many copies of the *History* found their way into the trenches on both sides of the conflict. The horrors of the war, the size and complexity of its battles, and the feeling that it marked a turning point in world history led various readers to turn with fresh eyes to Thucydides and to draw new parallels between the ancient and the modern world. W. A. Thorpe, a British man of letters who worked at the Victoria and Albert Museum, noted in his essay *Thucydides and the Discipline of Detachment*, which began life as a review of *Historical Reality*,[5] that Abbott's book was the 'fruit' of this Great War turn to Thucydides (1926: 630–1). Abbott himself notes that the war had led to a new appreciation of the Athenian historian. Speaking of the famous funeral speech, for example, he recalls that Pericles intended to depict Athens as men liked to see her and to glorify the men who had laid down their lives for the city. 'Both aspects of the speech were utilized in England at the beginning of the Great War. The first inspired our public speakers and writers to imitation almost amounting to plagiarism; the second was reproduced in a leaflet and sent to our soldiers and sailors' (Abbott 1925: 189). Abbott then explains that one soldier who read the speech in the trenches at Gallipoli referred to it as 'the supreme tribute' to fallen comrades. That soldier was Orlo Williams (1883–1967), a junior officer in the British army, who had had his first experience of combat at Gallipoli in 1915. Before the war, he had been educated in the Classics and would later become clerk of the House of Commons, but he was in no way a professional scholar. Nevertheless, he was a bookish fellow and after the war remembered vividly his experience of reading Thucydides while in the trenches in the Dardanelles. Williams writes of experiencing Thucydides while sheltering from the maelstrom of battle in his dugout:

> In this spirit I made again the acquaintance of Thucydides, who kept me going many weeks of the Dardanelles campaign, amazed at the modernity of his

outlook and the extraordinary political insight reflected in his set speeches. Again and again an exclamation was forced to one's lips by an expression particularly apt to the conditions of 1915. That wonderful chapter of condensed acumen, for instance, in which he shows that the general political feature of States determined their sympathies in the direction of Athens or Sparta, as the case might be, could have been applied with hardly a word changed to the factors which determined the sympathies of nations in 1915 toward the Allies or the Central Powers. It was impossible not to leave Thucydides with the conviction that he is unsurpassed among political historians, and that, in particular, the funeral oration of Pericles is the supreme tribute to the fallen soldiers of a free State for all time, leaving nothing to be said, no emotion unexplored, and no grace of expression to be added. The peculiar applicability to our own expedition of the account of the Athenian expedition against Syracuse was happily hidden from me till later.

Williams 1919: 469

This quotation is from an essay published in 1919 in the *New Statesman*. In the essay, Williams remembers the various books he read while on campaign with the British army in the eastern Mediterranean to relieve the tedium of long campaigns. Perhaps it was the geographical location which first recommended Thucydides to Williams. It was in the northern Aegean that Thucydides himself fought in the Peloponnesian War before his Spartan opponent Brasidas defeated him (4.104–6). Gallipoli was also close to the Thracian mines that Thucydides inherited from his family and, surely, was one of the locations he retreated to during his ignominious exile from Athens (Burns 2010). The quotation, moreover, points to a number of key themes that will come up again in both British readings of Thucydides generally and in Abbott's monograph specifically. First, one can see how easily Williams found it to draw a direct analogy between ancient and modern politics as presented by Thucydides. Just as the Greek states had lined up behind Athens and Sparta in 431 BC, so too were European states falling in behind Britain/France and Germany in 1914. I will argue later in this chapter that Abbott too draws the same equivalence repeatedly. He looks to understand power politics through a Thucydidean vision that poses modern European states as equivalent to ancient city-states such as Athens, Sparta and Melos.[6] Second, in this period, Thucydides himself is held up with increasing frequency as a profound political commentator. As Williams explains, it is not just that there is congruence between ancient and modern events, but the 'modernity' of Thucydides' outlook and his 'extraordinary political insight' provide material that helps readers to understand the traumatic events that are unfolding around them. Third, there is the personal element in Williams' 'acquaintance' with Thucydides. The geographical situation that he found himself in, as well as his direct experience of combat, lead him to Thucydides' thought. This experience was far from unique in the years between 1914 and 1918. Soldiers on the front, as well as civilians at home, felt drawn to Thucydides by their personal experiences of the war.

Many readers of Thucydides felt that there was a very specific parallel between the Peloponnesian War and the Great War. Both wars were of such magnitude, such violence and had such a profound effect on politics and thought that they were believed to be alike. For example, in his 1918 lecture on *Aristophanes and the War Party* (published in 1919), Gilbert Murray argues that the Peloponnesian War was a 'world war' as far as the Greeks were concerned because it touched their entire world, and that the division of political parties within each *polis* reflected the division of parties in modern Britain and Germany (Murray 1920; cf. Th. 1.1).[7] The Peloponnesian War, of course, was not unique in this regard. Other writers in the trenches turned to Homer and the Trojan War (Vandiver 2010), or the Latin poets that many knew so well from school, others to the conflicts that defined the relationship between England and France in the middle ages (cf. Machen 1915). Yet Thucydides certainly occupied a small but significant niche among readers. The Scottish writer Compton MacKenzie recalled reading Thucydides, alongside Virgil, at Gallipoli (Vandiver 2010: 62),[8] and Winston Churchill was given two editions of the *History*, one from Lloyd George, when he exiled himself to the Western Front after the failure of the Dardanelles campaign (Schelske 2015: 85–6). In the archives of Trinity College, Cambridge, there is also a series of letters between a certain G. K. M. Butler (a soldier on the front) and H. M. Butler (his father and a noted Cambridge academic) expressing thanks from the former to the latter for sending a copy of Thucydides and a copy of the fellowship examination questions on Thucydides (MS. JRMB 5/1/45, 5/1/52, 5/10/110). Enoch Powell even recalled hearing of a letter from Butler to his son comparing 'Prussian' aggression towards Belgium with Athens' subjugation of Melos (Churchill: 1/6/19: 9). Morley has recently demonstrated the variety of responses to Thucydides during the war itself. The *History* was mined for parallels to the current conflict (Morley 2018b: 415–17), Thucydidean quotations were used in Britain as propaganda, and quotations from the Funeral Speech found their way onto London omnibuses and war memorials across the empire (Morley 2018b: 426–8; cf. Londey 2007). The effect of such uses of Thucydides were, no doubt, to spread his thought further and wider among the general public than ever before. A common theme running through many of these wartime engagements with the *History* is the experience of the contemporaneity of Thucydides.

The feeling that Thucydides was relevant during the Great War was not limited to soldiers at the front. Academics such as William Hutton at Toronto and T. R. Glover at St John's College, Cambridge, published works on Thucydides[9] that specifically drew parallels between the Peloponnesian War and the Great War (Hutton 1916: 241–2; Glover 1917).[10] Perhaps the closest approximation to Abbott's presentation of Thucydides as an empirical realist is Glover's analysis of Thucydides, produced at the very height of the war. Terrot Reaveley Glover (1869–1943) was a lecturer in classical literature at the University of Cambridge and a fellow of St John's College. He was a well-known Latinist who became the University Public Orator in 1920, a position that entailed giving orations in that ancient language. Outside of academia, Glover was most famous as a Baptist preacher who gave sermons across the country. He was noted for his traditionalist views of hymns (Aubrey 1953). It was as a Baptist that Glover was best known among the British public. He spent the early part of the war in Cambridge, giving lectures on Greek history to a much-reduced undergraduate audience of nine women and ten men.[11] As the war ground on, however, he appears to have felt conflicted over his liberal and Christian views. He began to ask himself could one still love one's enemy during a total war. Glover was certainly no pacifist but he also took measures to protect conscientious objectors. On the political issues, he sided with Sir Edward Grey, the Foreign Secretary, in so far as he believed that Britain was honour bound to protect her allies. In 1915, Glover partially removed himself from such tensions when he went to India to take up a commission with the YMCA for a year. Before he departed for India, however, he submitted to the publisher Methuen the manuscript for a history of Greece titled *From Pericles to Philip*, which was eventually published in 1917. The book was something of a commercial success and was reprinted in 1918, 1920 and 1926. This work represented Glover's first real foray into Hellenic studies. He takes as his subject the changing nature of the polis *and* its effect on the Greek interstate system. The book is not a narrative history but effectively a study of the change in political order in ancient Greece from the Peloponnesian War to the rise of Philip of Macedon. Ultimately, this can be summarized by the tension between Isocrates' favoured view of political organization of the Greeks, a grand *koine* of all the *poleis* led by a monarch, and Demosthenes, who argued for the continual independence of the city-states. As Glover worked through the manuscript in 1917 he was again struck by the similarity of the experience of the Greeks during the Peloponnesian War in the early fourth century BC and that of his own age (1917: ix).[12]

In Glover's work, Thucydides is presented as first and foremost an upper-class Athenian: 'That his youth and education were essentially Athenian is plain to read on every page of his work. All the main impulses and interests of Athens are there – rhetoric, tragedy, philosophy, empire, autonomy, and political theory. He owes his education to sophists, poets, philosophers, soldiers, and statesmen – to Athens' (Glover 1917: 62). Glover (1917: 63) imagines that Thucydides' personal views were rooted in this aristocratic milieu and that he was a supporter of moderate democracy, peace and a *modus vivendi* with Sparta. He even went so far as to imagine that when Thucydides was elected general it was on Nicias' ticket (1917: 73). Glover further claims that exile must have changed Thucydides in many ways. It allowed him to gain access to non-Athenian accounts and to differing points of view. More significantly, it allowed him to wander from place to place, 'penetrating' deeper into the realities of life. Exile allowed Thucydides to get 'outside the parish, outside the island, beyond the conventions, the traditions, and the common values, as year after year he sees the cities of many men and learns their mind. Solitude drives him into reflection, and intensifies a native severity of thought. He comes back to Athens a stranger, a man forgotten, to a changed city' (Glover 1917: 69). It is the experience of exile, therefore, that gives Thucydides the true opportunity to develop his realism. This realism is then put to good use to probe the moral tensions at the heart of Athenian society and empire. Speaking of the funeral speech, Glover notes that Thucydides' own character allows him to combine clearness of insight and self-restraint 'almost unexampled in literature' to analyse the 'national mind' of Athens (Glover 1917: 81). Nothing escapes Thucydides, all is recorded with 'relentless precision', leading many readers to remark on his coldness and detachment, to remark upon his clear, keen intellect unclouded by 'likes and dislikes', by 'feelings or sympathies'. 'They are wrong. Thucydides is greater than they think' (Glover 1917: 81). Thucydides' empirical realism, expressed by his factual accuracy and strict adherence to a historiographical programme, therefore, allows him to suggest, but not preach, political doctrines.

Glover's effort to understand the relationship between Thucydides' empirical realism and his moral and political outlook appears to have roused feelings of sympathy in the readers of *From Pericles to Philip*. In 1918, Lady Courtney wrote to Glover explaining that it was the last book she and her husband, a famous Liberal politician opposed to militarism and imperialism, read together before he died (Wood 2015: 115–16). There is also a letter, preserved in the archives at St John's, from a certain J. D. Maynard of Birmingham, one of Glover's Baptist acquaintances (Glover 5/5/15), who explains that he has stopped reading the newspapers because he has found in Glover's book and in Thucydides a better way to understand the war and politics in 1918.

> Dear Glover,
>
> I went to tell you of my appreciation of 'Pericles to Philip'. The evidence is that I first got it from a library but soon took back the library copy and I bought it for myself. I had been reading Thucydides (Jowett's translation), and was struck by the fact that in essentials it was the history of this war. Also by what you notice, viz. the absence of any ethical notions from the speeches of the politicians.
>
> How close is the parallel between the position at Sphacteria and that at the end of 1916 – when the enemy would have made peace, but we insisted on the knock out blow! Will the ultimate result be the same?
>
> Me finds our statesmen too – is not Lloyd George Cleon? And Thucydides describing Cleon, like, say, Landsdowne describing Lloyd George? I remember hearing you on Herodotus and Euripides long ago. But in the war chapters you are, like Thucydides, writing of the present war. Last autumn I was reading daily and weekly papers a good deal, but since I have taken to Thucydides, and you, I have found the need otherwise supplied, in a way very helpful to thinking.
>
> We extreme pacifists are a new feature (I mean those of actual conviction – not with spirits afraid, if there are such) to which I suppose Greece offers no parallel. I think it will have to be our part to formulate a 'theology of history' – like Jeremiah – on which a new and humble Europe may form up.
>
> Yours in common
> J. D. Maynard

This is a remarkable letter. One can well imagine that Maynard is not a university-educated man from his English (e.g. 'Me finds . . .'). However, through Glover he discovers Thucydides, and like Glover, Maynard is immediately struck by the comparison between the ancient and modern wars and the lack of morality in Thucydides' speeches, at least those offered by Cleon. However, Maynard goes further, feeling the urge to draw close parallels between particular episodes in Thucydides and the modern war. Britain, like Athens, refused to make peace when the political situation was favourable. Moreover, both states are led by statesmen devoid of morality who harangue for war. Indeed, Maynard even claims that he has given up reading the daily papers to rely instead upon Thucydides and Glover. In other words, he is imagining that history is repeating itself and that he need only consult the past to understand the present. Although this particular line may just be a way to praise Glover's writings, it certainly demonstrates a willingness to consider the contemporary relevance of

Thucydides and Greek history. Maynard, furthermore, believes that there is a limit to the value of the Greek example. As an 'extreme pacifist', he believes the Bible is the only text on which a new European political order can be erected. In sum, in this unique letter, we have the very rare example of a non-academic reading of Thucydides. It is inspired by Glover's reading of Greek history, but it also represents a serious effort to experience the contemporaneity of the Peloponnesian War and the Great War. Yet, in Maynard's estimation, Thucydides has nothing to offer the post-war world. The lack of morality in the text means that the *History* is insufficient to help form a new 'theology of history', by which he presumably meant a refashioning of the European political order through the light of Christ.

Thucydides and historical realism

Let us now return to the *Study*. Although a product of the Great War, Abbott intended his reading of Thucydides to push past that of Williams and Glover outlined above. He intended not only to draw parallels between the two conflicts but also to offer a reading of the text that could help educate modern students of politics. In other words, he wished to explore what role Thucydides' thought, methodology and opinions might be able to play in the post-war reorganization of European politics. Abbott, for his part, was no professional Thucydides scholar. He possessed no advanced training in either classical philology or ancient history. His Greek, both ancient and modern, was, no doubt, excellent, but there is little evidence that he had been trained in advanced textual exegesis. He graduated with an undergraduate degree from Emmanuel College, Cambridge, in 1899. The university then offered him money to head to Macedonia and Greece to collect anthropological information about the present inhabitants of south-west Europe, where he made extra money as a foreign correspondent for various newspapers. Abbott later became a war correspondent covering the Balkan Wars. He published a number of other books, all of which dealt with the contemporary society and politics of Greece, Macedonia and Turkey (see, for example, Abbott 1900, 1909, 1912, 1916, 1917, 1922). It was not, however, his experience of modern Greece that led him to Thucydides, nor his university education. Rather, he admits in the preface to *Historical Reality* that it was during the Great War that he 'renewed his acquaintance' with the Greek historian.[13] As he did so, a dawning realization led him to appreciate the 'applicability' of the *History*'s contents to current circumstances: 'yesterday and to-day appeared to meet in his pages and illumine each other' (Abbott 1925: v). In other words, Abbott thought of his own turn to Thucydides as a moment of sudden illumination when the ancient world helps one to understand better the modern world and the modern the ancient. In Abbott's own words, 'The thought then came that a clear and concise presentation of a writer who deals in so masterly fashion with foreign policy and democracy, imperialism and the struggle for power, might be of interest, perhaps even of practical use, at a time when such problems engage more than ever public attention' (Abbott 1925: v). For that reason, he undertook to write a book that taught students how to read Thucydides, to elucidate the contours of his thought and to offer a portrait of Thucydides as a man (Abbott 1925: vi; cf. Taylor 2010: 6).

Abbott works out his claim that Thucydides' historical and literary presentation of events approaches 'reality' and 'realism' over the course of his entire book. It rests on a number of assertions: that Thucydides possessed a scientific method; that he attempted to get at the truth of events 'rationally'; that his literary style is 'unadorned'; and that the speeches were not true recreations of ancient oratory but vehicles for the expression of his own political thought.[14] The character of Thucydides as a thinker, his methodological approach to history, and his literary art are clearly important to Abbot: entire chapters are devoted to Thucydides' 'Scientific Method', 'Detachment', 'Art' and 'Style'.[15] Abbott positions his vision of Thucydides within the latest German and British scholarly debates. The German debate in which Abbott intervenes is the *Thukydidesfrage*, or the question over the date of the composition of the individual components of the *History*. F. W. Ullrich argued that Thucydides composed the first ten years of the *History* in ignorance of the later history of the war. As the war unfolded, Thucydides continued to take notes but did not sit down to 'write up' the remainder of the *History* until after Athens had been defeated. Against this theory, a number of scholars led by Classen argued that throughout the war, from 431 to 404 BC, Thucydides took copious notes, and that it was only after the fall of Athens that he began to write the *History*. Abbott prefers Ullrich to Classen's arguments, believing the latter to be 'if not impossible, singularly unreal' (Abbott 1925: 172–3). Here Abbott is engaging with German scholarship from the nineteenth century and ignoring the newer work of Schwartz (1919), which can be attributed to Abbott's primary role as a war correspondent and journalist, rather than a classical scholar. However, Abbott goes further than Ullrich in his belief that Thucydides was not only taking notes throughout the Peloponnesian War but also writing the *History* as the events themselves unfolded.

The second debate Abbott was responding to was that over the real cause of the war; that is, the desire of the 'party of the Piraeus' for conquest and money, initiated by Cornford (Abbott 1925: 49–51). Interestingly, Abbott does not criticize Cornford for his portrayal of Thucydides as a tragic writer, even though he is at pains to argue for his use of the 'scientific' method throughout the book. However, he dismisses out of hand Cornford's assertion that Thucydides had misunderstood the real economic causes of the conflict by maintaining that it is only after the death of Pericles (cf. 2.65) that the *demos* began to consider seriously the policy of western expansion (Abbott 1925: 51–5). Having established his position on these debates, Abbott is then free to discuss his central argument: the nature of Thucydides' historical and political realism and the way modern students can derive philosophical and political insight from an ancient text.

Abbott presents Thucydides' realism as rooted in both his own intellectual abilities and the tumultuous times in which he lived. In Abbott's mind, the generation that Thucydides lived through endured one of the worst crises in history, which disturbed all but 'the strongest' of minds. For nearly thirty years, the whole Greek world was driven by acute political passions into a ferocious conflict: passions which were hardly comprehensible to modern man 'though our forefathers of the seventeenth century might, and Frenchmen of the Revolution period would, have understood it' (Abbott 1925: 162). The relatively small geographical area of Greece intensified political passions, personal animosities and the war between Athens and Sparta. 'The whole national life, public and private, was poisoned' (Abbott 1925: 162). The depth of violence unleashed by the war pushed out older moods of thought. 'Idealists saw things which astonished them; moralists were no longer sure of themselves' (Abbott 1925: 162). The only man who saw through the confusion was Thucydides. He achieved this intellectual feat by abandoning idealism and moralism, adopting a cold hard realism instead.

> Thucydides ... having started with no illusions, either as to divine providence or as to human wisdom, suffers no disillusion. Amid the wrecks of men and cities he steers a clear course; in this tossing sea of madness he holds fast to his own sanity: his feet ever firm upon solid fact. He confronts events as a scientist confronts Nature: aware that what is happening has happened before and will necessarily happen again in the future.
>
> Abbott 1925: 163

'Science', in the sense of dispassionate and accurate observation, therefore, is key to Thucydides' historical realism. Both terms focus on what really is and exclude moral and ethical considerations. Science and realism allow Thucydides to be dispassionate. Abbott opens his account of Thucydides' 'scientific method' through an analysis of the prefatory *archaeology* (1925: 25–31). He notes that Thucydides attempts to reconstruct the past based on probability, a methodology that twentieth-century scholars argue is no guarantee of capturing reality. Therefore, for example, Thucydides believes that he can identify the names of modern tribes and peoples from the names of ancient tribal chiefs. Modern scholarship has shown that 'national names' are often derived from chiefs who never existed. Thucydides' method, therefore, is deficient, but this is not discreditable to him. 'Knowledge advances by steps not leaps' (Abbott 1925: 26). Writing in the fifth century BC, Thucydides could not have anticipated modern scholarly techniques. Yet the key point is that Thucydides attempted to take a dispassionate rational look at the past. He used the discoveries made in graves to make rational deductions about the past. Yet, at the same time, he did not let his scepticism run wild and simply deny the existence of the Trojan War. He attempted to understand it from the perspective of his contemporary world as a war of conquest and empire. He even uses a process of rational deduction to argue that the Trojan War, which was the greatest that the Greeks had then embarked upon, was not as big as either the Persian or Peloponnesian Wars. Abbott (1925: 30) asks 'could any argument be more modern, any method more scientific?'

Moreover, in dealing with the events of his own day, with the Peloponnesian War, Thucydides' standard 'is as strictly scientific as the nature of the subject permits' (Abbott 1925: 32). The important caveat, 'as the nature of the subject permits', is there because Abbott is at pains to argue that human affairs can never be recorded and discussed with the same exactitude as the facts of the physical sciences. He argues that Thucydides understood tolerably well the distinction between 'subjective' and 'objective' based upon the claim at 1.22 that he had attempted to arrive at the best sources where he had himself not been the witness to events or the hearer of a speech. This represents an important aspect of Thucydides' scientific method, but one which often leaves the reader with the task of disentangling what Thucydides presumably saw himself from what he only heard from other sources: a task not helped by the fact that Thucydides often conceals his 'laboratory work' (Abbott 1925: 35). Although where Thucydides' narrative can be checked against modern archaeological and epigraphic finds, his accuracy is not found wanting (Abbott 1925: 39).

Abbott's Thucydides, therefore, fully satisfies Morley's (2018b) definition of an empirical realist. The speeches initially represent a problem for Abbott because they clearly do not fit into the paradigm of Thucydides as a scientist as they are not copies of the actual words delivered. Thucydides, of course, acknowledges this in a famous passage (1.22), where he claims that it was often difficult for him to remember what was said, or he only had had reports of the speech to go on, so he sometimes wrote down what seemed to best fit the occasion. Here verisimilitude takes the place of verity. On this point and in line with his scientific comments, Abbott writes simply that 'This is disconcerting' (Abbott 1925: 39). Abbott's answer is to sidestep the speeches' historical value and instead argue that they form 'an invaluable storehouse of political thought' (1925: 42) in which hardly a problem of statesmanship is left untouched. By way of example, Abbott points to the following speeches. The speech of the Corcyrean envoys beginning at 1.32 shows how an island state can suddenly 'wake up' to the dangers of isolation; the perils of larger states attempting to rule smaller neighbours through division (6. 77, 79); Pericles' explanation of the advantages of sea power (1.142, 143, 2.62); and the Mytilene debate points to the merits of severity and magnanimity towards rebellious subjects (3.39–40, 44–8). The speeches allow the reader to see how the Greeks themselves reacted to events, often by offering opposing views. They are infused with 'reality' in the sense that the speakers present their views of not only current events but also broader political themes (Abbott 1925: 188–9). They allow Thucydides, therefore, to present detailed analysis of broad political issues that could not be easily inserted into his strict chronological narrative of events. 'On no part of this book has Thucydides lavished more labour, and no part of his labour has been more fruitful in suggestion to political thinkers of later ages' (Abbott 1925: 42). The speeches, therefore, are the points at which Thucydides departs from his usual scientific method but also represent the greatest expression of his literary style and provide a storehouse of his political analysis.

In Abbott's view, however, not all speeches are equal. He dismisses the Melian dialogue as 'among the writer's most notable and disappointing performances' (Abbott 1925: 192). Abbott's attitude to the dialogue may strike readers as strange. After all, for contemporary realist scholars the dialogue is often taken as a paradigmatic text in which Thucydides lays out his hard-headed vision of political realism (see, for example, Donnelly 2000: 23; Frankel 2013: 177). The Athenian rejection of ethical norms and their insistence that their power justifies their policy in an anarchical world with no supranational government to restrain their actions appeals, at first glance, to many realists as being a well-written and succinct view of the consequences of the pervasive anarchy of international politics. The political message of the Athenians in the dialogue also appealed to

Abbott. Famously the ancient rhetorician Dionysius of Halicarnassus claimed that the language employed by the Athenians in the dialogue was below freemen and only worthy of oriental despots. Abbott dismisses Dionysius' criticism as the product of rhetorical fashions current in the reign of Augustus. In contrast, the Great War generation reads the Melian dialogue with different eyes and can readily understand the interplay between great powers and small neutral states. Abbott's real criticism of the dialogue is literary. Parts of it are direct and powerful, such as the 'immortal definition' of the 'rights' of the weak at 5.89. 'The rest – mere degrees of flabbiness: here confused, there loose and wordy, as if the pen ran away with the author' (Abbott 1925: 193). Literary art, therefore, is important to Abbott's estimation of Thucydides' politics and is seen as a key component of his scientific attitude, rationality and realism. Had Thucydides merely produced an accurate record of what really happened, then his work would have been nothing more than 'a useful book of reference like those written by Polybius and other historians of a later age, who heeding the master's precept too well and his practice not enough, laboured, by a single-minded devotion to accuracy, to make their works valuable for all time – and succeeded in making them unreadable in all times' (Abbott 1925: 167). Thucydides' *History*, therefore, attained political relevance precisely through its artistic prowess.

This is not to say that Abbott sees Thucydides as absolutely impartial. Grote may have gone too far in defending Cleon from Thucydides, but to Abbott it is clear that much of the criticism is fair (1925: 93–109). Thucydides could hardly be said to be impartial in his treatment of Athens. The lesson Thucydides provides on democracy, Abbott contends at the end of his second chapter, is the wholly conventional interpretation that it was a 'childish experiment' and 'its sole value for posterity is that of a warning' (Abbott 1925: 147; cf. the anti-democratic tradition of thought outlined in Roberts 1997). This argument, of course, attempts to reconstruct Thucydides' personal opinions and modifies Abbott's earlier claims about his vaunted impartiality. However, as Abbott explains, all historians and philosophers who have critically engaged with Athenian democracy have in some sense been biased. The ideal 'unbiased' historian never existed, certainly not in recent British literature. Grote was overly zealous in his praise for democracy (cf. Kierstead 2014), while William Mitford, an early nineteenth-century historian of Greece writing under the shadow of the French Revolution (cf. Sachs 2016), often lost his 'sobriety' when treating the fifth-century Athenian regime. The uniqueness of Thucydides, for Abbott, is that when considered among other ancient historians he comes out of such a comparison '*facile princeps*'. The impartial streak in Thucydidean thought only serves to prompt the reader to engage more critically with the text, enhancing the experience of reading and engaging with the political views put forward. Thucydides' literary medium is, therefore, essential to his political message.

Thucydides and political realism

So far we have seen that Abbott had few qualms about claiming that Thucydides was an empirical realist who accurately recreated human events, psychologies and institutions. However, I claim that Abbott thought Thucydides was also a doctrinal realist – that is to say, someone who presented realism as a political system. This vision of Thucydides' political realism, however, requires careful understanding and deconstruction on the part of the reader.

In Thorpe's *Detachment* essay (1926), which I noted above began its life as a review of Abbott's *Thucydides*, it is claimed that the Athenian historian is a political realist because he is the product of the sophistic movement and because he comes from the stock of the hard-headed people of northern Greece, mixed with Thracian blood. Abbott, I believe, would have agreed with this analysis as far as it goes, but would have added that to really understand Thucydides' realism, both literary and political, one needs to get to grips with his presentation of the nature of man. Abbott claimed that the Athenian historian is a 'scientist' because 'the uniformity of human nature is a cardinal point in Thucydides' mind; another point is that events have always followed the same orderly sequence' (Abbott 1925: 31). In Abbott's lively account of his time in North Africa at the time of the Italian invasion, published as *The Holy War In Tripoli* (1912), however, there is a very clear sense that humanity is enormously varied. Abbott draws a clear distinction between the 'civilized' European nations and the Arabs and Berbers who lived in North Africa.[16] And yet Abbott's claim that Thucydides is a scientist, an empirical realist and political interpreter for the ages rests on the conceit that human nature is fundamentally the same in all ages and that history represents a recurrent series of events, allowing cogent parallels and analogies to be drawn between different events and conflicts. The most significant aspect of Abbott's interpretation of human nature in Thucydides is that it suggests that history repeats itself. If human nature does not change then, as Thucydides writes, the same or similar events will recur.

> Under all surface diversities mankind possesses the same attributes, mental and moral. The external conditions also vary only within limits. Hence it follows that,

by studying the present, we can understand the past and anticipate the future; for, since the factors – circumstances and human nature – from the conjunction of which historical phenomenon result, do not change in essence, the future will, in effect, repeat the present. It will be noticed that this view excludes the modern idea of amelioration not less than the ancient idea of degeneration. To the historian's mind a millennium is as foreign as a golden age. He has no use for theories which have no real basis in observation.

Abbott 1925: 75

The claim that history is fundamentally unified denies the possibility of real change. There is no improvement or decline. States, religions, beliefs, of course, come and go, but human nature remains constant and unchanging. Thucydides' views, of course, are not necessarily those of Abbott. However, I think we can also see here the influence of the Great War on Abbott's thinking. Before the war, Abbott was enamoured and in awe of the very different culture of North Africa that he found himself travelling through. The young man was drawn to the differences, the exoticism and adventure that was all around him. However, the experience of the Great War led him down a different path, one that led him to look with cynicism on human action.

Abbott's realist Thucydides looks to be, at first glance, similar to that of many contemporary realists in International Relations who argue that differences in culture, morality and society are so much window dressing which ultimately mean little in the harsh world of interstate relations (cf. the criticisms of this view by Lebow 2003). Rather, there is only the reality of power and the anarchic struggle among states to gain it or to avoid losing it. Like the neo-realists, Abbott denies differences between humans across time as 'surface diversities'. Similarly, his Thucydides views 'progress' as the mere increase in wealth, security and knowledge and the attendant improvement in morals and knowledge (Abbott 1925: 74), not a genuine development in human nature. Abbott quotes Bury (1909: 253ff.) when arguing that antiquity was innocent of the idea that the development of civilization accompanies a development in human nature. Human nature, in Abbott's reading of Thucydides, remains constant. It certainly adapts itself to changing external conditions such as political institutions and education. Therefore, communities may be moderated by their ways of life, 'but the modification does not go very deep' (Abbott 1925: 75). Thucydides is adept at distinguishing what is superficial in human affairs from what is essential and immutable. This insight allows him to abstract from the uniformity of human nature and the fact that, under similar circumstances, similar events are likely to recur. In other words, Abbott has taken Thucydides' claim that similar events will reoccur in the future according to an unchanging vision of human nature, *kata to anthropinon* (κατὰ τὸ ἀνθρώπινον, 1.22.4), to present history as a unity. The *polis* may disappear to be replaced by the nation state, but humanity remains fundamentally the same.

Abbott is arguing that Thucydides' realism is more than merely historical or scientific. His realism proceeds beyond the simply empirical to form a 'philosophy of history'. This is not a 'popular' philosophy, because it is painful for those of a sentimental or idealist stamp, nor is it an 'academic' philosophy, because it 'contains none of those recondite tenets which so often invite our attention and elude our comprehension' (Abbott 1925: 76). In other words, Thucydides does not blind his readers with lengthy philosophical discourse. Neither, Abbott claims, is Thucydides' philosophy of history the 'simple facts of life' (Abbott 1925: 76). Thucydides' philosophy is simply a realist depiction of human nature that focuses on the psychological motivations of self-interest, honour and fear. Kinship and morality are mere cloaks hiding the true motives of men and states. Democrats are not drawn to democrats, nor Ionian to Ionian. The desire for power may be cloaked in rhetorical appeals to faction or race (Abbott quotes 1.124 and 6.80, 82 on this point), but self-interest is the true driver of political action, 2,500 years ago and today.

> On the whole, it may be said that, in the historian's view, there are no wars of races or of ideas, but only wars of interests. Where the conflict is between faction and faction, the representative leaders may pose as champions of constitutional ideals; but, while fighting in the name of a principal, they really fight for a prize. The same as to the conflict between state and state. Although affinity of race or of institutions may have some little influence, in general the policy of states runs on other than sentimental or idealistic lines. Its goal is power, pursued for the gratification of covetousness and ambition.
>
> Abbott 1925: 71

Abbott finds in Thucydides a description of self-interest as the ultimate driver of all political action. Interestingly, Abbott sets the interpretation against the sentimental or idealist line of thought more than a decade before Carr will publish his devastating critique of interwar international thought (Carr 1939). He accepts this realist view of politics as an inescapable truth. It was the governing principal in Thucydides' time and remains so today. The best that scholars of international affairs, as well as citizens, soldiers and statesmen, can do is to recognize this reality and to act accordingly. However, it should be noted that Abbott does not set this view of human nature in Thucydides against any 'idealist' scholar of International Relations. Instead, he positions his Thucydides against a series of classical scholars who, Abbott believed, had fundamentally misunderstood the role of realism in the *History* and the true political lessons contained within it (Abbott 1925: 231–2). Abbott names J. P. Mahaffy, a Victorian professor of Classics in Dublin, famous for teaching Oscar Wilde, who had recognized Thucydides' dark depiction of human nature but had found the Greek historian too severe (1874). He also points to Gilbert Murray, who had painted a picture of Thucydides as a 'passionate patriot' lamenting over the fall of Athens (1903), and Thomas Arnold, who had found in Thucydides 'an earnest preacher' of morality who would have done infinite credit to the school master had he been educated at Rugby school (Arnold 2010). Finally, Classen had devoted his life to the study of Thucydides and in his enthusiasm had reduced him to the level of a 'Lutheran pastor'. Each of these scholars had either found in Thucydides things that were not there, or complained of finding things in the text that they believed should not have been there. 'Thucydides is too devoid of atmosphere for either the patriot or the artist or the moralist to feel at home – to satisfy the conditions which their souls crave, he must be recreated in conformity with their own mental cast' (Abbott 1925: 232). Abbott's scientific and realist reading of Thucydides, by contrast, reveals exactly what is in the text, nothing more nor less, rendering these older readings obsolete.

There is one final point to make. Political realism was not simply a bone of contention among competing scholars. It was also, for Abbott, crucial to a functioning democracy. During the war, Abbott (1916) published a book in which he attempted to lay out the 'reality' of modern Greece's attitude toward the Great Powers and the divisions in British and French policy toward Greece. This book, *Turkey, Greece and the Great Powers: A Study in Friendship and Hate*, attracted much criticism in both literary and political circles and among Abbott's friends. In the preface to *Greece and the Allies, 1914–1922*, Abbott recalls how two pieces of his journalism saw the light of day and the third was suppressed for the same journal. Even the Home Secretary became involved over worries about Abbott's suggestion that Britain and France were not united in their policies towards Greece and south-west Europe. The experience reinforced in Abbott's mind the personal price of truth and the idea that a simple realist telling of facts was always useful. In other words, Abbott's personal experience of 'speaking truth to power' left him with first-hand knowledge of its personal cost but also of political realism's indispensability in a free and democratic society.

Self-interest in Thucydides

Let us now deepen our engagement with Abbott's realist interpretation through an analysis of his approach to political psychology, particularly the role of self-interest and fear in Thucydides. Abbott was impressed by the candour Thucydides gives to his various Athenian speakers when they are justifying their acquisition of empire. Among the speeches given by the Athenian envoys to Corinth and Melos, as well as those given by Pericles, Cleon and Diodotus in Athens, there is no appeal to idealist principals – 'no cant, no hypocrisy' (Abbott 1925: 141). The Athenians justify their empire in unguarded terms. They state explicitly that their desire to rule and exert power over the Aegean springs from 'a love of glory' and a 'love of profit'. Their role is based on power and military might alone, and in support of this assertion Abbott quotes the idea that 'the weaker must be kept by the stronger', which he attributes to 1.75–6 and 5.105. After honour and profit comes fear. It is dangerous for a tyrant city to let her empire go, or to let her power slip, as both Pericles (2.63) and Cleon (3.37, 40) frankly acknowledge. Abbott's focus on honour, self-interest and fear as the primary motivations in Thucydides echoes a common theme in realist readings of Thucydides. After fear and honour, the Athenian desire to acquire and maintain their empire is presented as the third great political/psychological motivation in a speech given by their ambassadors to the Peloponnesians on the eve of the outbreak of the war (1.75). Indeed, for many modern commentators, it is Thucydides' focus on self-interest that gives the work such value (Sahlins 2004: 3).[17] Self-interest is a psychological driver that, for Abbott, is easy to understand and apply to modern states and political factions without having to worry about differences in culture and society or the role or norms and laws. All states desire wealth and, most of all, power. Yet, as Crane reminds us, Euphemos' speech at Kamarina and the Melian dialogue point to the limits of self-interest in politics (1998: 263). Connor argues that as the Sophists became more visible in Athenian society, the concept of self-interest became more prominent. Thucydides, reacting against this movement, does not simply affirm or deny the primacy of self-interest, but rather he subverts his readers' expectations to probe the concept's uncertainties and limitations (1984: 14–15).[18] For Abbott, Thucydides describes with reality and accuracy the central place of self-interest in the hearts and motivations of men in the manner of a 'cynical pessimist'. The word cynical here introduces a moral note to the analysis and, perhaps, separates Thucydides' views from his teachings. Thucydides takes no joy in describing the world as it really was, but felt that it would be a beneficial and useful enterprise for future readers to help them see the reality of interstate politics with no illusions. Abbott summarizes Thucydides' political realism in the following words:

> Generally self-interest is the mainspring of human conduct, and goodness a matter of condition. The average man, when well off, is comparatively good; but his virtue will not bear the stress of adversity. The fear of God ceases to restrain him as soon as he finds out – and this is easily done – that God treats the good and the bad alike. Stronger than the religious conscience – though operative only in a few cases – is the sense of honour (literally of disgrace): the sense which not only makes some men ashamed to do what is base, but even impels them to self-sacrifice. Such, stated in bare terms, is the result of Thucydides' induction. The experience of over two thousand years has not disproved its justness.
>
> Abbott 1925: 159

Yet Abbott cannot bring himself to present Thucydides to readers and students as a proponent of this view. Thucydides, for Abbott, is not Machiavellian. He does not endorse the blind pursuit of wealth and power, whatever the cost and for no reason other than self-interest. These are Athenian views but not Thucydides' own.

> Yet (I think I am stating what is not a mere matter of personal opinion) the politician who would look to Thucydides for countenance of the doctrine that, in international relations, the desire of self-aggrandisement not only is, but ought to be, the rule, would look in vain; while any candid student will find implied the wrong-doing – a sense of right for its own sake – as strong as it is passionless. This disinterested righteousness can hardly be formulated; for neither the sanctions of religion nor the speculations of the schools – the two fountains from which ethical formulas are drawn – enter into it. But Thucydides, without formulating, brings it home, to those at all events who can read a lesson for themselves, as no preacher or propagandist has ever brought it. His very reticence – like the reticence of Nature herself – is a tacit affirmation, which tells in the end much more than strenuousness of speech, and has the property of invigorating the reader. Everything local, personal, and petty is stricken down in the presence of this high sentiment: and he who chafes at the ethical contradictions of national creeds feels himself at last addressed on grounds which will remain when all else has passed away.
>
> Abbott 1925: 165–6

Thucydides' realism leads him to depict accurately the role of self-interest in politics, but that realism, coupled with his reticence about passing moral judgement, acts as a condemnation of such actions to all students intelligent enough to understand the lesson. Abbott is here being equivocal. He is clearly advocating a vision of Thucydidean teaching that excludes moral and political considerations, yet maintaining that the historian himself merely describes this worldview without endorsing it. Yet here Abbott himself is also pulling back from accepting an entirely amoral view of international politics by arguing *ex silentio*. Perhaps he felt that he knew Thucydides' mind after living with the text for so long, or, alternatively, perhaps it was his own experience of war and politics that led him to such a conclusion. However, most likely it is Abbott's attempt to understand what may be termed the realist paradox in the reception of Thucydides.

The literary realism of Thucydides is shocking but also the source of the *History*'s political power. Thucydides conveys the impression of telling us how the world really is. In times of trouble, such as in the wake of the Great War, readers turn to Thucydides to understand that such terrible events have happened before and will happen again – perhaps even how to weather such calamities and rebuild political orders afterwards. At the same time, however, many readers do not want to believe that Thucydides himself was an amoral historian, writing to instruct the would-be politician to be motivated by self-interest and nothing else. As Abbott put it, 'many have imagined the historian as a brain without a heart, as deficient in moral sentiment as he was pre-eminent in intelligence' (1925: 164). The above long quotations, therefore, are Abbott's attempt to have his cake and eat it – to present Thucydides as the dispassionate political realist but also to argue that because he never lectures his readers on moral lessons he is a very moral thinker. It is an attractive argument in that few, I believe, would care to think so ill of Thucydides' moral beliefs.

Fear in international relations

Let us now turn to the second important psychology in Abbott's realist Thucydides: fear. It is perhaps the most complicated of the human passions because its operation is dependent on external circumstances. Athens fears the loss of her empire, Sparta the rise of her rival, while lesser states fear the attention of both. These external factors shape how actors perceive their situation giving rise to fear. Nevertheless, it was imperative to understand fear because it had led, demonstrably, again and again to wars breaking out in modern Europe.

> Thrice has modern Europe been rent by a conflict in essence similar to the Peloponnesian War. Once from 1689 to 1712, again from 1798 to 1815, and again in our own day. The cause of all these struggles might, after changing the names,

be summed up in Thucydides' phrase: 'the growth of the Athenian power which alarmed the Lacedaemonians and forced them into war' (I. 23).

Abbott 1925: 3–4

Abbott here refers to British wars against the France of Louis XIV and Revolutionary France, and the Great War. Each involved grand alliances that drew in many European nations and eventually spread across the globe. There is an obvious parallel here with the 'Thucydides trap' as formulated by Allison (2017b). In Greece it is the growth of Athenian power that leads to war with the Spartans. Similarly, Abbott argues that in modern history Louis XIV, Napoleon and Kaiser Wilhelm II, like Pericles, were not content to let their states remain equal with their peers. Rather, they aspired to domination. Thucydides, in Abbott's estimation, not only describes an ancient war but accounts for the causes of many subsequent conflicts, just as Allison argues today. However, Abbott and Allison's arguments are subtly different. Allison draws attention to the 'fear' (*phobos*, φόβος) that the rise of Athens provoked in Sparta as a key cause of the war. Abbott, instead, argues that the other 'Greek states' – not just Sparta – rose 'in obedience to the instinct of self-preservation and in accordance with the perennial principle of foreign policy called nowadays "balance of power"' (Abbott 1925: 4). In other words, the rise of Athens is not just a problem for Sparta but for all the Greek city-states. For Abbott, Thucydides had understood perfectly the idea of the balance of power and the threat that Athens' rise posed to its operation in classical Greece.[19]

This claim is rooted in the idea that, for Thucydides, a number of factors come into play when describing the cause of war, but that the most significant is human nature: 'it is impossible to deal with matters historical except in terms of human mentality and psychology' (Abbott 1925: 56). For example, Abbott believes that in Thucydides' interpretation political circumstance is the primary cause for the Spartan regime (4.80), but the national character formed by that regime (1.84) was the immediate cause of Spartan inaction and dilatoriness (2.94, 3.92, 8.96). In other words, the geographical and social situation of Sparta creates her regime's character, which in turn leads certain psychological traits to rise to the surface (Abbott 1925: 57; cf. Jaffe 2017a). When combined with the rise of Athenian power, this naturally leads to 'alarm' among the Spartans (Abbott 1925: 58). Abbott's views here echo Allison's *trap* only in so far as he believes that alarm, or fear, causes war again and again throughout history. But they differ in that Abbott focuses not on a rising and established power but the historical, cultural and social make-up of a state, which conditions how fear arises and is expressed.

In a footnote, he points to the role of fear in the outbreak of hostilities between Britain and France in 1803 and among the Great Powers in 1914.[20] However, there are important differences. Abbott emphasizes that the alarm Sparta felt was also the product of her regime and its geographical setting. Abbott thought that human nature was eternal and immutable, but also that geographical and social circumstances bought out certain aspects of that nature at certain times. These circumstances are obviously distinct in the Greek and early nineteenth-century European cases. In making this claim, Abbott's arguments begin to look like recent critiques of the realist Thucydides that have emphasized the role of norms, society and culture in defining how states conceive of power and what strategies should be employed to attain it (Lebow 2001, 2003; Forde 2012). The essential oneness of human nature results in a view of history in which there are patterns and characteristic modes of behaviour that are observable in international politics. For sure, battles, plagues and famines happen, and states and empires rise and fall. But these are all so many ripples on the surface of history. Underneath, human beings remain essentially the same, continually driven by self-interest. This observation allows Abbott to claim that Thucydides' thought is useful to the student of modern politics because similar events keep recurring in this linear view of history. The key lesson Abbott wants his readers to take away is that states will often try to disturb the political equilibrium in which they find themselves and will often aim to dominate their neighbours.

Abbott's claim that the Peloponnesian War closely parallels three modern wars that each tore the European continent apart reinforces his view that little changes in human nature from one generation to the next. He allows that there is a vast difference in scale between the ancient and the modern conflicts but no real difference in the essential quality of human nature driving those wars. Quoting Hume (1994: 65–6), unattributed, Abbott argues that 'Ancient Greece is presented in miniature [as] a world politically analogous to modern Europe – a number of sovereign states whose conflicting interests admitted of merely temporary diplomatic combinations' (Abbott: 1925: 5). Here we see Abbott espouse another central tenet of contemporary political realism: the belief in the anarchy of the international system. Classical realists, following Morgenthau, often believe that international politics is defined by a struggle for supremacy and power that is 'universal in time and space' (Morgenthau 1948). Drawing upon Thucydides, Hobbes and Machiavelli, realists view this struggle for power as rooted in states' desire for survival and, then, the dominance of their peers (see, for example, the histories of realism by Donnelly 2000; Frankel 2013). For

Abbott, the actions of the Greek states are defined not so much by the drive to survive but by parochial self-interest. States such as Athens were driven by ambition to attempt 'world domination'. The 'parochial' desire of the other Greek states for independence led them to resist the unifying project of Athens, just as the 'parochial' tendencies of modern European states had led them to resist Napoleonic France or the Kaiser's Prussia (Abbott 1925: 57). When Sparta, or England, entered into war to stop the unifying ambitions of an Athens or a France, it was not for ideological reasons but rather because protecting the independence of the smaller states was in the national interest. Even Sparta's sparing of Athens following her victory in the Peloponnesian War (recounted by Xenophon *Hell.* 2.2.19–20) does not represent genuine altruism but an attempt to use Athens to counterbalance the power of Corinth and Thebes (Abbott 1925: 67). Abbott does allow that Thucydides points to Greek willingness to submit disputes between city-states to arbitration (he cites 1.28, 29, 34, 140, 145), but notes that the political 'machinery' of the Amphictyonic Council, an interstate council which governed the pan-Hellenic sanctuary of Delphi, was usually only deployed to serve the interests of one larger state or another, just as the League of Nations represented a cover for the self-interested policies of the Great Powers of Europe against the smaller states of Africa and Asia.[21] Following this line of thought, Abbott believed that Britain's championing of Greek entrance into the League in 1920 was occasioned not by altruism but a desire to weaken Turkish influence (Abbott 1922: 5). International politics, therefore, remained unconstrained by any legal apparatus. Power remained the sole arbiter of disputes. Larger states looked to dominate their smaller peers who in turn searched for security, leading to an interstate system characterized by anarchy and the domination of the powerful over the weaker.

The fear that the rise of Athens provoked in Sparta is taken by Abbott as the 'truest' cause of the Peloponnesian War. The economic motive of the party of the Piraeus proposed by Cornford (1907) and then dissected by Grundy (1911) and Dickens (1911) is dismissed with a contemporary analogy: 'We, in these times, have seen that the commercial spirit played only a secondary part in the Great War: some of the Powers did not fight for markets at all, and others fought for other things besides markets' (Abbott 1925: 68). Similarly, the affairs of Epidamnus and Potidea are labelled the 'occasions' of the Peloponnesian War and compared to the 'Servian' (sic. Serbian) and Belgian affairs, which were the direct causes of the outbreak of the Great War. These affairs are not causes but act as catalysts that accelerate an already inevitable crisis.

Conclusion

To reiterate the main claims of this chapter, Abbott's *Thucydides: A Study in Historical Reality* stands as a key moment in the British turn to Thucydides. It is the first attempt in English to consider Thucydides not only as an empirical realist or as a keen observer of human nature and psychology, but to argue that the *History* represents a timeless example of literary and theoretical realism. Moreover, Abbott composed this book with students of politics as well as classical studies in mind. It is, in other words, an attempt to offer Thucydides' realism to political scientists and even to statesmen and men of affairs.

Abbott closes his book with a short chapter titled 'A Possession Forever', a clear reference to Thucydides' claim that his work will be a *ktema es aiei* (1.22). It is clear that Abbott imagined that Thucydides' work represents a possession as political philosophy. The congruence of Thucydides' realism and his uncompromising depiction of human nature elevate the work from mere chronicle to a great artistic and philosophical artefact and a vehicle for teaching the true nature of politics. For Abbott, 'There is a beauty in romance; but a grander beauty in stark, ruthless, uncompromising verity. This is the kind of beauty that the singularly proud and reserved author of the *History* discloses' (Abbott 1925: 232). Thucydidean realism is finally, therefore, revealed to have an aesthetic quality for those insightful enough to grasp it. The beauty of Thucydides' narrative raises the *History* up to be a possession forever, a text that is of perennial utility to those intelligent enough to understand its lessons. However, Thucydides' literary art is of a rare character, and it has not often been equalled by later writers, but it is by no means an isolated phenomenon. 'Its replica is to be found among brain-workers the world over; though seldom among those of whom the world hears' (Abbott 1925: 232). In other words, there is an unidentified group of realists, treading in the footsteps of Thucydides. Contemporary realist scholars often point to a tradition of such thought, beginning with Thucydides and continuing with Machiavelli and Hobbes. Abbott declines to name these 'brain-workers' who should stand company with Thucydides.

This is not to say that Thucydides had a 'didactic purpose' in any 'narrow sense of the term'. For Abbott, Thucydides is not writing a statesman's manual (cf. Wendt 2016) nor a handbook of politics, precisely because he avoids direct instruction or authorial exposition. We saw earlier that in Abbott's estimation it is in the speeches that the purest form of Thucydides' political philosophy is to be found. The speeches, of course, often form pairs that explore issues from diametrically opposed points of view. Therefore, it is impossible to say that

Thucydides believed *x* or *y* or that a particular reading is the interpretation he wished his readers to take away from the *History*.

> A thousand opinions may be formed about the meaning which he attached to this world – military, political, ethical. But, although it teaches many lessons, the *History* is not written to enforce any particular lesson. Thucydides lets his story tell itself in the deeds and words of those who act it out. He must therefore have meant that it is the thing itself which will have use and value for all time.
>
> Abbott 1925: 234

This is hardly an original opinion. Already in the seventeenth century, Hobbes had claimed that Thucydides never digresses to give moral lectures to his readers (1989: xii). Nevertheless, Abbott finishes the book by noting that it is Thucydides' fierce intellect and the beauty of his prose that has led to the *History*'s deserved fame down the centuries.

> And so it comes about that, while Thucydides did not put forward any claim to imperishable fame, Time the supreme arbiter has established it. His authority endures, unimpaired by changes in literary taste or academic doctrine. His practice puts all creeds to shame, and questions whether history is a science or whether it is an art lose their pertinence in sight of his performance. Those among us who are least in sympathy with the writer's temper feel constrained to do homage to the forces of his intellect; while those who approach him predisposed to receive what he has to give part from him abashed by his wisdom: he seems to have penetrated into the inmost recesses of the human heart – to have left nothing relating to the eternal strife of man unprobed and unexplained. Wherefore scholars still admire, even though they may not always understand, and statesman still use, the History which Thucydides the Athenian wrote two thousand and three hundred years ago.
>
> Abbott 1925: 235–6

5

Thucydides, Historical Change and Contemporaneity

Arnold Toynbee (1889–1975) was one of the most prominent public intellectuals in the mid-twentieth century Anglo-American world. His voluminous writings covered history, the philosophy of history and international policy. After the Second World War, his cultural and intellectual standing only increased as he came to be seen as a wise sage advising against the dangers of nuclear war and ecological catastrophe. Toynbee's reputation as a public intellectual was such that in March 1947 he became *Time* man of the year. Before the Great War, Toynbee lived in a Victorian world of order and stability that he imagined might last forever. Britain's declaration of war on 4 August 1914 shattered this belief. Toynbee did not fight. He avoided conscription on at least three occasions on medical grounds, although it was almost certainly fear that kept him from the front. Nevertheless, the war was a personal calamity for Toynbee that would lead him away from the exclusive study of the Classics to focus, instead, on a comparative history of all civilizations. It is also at this moment of change and disaster that Toynbee discovered the contemporaneity of Thucydides. He would later recall:

> I discovered [the Greeks'] contemporaneity for myself by the aid of a different clue when the outbreak of the First World War caught me teaching Ancient Greek history at Oxford. For the experience of a war in which the spiritual as well as the political destinies of Western Christendom were manifestly at stake brought to life for me the sense and feel of phrases in the work of Thucydides which I had read hitherto with blind eyes because, so far, I had not been in possession of the psychological key to them. I realised in 1914 that the experience which was overtaking my generation now in the course of Western history had overtaken Thucydides' generation in the course of Hellenic history by the time at which he wrote his book. In other words, the age of Thucydides, so far from lying behind me in my past, had been standing all that time in front of me in my future until now, when I was just beginning to catch Thucydides up through meeting in my own life with Thucydides' experiences.
>
> Toynbee 1950: 8–9

This engagement with Thucydides should not cause surprise. Toynbee's intellectual and social origins lie firmly within the academic discipline of Classics. Before the Great War, he was a student at Balliol College, Oxford, where he studied under Alfred Zimmern. He was also on good terms with Gilbert Murray, eventually marrying his daughter Rosalind (McNeil 1989a: 38–63). However, at Oxford Thucydides emerged not as a writer of purely antiquarian interest, but as a great thinker who speaks to the contemporary moment. As Toynbee explains in the above quotation, the feeling of contemporaneity that Thucydides elicits in his readers is of the utmost importance to the reader's experience of the text. It is also very important to the wider concept of the Thucydidean turn. Edward Keene (2015: 364) argues convincingly that Toynbee's Thucydides may well be the primary source for many early American International Relations scholars, from whose work later scholars would establish the Athenian historian as the first political 'realist' in the 1960s and 1970s. Toynbee was certainly a highly visible figure to American scholars. For much of the interwar period (1918–1939) he was Director of Studies at the Royal Institute for International Affairs,[1] a forum for the research and discussion of international relations in London, where he published the annual *Survey of International Affairs*.[2] Furthermore, his *Study of History*, a ten-volume personal view of the history of the world,[3] achieved widespread popularity and was a direct influence on early International Relations realists such as Louis Halle and Raymond Aron, and facilitated their discovery of Thucydides (Keene 2015: 364–5).[4] For Keene, it is Toynbee's experience of the 'contemporaneity' of Thucydides that most attracted later scholars.

Thucydides did not provide Toynbee with simple historical parallels that would attract later writers, such as the bipolar relationship between Athens and Sparta, the conflict between a sea power and a land power or the ideological differences between democracy and authoritarianism. Nor did Toynbee look to Thucydides for relevant strategic insight into the contemporary world. Instead, 'Thucydides inspired a much larger question of world history as a comparative study of the rise and fall of civilizations' (Keene 2015: 364–5). Toynbee's most famous and influential work was his massive multi-volume *A Study of History*.[5] This work is not itself a work of history but a series of extended reflections on global history. Toynbee thought that the fundamental unit of study in history is the 'civilization' and that the only way to understand it was through comparative study. Toynbee hardly gives Thucydides pride of place in *Study*. He is frequently mentioned, to be sure, but often in the company of other significant historians and philosophers. For example, in volume 3 Toynbee offers an analysis of 'the growth of civilization', which includes a short discussion of Thucydides among a list of around two dozen other significant thinkers including ancient historians, the Buddha, Lenin, Machiavelli, Muhammed, Peter the Great and Confucius.[6] I shall argue in this chapter that, without doubt, Toynbee's idea of the rise and fall of 'Hellenic civilization' is of crucial importance as the paradigm through which the history of all other civilizations is worked out (McIntire and Perry 1989: 22–3), but Thucydides' role in this grand view of history is only comprehensible when understood alongside other classical texts.

Toynbee's unique approach to the study of both history and international relations proved controversial in his lifetime. His early support for the League of Nations and his later attitude to appeasement drew criticism from E. H. Carr, who saw Toynbee as the quintessential utopian in the *Twenty Years Crisis* (1939: 100–3).[7] Similarly, in the 1950s and 1960s, as Toynbee finished the final volumes of *A Study of History*, a number historians such as Pieter Geyl, A. J. P. Taylor and Hugh Trevor-Roper lined up to attack Toynbee's ideas. Historians were particularly critical of the supposed rigidity of Toynbee's focus on civilizations and his later belief that religion could solve the world's great political problems (Geyl, Toynbee and Sorokin 1949; Geyl 1955, 1956a; Taylor 1956; Trevor-Roper 1956). Indeed, Geyl even hailed Toynbee as less a historian and more a prophet (1956b), thereby damning his scholarly rigour while acknowledging his role in world affairs. Despite recent attempts to survey Toynbee's oeuvre with fresh eyes and reassess his position in intellectual history (e.g. the papers collected in McIntire and Perry 1989; Hall 2014; Kumar 2014), he remains a controversial figure today. Accordingly, modern scholars of both the Classics and Political Sciences may find Toynbee's ideas of Thucydides and his vision of Graeco-Roman (or Hellenic) civilization somewhat bizarre. Although we are comfortable today speaking of the Classical World, few would argue that there is a unified, monolithic civilization that stretches from Mycenaean times to the fall of Rome, which came to cover a geographical area that extended from Scotland to Egypt. My aim in this chapter is not to pass judgement on the validity, or otherwise, of Toynbee's historical vision. Rather, I aim to explore how Toynbee came to think of Thucydides as a contemporary through his voluminous writings on history, the classics and modern politics and the place that Thucydides occupies in his view of history and international politics. In thinking through Thucydides' contemporaneity, Toynbee leaves aside for the moment the issues of psychology in the *History* to focus, instead, on ideas of historical time. In other words, Toynbee considers in greater detail than any other British scholar analysed in this book the relationship between his day and Thucydides' as well as the ideas of historical time found within the *History* itself.

Toynbee's presentation of the contemporaneity of Thucydides left readers with the impression that classical civilization and Western civilization were undergoing similar cycles of history. Therefore, Thucydides' depiction of the breakdown of the Greek world is a parallel to interwar politics or, later, to the Cold War. Thucydides' text, to a certain extent, invites such readings. At 1.22, Thucydides invites his readers to read the *History* as a useful aid for future political events because the human thing (*kata to anthropinon*, κατὰ τὸ ἀνθρώπινον) being what it is, events are likely to be the same or similar in the future. This is not an absolute assertion that Thucydides adopted a cyclical view of history as we find, for example, in Polybius. However, it does at least leave the door open to the possibility. That said, Thucydides also introduces other ideas of historical time into his text. At 1.1, for example, he claims that the war was the greatest *kinesis* (κίνησις) to have ever affected the Greek and barbarian world. This word can mean movement but also change. It is not clear, then, whether Thucydides imagined that events were moving in a predictable manner or if he supposed a more unpredictable pattern to events (cf. Meier 2005; Rusten 2015). Thucydides' view of historical time continues to divide Classicists and Ancient Historians. For Arnaldo Momigliano (1966; cf. Greenwood 2015: 44), Thucydides had no cyclical view of history. While Virginia Hunter (1973), following Cornford, points to the role of identifiable 'moral cycles' in Thucydides, which she equates with a 'demythologised' Herodotean cyclical view of history. For Hunter, Thucydides studied Herodotus' account of the fall of Xerxes carefully and then substituted the Persian tyrant for the Athenian *polis* and removed the religious overtones (1973: 167, 181). Pierre Vidal-Naquet (1986: 46) offers a synthesis view, which argues that Thucydides' view of historical time is at once both cyclical and linear. It is cyclical, or in Vidal-Naquet's term, 'permanent', because events are likely to repeat, and linear because events could change as the cycle comes into contact with different situations and contexts.

Turning to the reception of Thucydides' idea of time and change in contemporary International Relations we find that the cyclical view of history is particularly important, if controversial. Lebow (2003) predicates his study of Thucydides on the fact that the Greek historian is describing the rise and fall of states. Looking further back, we find that realists such as Gilpin (1981) ground their reading of International Relations generally and Thucydides in particular on the rise and decline of hegemonic states. Even Allison's Thucydides trap falls into this paradigm in the sense that it presupposes a continually recurring 'event' in the shape of the fear of a rising power leading to war. However, viewing Thucydides as a proponent of cyclical history risks trapping him within an interpretive discourse and disallows the possibility that he might have other, important, insights to offer readers into the nature of historical time. Benjamin Frankel (2013: 349–50), for example, holds Thucydides (alongside Polybius and Machiavelli) as a key proponent of cyclical history, with which he contrasts the 'historicism' of figures such as Kant, Hegel, Marx, Lenin and Fukuyama. The incorporation of theories of historical time into International Relations scholarship, and the tension between the cyclical view of history and the linear, is still far from settled, as a recent paper by Joseph MacKay and Christopher David LaRoche (2017) makes clear.

Toynbee's reading of Thucydides makes an important contribution to this debate, because he offers an interpretation that focuses less on how Thucydides thought about rise and decline than how Thucydides himself fitted into the broader cycle of the history of Graeco-Roman civilization. Thucydides' contemporaneity rested on the supposition that he stood at the same moment in his civilization's life cycle as Toynbee himself did in the modern Western iteration of civilization. Certainly, Thucydides was a great thinker, because he grasped the wider import of the change that was occurring around him. This point is alluded to when Toynbee talks of experiencing the contemporaneity of Thucydides, but is worked out much more fully in his description of the rise and fall of Graeco-Roman civilization in both the *Study* and his other historical writings. Here I note a further point that will arise throughout this chapter. Thucydides is a critical, even crucial, writer for Toynbee. Nevertheless, he can only describe one especially important moment in the grand sweep of the history of civilization. For that reason, we find Toynbee reading Thucydides alongside a host of similarly important classical texts, particularly Aeschylus and Lucretius. Toynbee's positioning of Thucydides in the broader sweep of classical history raises the possibility that the Athenian historian's view of interstate relations is only one among many produced from his civilization and that the true value of the *History* lay in understanding its unique voice among other classical texts. In other words, it is important to tease out what is useful, what is contemporary in Thucydides, while identifying the same in other texts.

Thucydides and the cycle of civilizations

As long ago as 1955, the noted British philosopher Ernst Barker argued that Toynbee's primary ancient influence was Polybius and his conception of cycles, and that Toynbee throughout his life made much more use of Hellenistic than classical Greek history (Barker 1955: 8). However, there is strong evidence that Thucydides (alongside Aeschylus and Lucretius) was key to Toynbee's idea of the cyclical history of civilization as early as 1921. In that year, Toynbee delivered a lecture before an assembled audience of *Literae Humaniores* undergraduates at Oxford, which was then published as a stand-alone pamphlet (Toynbee 1921a) and, in a slightly modified form, as part of R. W. Livingstone's collected volume, *The Legacy of Greece* (Toynbee 1921b).[8] In those essays, Toynbee attempted to justify his vision of Greek and Roman history as the history of a 'Hellenic' civilization, which stretched from 1100 BC to the seventh century AD.[9] This civilization, Toynbee was already claiming, had undergone a process of rise and fall, which could be understood as a drama divided into acts and scenes, that held relevance to those students interested in the future of modern 'Western civilization'. As Toynbee notes, the Great War made the task of understanding Western civilization much more urgent. To understand the origins of Western civilization was also to uncover the origins of the Great War and, hopefully, to avoid future conflicts. The ancient Greeks, as a completed civilization, demonstrate how such a study might be undertaken. As we shall see in this section, both essays present Thucydides as integral to Toynbee's wartime engagement with antiquity, but he is hardly alone: Thucydides' writings cover only a small part of the history of 'Hellenic' civilization and, important as he is, other ancient writers such as Aeschylus, Plato, Lucretius and others are considered to be equally important.

To understand better Toynbee's idea that classical and modern history were running parallel to each other, we first need to consider in greater depth his idea of civilization. Toynbee concluded in the shattered remains of Europe that the nation state was not the smallest 'intelligible unit of history'. Instead, he argues, the fundamental object of historical inquiry should be the civilization. Already by 1920 he had sketched out in a very rough way the ideas that would form the basis for the first six volumes of the *Study*, in which he would attempt to define what a civilization[10] is and outline the laws that governed the varieties of human experience and the unity of human nature. In short, Toynbee believes that all civilizations pass through four states: 'growth, a time of troubles, the universal state, and decay'.[11] Growth is the product of a process Toynbee labels 'challenge and response', in which a creative minority respond effectively to environmental challenges with cultural or technical solutions (Hall 2003). These responses allow the civilization to survive and eventually thrive. If a culture manages to live in equilibrium with its environment (Toynbee names the Minoans, Inuit and Steppe peoples), then it will never progress to become a civilization.[12] If a civilization does manage to progress, then it undergoes periods of expansion and contraction, integration and differentiation. A second process then begins, which Toynbee labels 'withdraw and return'. The creative minority alternatively withdraws into contemplation only to later return to action in a pattern of equilibrium. Over time, civilizations begin to decline, for a range of reasons, including loss of creativity and an overreliance on *mimesis*. For Toynbee, 'Civilizations die of suicide, not by murder.' There is, therefore, an inevitability to the rise and fall of a civilization, but the specific pattern, the turn of events that define this process, varies depending on the situation – as does the life span of the civilization. Toynbee's idea of 'withdraw and return' allows different civilizations to pass or fail a varying number of crises, depending on local circumstances, before they finally die. Toynbee's diplomatic work, no doubt, influenced this idea of a civilization. At the 1919 peace conference, he was involved in the question of what should happen to the Ottoman Empire and the Arabs, and the possibility of a Jewish homeland. This experience gave Toynbee a developing sense of the differences and similarities of the civilizations that surrounded him.

In the 1921 essays, Toynbee's definition of a civilization is, at best, vague. He argues that 'the study of civilization is no different in kind from the study of literature. For in both cases you are studying a creation of the spirit of man or, in more familiar terms, a work of art' (Toynbee 1921a: 5). Civilizations, therefore, differ only from arts such as poetry and statuary by degrees, as both are the works of the human spirit. They are, moreover, exceedingly rare. While Western Europe has produced hundreds of 'societies', it has only produced three 'civilizations', namely the Minoan, the Graeco-Roman and the modern Western.[13] Toynbee has not yet attempted to justify why he sees Graeco-Roman civilization as a unity or attempted to justify any differences with the Minoan or Western civilizations, as he will later do in the *Study*. In the later iteration of his paper, he adds that Western civilization is the child of the Hellenic in the sense that it inherited its political structures and institutions from the ancient world. Even the Crusades represent a Western longing to return to its oriental home (Toynbee 1921b: 293). Nevertheless, the key theme of equivalence is already taking centre stage alongside the metaphor of history as drama. It is because civilizations follow the same historical (we might say dramatic) course that they are 'useful' to study today.

The most influential writer in Toynbee's reading in the years immediately after the Great War was, almost certainly, Oswald Spengler, the great German historian who had published *Der Untergang des Abendlandes* (known in English as *The Decline of the West*) in the summer of 1918 (cited in the bibliography as Spengler 1991). Spengler imagines that civilizations, like biological organisms, had a natural life cycle. They grow, reach maturity and then begin to decay. This book had little immediate influence in Britain owing to a general anti-German sentiment (McNeill 1989a: 98). However, Toynbee's friend Lewis Namier lent him a copy in the summer of 1920 (Spengler 1991). Twenty-eight years later, Toynbee recalled the influence of the book upon him in terms similar to his memory of the effect Thucydides had had in 1914. Spengler posed questions for Toynbee that afforded no easy answers. He offered in his book 'flashes of insight', such as his focus on civilizations as the fundamental unit of historical enquiry, rather than 'arbitrarily insulated fragments' such as nation states and societies (Toynbee 1948g: 9–10). Moreover, Toynbee was drawn to Spengler's pessimism about the future of Western civilization. Yet Toynbee also saw Spengler's book as an opportunity. The German historian, he believed, had been too rigid in his analysis of the rise, decline and fall of civilizations as a uniform process that followed a 'fixed timetable'. Instead, Toynbee began to wonder whether 'English empiricism' might do more to describe the different ways in which civilizations were formed and the various processes that led to their decline and fall over time based upon observable facts (Toynbee 1948g: 9–10).

Spengler posed a question of historical change that Toynbee sought to answer: if we can answer how and why civilizations fall, might we also be able ascertain over what time frame? We have already seen that Toynbee linked Thucydides to ideas of change and decline in the history of civilizations in the 1940s and 1950s. It is interesting to note, therefore, both the similarities and differences between the British and the Greek historian in their approach to this fundamental historical question. The understanding of movement, change and transformation has been a central question of historiography ever since Thucydides described the subject of his work as 'the greatest *kinesis* [movement, change, mobilization][14] that ever affected the Greeks' (1.1). For Toynbee, change is at once linear and cyclical. In the first six volumes of the *Study*, he explains that the rise and fall of individual civilizations follows a cyclical path. However, in the seventh volume Toynbee turns to study the importance of religion in history (see in particular Toynbee 1954a: 420–7). Yet he also claims that the tragic destruction of each civilization leads to a 'linear progress' in religion. Western civilization was a product of medieval Christianity, and as God died in the West, at least according to Nietzsche, civilization began to decay. However, Toynbee believed that there was still the possibility that elites may fashion a new, higher religion that might span the globe, thereby following the pattern of 'withdrawal and return'

(MacDougal 1986: 24). Toynbee combined in one fell swoop the classical idea of the cycle of history with the modern concept of progress.

William McNeill, Toynbee's intellectual biographer, argues that Thucydides occupies a difficult place in the *Study*. Thucydides certainly influenced Toynbee's idea of the tragic aspect to historical writing, almost certainly mediated through a reading of Cornford, as we shall see later in this chapter. At the same time, McNeill maintains that up until the early 1920s, Toynbee was most interested in the 'clash' between the Eastern and Western worlds, and accordingly was more deeply influenced by Herodotus (1989: 98), who treated the wars between the Persians from the East and the Greeks from the West. In later volumes, he turns to a comparative method in which he draws from a scientific approach an empirical accuracy, inspired by Thucydides, to offer an accurate account of the rise and fall of diverse civilizations. Thucydides is particularly relevant to Toynbee's idea of 'withdraw and return'. In his view, Thucydides is a member of the creative minority who withdraws from the field of public action following his exile, only to return as an historian (Toynbee 1948c: 217ff.; cf. Th. 5.26). Toynbee later explains that alongside Clarendon, Procopius and Josephus, Thucydides described how war could act as an instrument of change within a civilization. Specifically, Thucydides described a 'breakdown' of the promising Graeco-Roman civilization (Toynbee 1954d: 60–2).[15] However, Toynbee also imagined that Thucydides witnessed only the first in a number of crises that faced the ancient Mediterranean world.

Toynbee presents the stages that divided classical history as akin to a drama. The unfolding plot of Hellenic history is, in the manner of a play, separated into three acts and a number of different scenes (1921a: 15–17; I quote here Toynbee's own table):

Act I (11th cet.–431 B.C.)

1. Synoikismos (formation of the city-state, the cell of Greek society), 11th cent.–750 B.C.
2. Colonization (propagation of the city-state round the Mediterranean), 750–600 B.C.
3. Economic revolution (change from extensive to intensive growth), 600–500 B.C.
4. Confederation (repulse of Oriental universal empire and creation of an inter-state federation, the Delian League), 500–431 B.C.

Act II (431 B.C.–31 B.C.)

1. The Greek wars (failure of inter-state federation), 431–355 B.C.

2. The Oriental wars (the superman, conquest of the East, struggle for the spoils, barbarian invasion), 355–272 B.C.
3. The first rally (change of scale and fresh experiments in federation – Seleucid Asia, Roman Italy, Aetolian and Achaean 'United States'), 272–218 B.C.
4. The Roman wars (destruction of four great powers by one; devastation of the Mediterranean world), 218–146 B.C.
5. The class wars (capitalism, bolshevism, Napoleonism), 146–31 B.C.

Act III (31 B.C.–7th cent. A.D.)

1. The second rally (final experiment in federation – compromise between city-state autonomy and capitalistic centralization), 31 B.C.–A.D. 180.
2. The first dissolution (external front broken by tribesmen, internal by Christianity), A.D. 180–284.
3. The final rally (Constantine – tribesmen on to the land, bishops into the bureaucracy), A.D. 284–378.
4. The final dissolution (break of tradition), A.D. 378–7th cent.

We can see in this table that without using the terms 'challenge and response' and 'withdraw and return', Toynbee is already thinking along those lines in 1921. Philip, Alexander, Augustus and Constantine all represent the return of creative elites to solve problems at the heart of classical civilization. This schema describing the overall rise and fall of Hellenic civilization remained essentially the same throughout Toynbee's life. The most notable aspect of the scheme is its phrasing in the vocabulary of drama. For Toynbee, ancient history divides chronologically into acts and scenes. Each scene drives the 'plot' forward in a particular way. For example, 431–355 BC, the period of which Thucydides describes the earlier portion, is defined by the failure of attempts to force the Greek city-states into a federation which, ultimately, paves the way for the rise of Macedon and the spread of Hellenic civilization to Eastern lands following the conquest of the Persian Empire by Alexander the Great. Toynbee was not above playing fast and loose with the precise chronological parameters of these divisions. Later in his paper, he would claim that it was the genius of Thucydides to realize that the Peloponnesian War formed a self-contained 'act' in the wider sweep of Greek history (Toynbee 1921a: 23; cf. Th. 5.26). Toynbee even suggested to his audience that everyone has to make their own analysis; that is, each student should divide the 'play' up in their own way. This temporal uncertainty does not diminish the salient point that the acts and scenes only make sense when placed within the broad sweep of Hellenic history. Indeed, Toynbee specifically argued that the main problem with the way ancient history was taught was its emphasis on fifth-century Greece and the breakdown of the Roman Republic because it focused only on two acts divorced from the connecting plot that stretched from the decline of the Mycenaean world to late antiquity. This is a much more flexible view of civilization than Spengler's more biological approach because it allows Toynbee to explain why Greek and Roman politics and civilization often appeared on the point of collapse, for example during the Peloponnesian War and the Roman Civil Wars, yet managed to regroup and reform until the final crisis of late antiquity.

Toynbee is here grappling with a problem that has so far not troubled the writers of the turn: exactly what is the relationship of a text written so long ago to the politics of today? Cornford, Zimmern and Abbott had all expounded upon Thucydides' genius but also relied on simple parallels between the fifth century BC and the early twentieth century. Toynbee goes further. He tries to establish concrete historical links between Thucydides and the present day. The idea that Greek history from the mythical past to the Roman conquest represented a knowable whole was familiar from the earliest days of the Enlightenment. His attempt was predicated on the idea that to gain anything of value from ancient history, one must understand that topic in its entirety. This idea had a long genealogy in British thought. The early histories of Temple Stanyan (1707, cited as Stanyan 1751), John Gillies (1786) and William Mitford (1784–1810, cited as Mitford 2010) had all adopted such broad sweeps, but they had also added breaks and discontinuities. For these historians, there was a difference in what it was possible to know of early Greek history before the more trustworthy accounts of Herodotus and Thucydides began. Moreover, these historians had seen the rise of Philip or the conquest of the Romans as effectively ending Greek liberty and therefore their narratives. George Grote (2010) similarly limited his influential *History of Greece* to affairs on the Hellenic peninsula and her colonies. Few in the eighteenth and nineteenth centuries had attempted to link Greek and Roman history together into one broad narrative. However, in the 1910s and 1920s the first volumes of the *Cambridge Ancient History* appeared. This multi-authored work attempted to offer a comprehensive scholarly history of antiquity from the Stone Age to the age of Constantine that was also accessible to the layman. However, even with the *CAH* we should note the differences with Toynbee's view of Graeco-Roman history. The *CAH* never attempts to identify a Graeco-Roman civilization and it starts and ends much earlier than Toynbee's interpretation of classical history. Toynbee here suggests that Graeco-Roman or Hellenic civilization spanned both the Greek and Latin peoples, stretched from the moors of Scotland to the Indus valley and ends only with the barbarian invasions and the rise of Christianity as late as the seventh century AD. In sum, he proposes a unity to classical history under the rubric of a single civilization.

Toynbee also intended this 'dramatic' conception of the rise and fall of a civilization to fulfil a didactic function. Like Thucydides, he imagines himself educating his own and future generations (cf. Th. 1.22). He argues in the paper that because Graeco-Roman history has been worked out to its conclusion, it is perhaps more valuable than the study of contemporary history because it allows the student to see how the play continues and finishes (Toynbee 1921a: 10–12). There is a strong assumption here that the Graeco-Roman and Western civilizations are equivalent and that the narrative of their respective rise and fall will play out not in exactly the same way but similarly in the sense that both faced a number of challenges and crises. We have already seen that the idea of equivalence was crucial to Toynbee's turn to Thucydides. The experience of the outbreak of the Great War provided a direct parallel to the Peloponnesian War. As the cycle of the respective histories revolved, they found themselves, at the moments of the Peloponnesian and Great Wars, to be running in parallel. The use of this parallel is further strengthened by the distance between the Greeks and us, which allows us to view the completed play without any partisan interest. Moreover, Toynbee holds that the quality of the literature of the Greeks and Romans means that their historical experience is more finely expressed than that of the modern Western civilization. 'I felt that these men had travelled along the road on which our feet were set; that they had travelled it farther than we, travelled it to the end; and that the wisdom of greater experience and the poignancy of greater suffering than ours was expressed in the beauty of their words' (Toynbee 1921a: 12). The Thucydidean lesson, alongside the lesson from all ancient history, emerges as not bound by the tenets of a particular school of thought, of say realism or idealism, but the overall course of the rise and fall of civilization.

Following this logic, we should be able to pinpoint the parallels between the 'act' described by Thucydides and the corresponding 'act' in the history of Western civilization. Toynbee offers, at precisely this point, a translation of Thucydides' famous *stasis* passage (3.82), which describes how party strife and civil war intensified in Corcyra and ultimately spread throughout the entire Greek world.[16] His translation makes an effort to contemporize Thucydides' words. Most notably, Toynbee renders the Greek word *stasis* as class war. In an age that saw Marxism spread throughout Europe and the rise of communism in

Russia, a term like 'class war' had a definite contemporary resonance of the struggle between the proletariat and the middle and upper classes. The Greek *stasis*, however, is a term that was surely known to Toynbee's audience or at least could have been explained in the text as a Greek word that implied dissension between *oligarchs* and the *demos*. Palmer (2017) suggests that linguistically it can be translated as civil war, civil strife, faction, or revolution. Price (2001) even goes so far as to suggest that Thucydides saw the entire Peloponnesian War as a *stasis*. For Thucydides, *stasis* denotes an entrenchment of opinions and political positions, in this case between democrats and oligarchs, that leads to a lack of compromise and an intensification of violence as well as a breaking down of the bonds that hold society together. *Stasis* is exacerbated in the Peloponnesian War by Athens and Sparta supporting democrats and oligarchs abroad, but its causes lie in the internal tensions within the *polis*, perhaps even among families (Allison 1997: 168). No doubt what attracted Toynbee to this passage is the claim that human nature ensures that such calamities will occur again and again, despite 'changes in circumstance'. The Great War, like the Peloponnesian, is an inter-civilization *stasis*. For Toynbee, writing in the immediate aftermath of the Great War, it is not the equivalence between the actions of Athens and Britain, or Sparta and Germany, that matter; nor the parallels between the causes of the two wars. Rather, both wars had a very significant effect on their respective generations. Thucydides writes that the Peloponnesian War 'moved' (*ekinethe*, ἐκινήθη) the entire Greek world, while Toynbee uses the word 'upheaval'. Both wars fundamentally changed the world. Evil and stupidity pushed out idealism and intellect, and the passions become ascendant. The world, in short, became a much a worse place. When Toynbee recalled in the 1940s and 1950s that he had experienced the contemporaneity of Thucydides in 1914, and that he believed the Greek past was Europe's future, he may well have been thinking of the effect of the war on the Greek mind as described in 3.82 and 3.83.

There is a second point to make. Toynbee presents Thucydides as only one among many classical authors to describe the effect of class war, or conflict more generally, on the Graeco-Roman mind. Antiquity produced many historians of 'troubled times' to reflect the various conflicts and civil wars that marked the history of her civilization. So, for example, Xenophon, who is rather 'unimaginative and self-complacent' next to the 'sensitive and emotional' Thucydides, conveys the same thoughts found in 3.82 in his description of the Battle of Mantinea (362 BC), in which he lost his own son Gryllus (Toynbee 1921a: 29-30; *Hell.* 8.5). Moreover, the 'class war' intensifies in act 2, scene 4, during the Roman wars of conquest, when 'the whole Mediterranean world, and the devastated area in Italy most of all, was shaken by the economic and social revolutions which the Roman wars brought in their train. The proletariat was oppressed to such a degree that the unity of society was permanently destroyed with a violent extinction by Bolshevik outbreaks' (Toynbee 1921a: 34). Toynbee also quotes a passage from the Roman poet and philosopher Lucretius, which argues that death destroys personality and that the soul is not immortal.[17] In the version of the essay in the *Legacy of Greece* volume, Toynbee writes that 'Lucretius wrote that about a hundred and fifty years after Hannibal evacuated Italy, but the horror is still vivid in his mind, and his poetry arises it in our minds as we listen. The writer will never forget how those lines kept running in his head during the spring of 1918' (Toynbee 1921b: 315). Again, this passage is less about power politics than the effect of conflict upon the mental state of a generation. Many of these other writers Toynbee found equally, if not more, relevant during the Great War.

Nevertheless, Thucydides exerts a great influence on Toynbee's idea of the role of tragedy in history before he had even begun the *Study*. Already in the 1920 lecture and the 1921 essay, Toynbee had claimed that 'I suspect the great tragedies of history – that is, the great civilisations that have been created by man – may all reveal the same plot, if we analyse them rightly' (Toynbee 1921a: 6). And 'When Greek civilisation may be said finally to have dissolved, our own civilisation was ready to 'shoot up and thrive' and repeat the tragedy of mankind' (quoted in McNeil 1989a: 97). Here we see the germ of the thought that would drive the *Study*, namely the idea that there is an equivalence between the history of various civilizations that the careful historian can recover and understand. Toynbee maintains that this equivalence is able to help thinkers understand the modern West's future. However, in defining Thucydides' idea of a civilization so far, we also need to understand what Toynbee believed was driving their history forward and the role of Thucydides in this aspect of his thought. I turn to this problem in the next section.

Toynbee on Cornford and the 'impersonal forces' of history

At first glance, Toynbee's division of Hellenic history into acts and scenes like a play recalls Cornford's assertion that there is a parallel between Aeschylus and Thucydides. Both writers use drama to understand Greek history. Toynbee was certainly well aware of Cornford's 'heretical' view of Thucydides. *Mythistoricus* was such a notorious book that Toynbee simply must have read it while at

Oxford. Recall that Zimmern, Toynbee's teacher and friend, had sent Cornford a letter congratulating him on the work, and personally and professionally Toynbee was an intimate of Murray who was also on friendly terms with Cornford. Perhaps Toynbee even met Cornford at some meeting or conference. The world of British Classical Studies, after all, was not that large. It no surprise, therefore, to discover that Cornford's idea of impersonal forces in Thucydides' *History* deeply influenced Toynbee. In a 1922 volume on *Greek Historical Thought*, he argues in the introduction that the unifying theme of Greek historiography from Homer to Procopius (a sixth-century Byzantine historian) is 'the creed, at once primitive and profound, of Pride, Doom, and the Envy of the Gods' (Toynbee 1959a: ix). This volume is a collection of excerpts from ancient historians and other classical texts translated by Toynbee. From this material, Toynbee hopes that his readers will gain 'the real religious outlook of Hellenism' from this volume, or 'far better from Mr Cornford' (Toynbee 1959a: x). Toynbee is speaking here of *hubris*, *nemesis* and *phthonos* (ὕβρις, νέμεσις, φθόνος). The first two are forces that Cornford argued took hold of Athens; the third refers to the envy of the Gods, which again Cornford spoke about at length (1907: 219, 233).[18] Toynbee believes that the Greeks did not have the Christian concept of good and evil. Rather, they feared that the jealousy of the gods might destroy their power and their possessions here on Earth. 'Their kingdom was emphatically a kingdom of this world. Pericles exhorted his countrymen to let the greatness of Athens "fill," not "pass," their understanding; the "salvation" debated at Melos meant bodily escape from massacre or enslavement and not the release of the soul from guilt' (1907: 219, 233). In other words, Toynbee argues that all Greeks, including Thucydides, saw certain religious and impersonal forces at work in all things and all different to those familiar from Christian beliefs, which led to moral cycles such as that faced by Xerxes in Herodotus' account of the Persian Wars. Greek man could not expect to escape either destruction or the envy of the gods. Yet Thucydides was in no way unusual in recognizing this pattern.

Toynbee's source for the idea that tragic or moral cycles were prevalent in Greek thought is almost certainly Cornford. In volume 10 of the *Study*, there is further strong evidence for the influence of *Mythistoricus* on Toynbee. There, he recalls how reading the book altered his conception of history:

> F.M. Cornford, in his Thucydides Mythistoricus, taught me to indicate, by the use of an abstract noun with its initial letter printed as a capital, the presence of one of those psychic principalities and powers – 'The Tragic Passions', as

Cornford calls them – for which there are no proper names in the sterilized vocabulary of a rationalist latter-day Western Society. Hilm and Aidôs, Civilization and Democracy and Industrialism, Archaism and Futurism, Time and Space, Law and Fortune, are a few examples, taken at random. This usage has, of course, its own drawback. On the analogy of personal names, it might be misinterpreted as conveying the false, and unintended, suggestion that these presences are personalities, when the truth is that they are non-personal emanations from a subconscious abyss of the Psyche that is the matrix of personalities as well. Yet a usage suggesting personification is at any rate less misleading than one suggesting that these entities are abstractions – as would be implied by printing the initial letters of the corresponding English words in lower-case type – for, though they are not personalities, they are charges of psychic energy that have power to work weal and woe in human affairs, and the lack of proper names for them in a latter-day Western vocabulary betrays a tell-tale lacuna in things in Heaven and Earth than are dreamed of in Horatio's western Philosophy.

> Toynbee 1954d: 231

There is a lot to unpack in this quotation. I would like to begin by noting that Toynbee has found in Cornford not only a way of reading Thucydides but also all of history. In Cornford's Thucydides, the personification of dramatic states drives forward the events of the *History*. As in the case of one of Aeschylus' heroes, these personifications lead Athens, Thucydides' dramatic hero, to her eventual doom. Toynbee, however, has expanded the list of personifications to include 'Civilization and Democracy and Industrialism, Archaism and Futurism, Time and Space, Law and Fortune' – in other words, to include personifications that have been at work in the twenty or so civilizations that Toynbee had identified including the modern West. For Toynbee, personifications are no longer limited to Greek ideas of blindness and pride. They now include the very modern processes of democracy and industrialization, and ideas that were commonly believed to have grown organically within Western society, for example, the French Revolution or the Industrial Revolution. Toynbee suggests these were, in fact, personifications of 'psychic principalities and powers' that arrived as external forces to shape the history of Western civilization. This argument flies in the face of much of what Cornford believed. I argued in Chapter 2 that Cornford draws a sharp distinction between Thucydides 'ancient' mode of thought and the modern ideas of evolution and economics. Yet Toynbee seems undecided as to what these personifications actually are. In Cornford's presentation of Thucydides, they are archaic deities, stripped by the rationalist

Thucydides of their religious significance, which are used to explain the psychological forces that drive history. Toynbee appears to argue that they are emanations from a group 'psyche', found in a civilization at certain points in its history. Toynbee is unclear whether this means that these psychological forces emerge fully formed from the collected consciousness of a civilization or arrive from external factors. A passage in volume 9 of the *Study* suggests that Toynbee thought of these personifications as, to a certain extent at least, irrational: 'If blind and irrational forces were in truth outside the pale of political history, most published works on political history, from Thucydides' History of the Atheno-Peloponnesian War to D. C. Somerwell's British politics since 1900, would have been thrown on the scrap heap' (Toynbee 1954c: 772). In common with Cornford, Toynbee thought that perhaps the archaic states *hubris*, *nemesis* and *phthonos* survive in the modern world, indeed in all civilizations, and that it is the historian's job to understand them.

It is certain, I believe, that Cornford's reading of Thucydides as presenting a moral cycle, as Hunter (1973) would term it, in his depiction of the tragedy of Athens had influenced Toynbee's reading of all Greek literature as early as the first years of the 1920s. This influence clearly remained with Toynbee throughout the following decades when he acknowledged it in volume 10 of the *Study*.[19] This engagement with Cornford represents an important aspect to Toynbee's thinking that has been understudied by previous scholars but goes a long way to explain his interest in both the cyclical view of history and his interest in Thucydides, specifically. Let us now return to the pressing question of how this idea of cyclical history defined Toynbee's turn to Thucydides and his feeling that the Peloponnesian War and the Great War were in a meaningful sense contemporary.

The contemporaneity of Thucydides

In Chapter 2, I pointed out that Cornford had been hesitant to insert specific contemporary parallels into *Mythistoricus*. In Chapters 3 and 4, I argued that the Great War swept away any similar compunction in the writings of Zimmern, Murray, Hutton, Glover and Abbott, among others. In the late 1940s and 1950s, Toynbee recalled that he too felt no hesitation in drawing parallels between Thucydides' description of Greek politics and the outbreak of the Great War. We should, however, be wary of assuming that Thucydides' contemporaneity had emerged fully formed in Toynbee's mind as the clouds of war gathered over Europe in 1914. No contemporary source corroborates the 1950 quotation that opens this chapter. Nevertheless, two aspects of Thucydides' life and thought may have attracted the young Toynbee in 1914. First, Thucydides himself sat out much of the actual fighting in the Peloponnesian War because of his exile following the loss of Amphipolis. Similarly, Toynbee, unlike most of his school and Oxford contemporaries, did not serve on the front (McNeill 1989a: 64–91). At Winchester, he had hated military drills almost as much as he had hated team sports. Toynbee was much more at home with his books. At the same time, Toynbee, like most of the 'officer class' in Britain, France and Germany, had imbued himself with the 'heroic' ideals of Homer and the rest of the classical inheritance. His sojourn in Greece in 1911–12 had entailed feats of genuine hardship and even a confrontation with a band of *klefts*, suggesting that Toynbee was motivated and able to meet this heroic ideal, at least as he conceived it (McNeil 1989a: 64–5). In the event, Toynbee never enlisted. Indeed, he even avoided conscription three times on medical grounds by citing a case of typhus he originally caught while in Greece. He preferred, instead, to contribute to the war effort by working for the Foreign Office and then contributing to the British delegation to the Peace conference of 1919. The war, however, profoundly affected Toynbee (Stromberg 1989). He and his mother could never shake the feeling that his actions were indeed cowardly, despite the protestations of the pacifist Murray to the contrary. In particular, Toynbee resolved not to return to Balliol after the war. He worried, no doubt, how he could look the few surviving students and fellows in the eye. Instead, he threw himself into his work, both historical and political. Like Thucydides, Toynbee was removed from the arena of action and, therefore, resolved to make himself useful through study.

Second, as we have seen throughout this chapter, his reading of Thucydides reinforced in Toynbee's mind the idea that historical time did not move only in a purely linear fashion but also repeated itself in a cyclical pattern. In a slightly different retelling of the anecdote that opens this chapter, Toynbee emphasized that at the outbreak of the Great War this sudden vision of the contemporaneity of Greek history altered his perception of historical time.

> The general war of 1914 overtook me expounding Thucydides to Balliol undergraduates reading for Literae Humaniores, and then suddenly my understanding was illuminated. The experience we were having in our world now had been experienced by Thucydides in his world already. I was re-reading him now with a new perception –perceiving meanings in his words, and feelings behind his phrases, to which I had been insensible until I, in my turn, had run into that historical crisis that had inspired him to write his work. Thucydides, it now appeared, had been over this ground before. He and his generation had

been ahead of me and mine in the stage of historical experience that we had respectively reached; in fact, his present had been my future. But this made nonsense of the chronological notation which registered my world as 'modern' and Thucydides' world as 'ancient.' Whatever chronology might say, Thucydides' world and my world had now proved to be philosophically contemporary. And if this were the true relation between the Graeco-Roman and the Western civilisation, might not the relation between all civilisations known to us turn out to be the same?

Toynbee 1948g: 7–8

Again, the cycles of the two great civilizations are presented as running parallel to each other at this momentous instance. Here Toynbee's account of his Thucydidean epiphany is much fuller than the 1950 version. There is a much greater emphasis on Toynbee's idea of time as repeating itself. Thucydides had walked the same path that the generation of 1914 now found themselves journeying along. Thucydides provides a certain measure of comfort to these fellow travellers. He has seen it all before. This leads Toynbee to the further thought that if Thucydides' world and early twentieth-century Europe were 'contemporary' then might both civilizations prove to be on the same path? In other words, could Thucydides and the history of Greece more generally be used as a guide to the future? Toynbee is here suggesting that political events follow a rotational pattern in which civilizations rise and fall following a definable and observable path that is comprehensible only through the careful study of their history. Of course, Toynbee is remembering this epiphany years later in 1948 when he has already worked out his vision of the rise and fall of civilizations over more than three million words in his *Study*. It is no surprise, therefore, to find that Toynbee also pointed to the contemporaneity of Thucydides in volume 10 of the *Study*. This volume lists at great length all of Toynbee's intellectual debts and the various influences on his work. There Toynbee once again draws attention to Thucydides' contemporaneity, but this time in connection within a 'cycle of history' which encompasses both the Great War and the outbreak of the Second World War (Toynbee 1954d: 93–4). Gone now is the reference to teaching Oxford undergraduates. In its place, Toynbee argues that his classical education led him, in 1914, to return to Plato's disillusionment with Periclean democracy and Thucydides' description of the outbreak of the Peloponnesian War in 431 BC. Toynbee found himself undergoing the same 'experience' as Thucydides, which led him to appreciate with fresh eyes the 'inwardness' of 'Thucydidean words and phrases that had meant little or nothing to him before' (Toynbee 1954d: 93–4). Toynbee, therefore, felt keenly that 1914 and 431 BC were two dates 'philosophically contemporaneous with one another' (Toynbee 1954d: 93–4). This feeling of contemporaneity is reinforced in 1939 as Europe lurches towards another even more destructive war. Toynbee is reminded that Thucydides' account of the Peloponnesian War was similarly a tragedy in two acts separated by an interval of illusory peace, in the same way that the Punic Wars (264–146 BC) and the Roman–Persian Wars (AD 572–628) were also punctuated by periods of illusory peace.

In volume 10, we once again return to Toynbee's experience of the contemporaneity of Thucydides, but now he offers much more detail. There is a repeating cycle of wars, namely the Peloponnesian War, the Byzantine–Persian Wars and also the global wars of the twentieth century. This time what unites them is not the effect that they have on the psychology of a generation but rather their double nature, the fact that they are divided by an interlude of peace that presaged only an intensification of violence in the second half of the conflict. The outbreak of the three wars represents the same moment as the wheel of history turns. The contemporaneity of 1914 and 431 BC helps Toynbee better understand Thucydides' thoughts and writings. One immediately thinks of Thucydides' claim that events will likely recur in the same or similar manner, *kata to anthropinon* (κατὰ τὸ ἀνθρώπινον), although it must be noted that Toynbee makes no mention here of human nature. The outbreak of the various wars makes the 'classically minded scholar' realize that the experiences of Thucydides might be the same as those that were about to overwhelm many in Western Europe, but there is no claim that human nature is fundamentally the same in all periods. We should also note that during the Great War, Toynbee was similarly struck by parallels with the Punic War (McNeill 1989a: 94) and that a whole host of classical texts had provided him some measure of comfort, particularly Lucretius and Aeschylus. As an Oxford educated classicist, Toynbee was almost certain to remember and draw comfort from a range of ancient writings. It is also in keeping with Toynbee's sense that history was running in a recognizable pattern. If the parallel between 431 BC and AD 1914 works because they are parallel points in an historical cycle, it makes sense that readers should also find parallels with, say, the last generation of the Roman Republic when Lucretius was writing, because of the notion of 'withdrawal and return'. All civilizations, in Toynbee's estimation, faced a series of crises, caused by the withdrawal of creative elites. We have seen that the classical world underwent a number of these crises, so it is unsurprising that in 1914, when the Western world faced her gravest day, Toynbee should refer to material from a number of different points in the life cycle of Graeco-Roman civilization.

Toynbee was far from the only writer in the 1940s and 1950s to point to the contemporaneity of Thucydides. In America, comparisons between 431 BC and 1939 became increasingly widespread.[20] Toynbee himself was present at a speech given by George Marshall in 1947 that referenced the Peloponnesian War and later recalled the effect that this speech had on him in volume 10 of the *Study* (Toynbee 1954d: 60–1, footnote 3). In Toynbee's account of the speech, Marshall was struck by the contemporaneity of Thucydides and therefore the relevance of the Greek historian to the modern world. Elizabeth Sawyer (2013: 118–124) points out that Marshall may not have mentioned Thucydides in his speech at all, but simply intended to draw a comparison between democratic Athens and the US. However, Toynbee himself clearly took the speech as a reference to Thucydides. He was not alone in this belief. Already in a 1951 article in *Life* magazine, the journalist George Campbell saw Marshall's speech as an endorsement of the value of Thucydides as a thinker on international politics (Campbell 1951: 96). Louis Halle's 1952 essay, *A Message from Thucydides* (Halle 1955), should also be seen as an iteration of the growing Anglo-American sense of the contemporaneity of Thucydides. Moreover, Halle's essays reveals a significant Toynbean influence. He quoted Toynbee's feeling of the contemporaneity of Thucydides in 1914 and adopted the idea that this moment represented a turning point in the reception of the Greek historian (Keene 2015: 364).

What unites these references to the contemporaneity of Thucydides is the sense that the Athenian historian describes a war in a broader sweep of history that is particularly relevant to the situation in which the West found itself in 1914, 1939 and 1945. In a sense, there is nothing terribly groundbreaking about this insight. Thucydides had claimed to write for readers who might find his account useful in the same or a similar situation. In other words, he flatters his readers to imagine that if they are intelligent enough then they might understand the true import of the text. Readers have been struck by the similarities between the terrible times Thucydides describes and the terrible times that they find themselves living in, from Thomas Hobbes' examination of monarchy and war (Hoekstra 2016) to Connor's rediscovery of the *History* during the Vietnam War (1984: 7–8). Toynbee's own turn to Thucydides is another notable entry in this tradition of reading the *History* for comfort and instruction in times of trouble. However, Toynbee's words also move beyond Hobbes and Connor to ask why it is that we find Thucydides germane to our contemporary situation. Toynbee is not content to simply say that at certain times, and for certain reasons, the same or similar events recur. His aim was to understand a pattern to the madness that lay before him.

Conclusion: A Thucydidean turn?

Toynbee's reading of Thucydides is significant in this book's account of the Thucydidean turn because he went beyond simply feeling the contemporaneity of Thucydides in the way that, say, Orlo Williams had. The parallels between ancient and modern events struck many writers. The jostling for power among rival states, alongside the division of power between land and sea powers, suggested an obvious equivalence between the Peloponnesian War and the Great War. Toynbee, I am sure, would have agreed, but he also recognized that understanding the contemporaneity of Thucydides could be strengthened and deepened by thinking critically about the nature of change in the text and in the arc of world history more broadly. The answer Toynbee proposed was to view world history through a series of comparisons between civilizations, using Graeco-Roman antiquity as both a test case and a benchmark. Thucydides was an important, but far from unique, influence on this grand project. To understand Thucydides correctly, Toynbee appears to suggest, one must both live in a time similar to his and grasp the significance of his period as just another moment in the rotation of the great wheel of history. That said, Toynbee was not dogmatic in his notions of historical time and was willing to concede that there was both immutable progress in the history of religions and cycles on a much smaller scale identified by Cornford in Greek thought.

Toynbee is, perhaps, the writer who experienced Thucydides' contemporaneity most keenly of all the figures surveyed in this book. As Keene reminded us, Toynbee's experience is important because Halle and Aron remembered it in the post-Second World War period. Toynbee revealed to his readers that Thucydides was not just a source of apothegms and parallels nor a lofty political philosopher that required years of technical training to understand – nor even a source of a 'methodology' that modern students could learn and apply to the modern world. He was both those things but also a text for troubled times – for moments when ancient wars become modern nightmares. Since Toynbee, readers have similarly been struck by the contemporaneity of Thucydides during the Vietnam War, Iraq, Afghanistan and now the supposed looming conflict in the Pacific (Allison 2017b). Thucydides has now become forever our contemporary.

6

Learning to Tolerate Thucydides

On a cold Saturday in January 1936, about two dozen delegates gathered in Westminster School in London to attend the final day of the annual general meeting of the Classical Association. Huddled together on hard wooden benches, they had congregated to listen to papers on the current state of research into the Classics in the United Kingdom. Today, the Classical Association AGM sprawls out over three days and boasts hundreds of attendees and dozens of panels. In 1936, proceedings were rather more humble. There were no panels. Instead, around fifty delegates sat through a series of talks on all aspects of the Classics from Thursday through to Saturday. After the meeting had ended, delegates reconvened in the school hall for a rather meagre meal of corned beef with a side of either ale or cider. Despite the less than salubrious surroundings, a remarkable paper was given during the conference on the current state of Thucydidean studies. At 11 am on the final day, Enoch Powell (1912–98), then a young scholar of ancient Greek who had won a fellowship at Trinity College, Cambridge, only two years before, ascended to the speaker's podium. Powell's expertise lay in the painstaking study of the surviving manuscripts of Herodotus and Thucydides. On that morning, however, Powell chose to speak about the effect of the Great War upon Thucydidean studies. His paper opened with the observation that, generally speaking, the war had had a devastating effect on classical scholarship: work had ceased during the fighting, a whole generation of scholars had been lost in the trenches, and the hardening of national borders had prevented the flow of ideas. However, there was one exception to this dire picture: Thucydidean studies. Indeed, Powell felt that the study of Thucydides had profited from the war. He claimed that in mere bulk, the seventeen years prior to 1936 had produced more literature on Thucydides than any preceding age, including the final quarter of the nineteenth century, which Powell labelled the 'heyday' of German scholarship.

Powell had little to say on the 'ephemeral' literature produced during the war itself, meaning the appearance of Thucydidean quotations on war memorials or propaganda.¹ Rather, his paper focused on the influence of the war on sober philological and historical analyses of the text. The beginning of the effect could be dated precisely to 2 November 1914 when a young German officer named Schwartz was killed at the front. 'To this event we owe a book which is the most momentous ever dedicated to Thucydides' (Churchill archives 1/6/19: 2). For that officer was the son of Eduard Schwartz, the renowned German scholar who, until that date, had been editing a monumental edition of the *acta* of the Ecumenical Church but now turned to the study of Thucydidean composition, 'seeking some relief from the pressure of misfortune' (Churchill archives 1/6/19: 2; Schwartz 1919). Powell does not say it explicitly, but he suggests that Schwartz, deeply affected by the war, turned to antiquity's greatest historian of conflict out of a sense of kinship: both men had seen and felt the terrible consequences of the greatest *kinesis* of their times. Schwartz's study focused on understanding Thucydides as a man and as a historian. Before the Great War, German scholars such as Wilamowitz and Classen had argued endlessly over the precise dates of the composition of various parts of the *History*, positing first and second drafts, in an ongoing debate called the *Thukydidesfrage*. Powell thought that Schwartz realized intuitively that a 'creative' historian like Thucydides could only write so authoritatively of an event when it lay completed before him. Thucydides had, in this interpretation, made notes and even drafts throughout the conflict but returned to a broken Athens only after the end of the Peloponnesian War to rewrite his project into a unified whole. Working in the shattered ruins of his beloved city, Thucydides began to revise the layers of his work, interpreting the Peloponnesian War through the prism of Athens' defeat.² This Athens appeared to Schwartz and other German writers much like their own shattered empire in 1917 and 1918. Schwartz had led scholars to see that the central edifice of the history was a bipolar political order divided physically and spiritually between Athens and Sparta.³ This dualism runs through Thucydides' work from the *Archaeology*, through the *Pentekontaetia*, into Pericles' speeches and then into the rest of the work. It divides Sparta from Athens, oligarchy from democracy, land power from sea power. Later German scholars – Powell named Max Pohlenz (1919 and 1920) and Schadewelt (1929) – were left to debate only the details of Schwartz's reinterpretation of the *Thukydidesfrage*, although the latter had also moved away from considering Thucydides as solely a 'historical scientist' to also analysing him as an 'historical artist'.

The intensification of scholarly interest in Thucydides was also felt in France and Britain. During the Victorian period, Powell thought that scholars such as Thomas Arnold (2010) and J. P. Mahaffy (1874) had treated Thucydides as belonging to an earlier archaic and violent world that had been superseded by Victorian advances in science, politics, morality and law. In the early twentieth century, Cornford, at least in Powell's interpretation, had treated Thucydides as an object of only antiquarian or literary interest. After the war, scholars could no longer afford to be so complacent in their confrontation with Thucydides' dark depiction of human nature. Accordingly, the 'highly' gifted French journalist Albert Thibaudet had written in 1922 *La campagne avec Thucydide* and George Abbott had published *Thucydides: A Study in Historical Reality* in 1925. A 'spiritual similarity' between the Great War and the Peloponnesian War inspired both these works. Moreover, both accepted and understood the harsh political world described by Thucydides. They even went so far as to embrace the effect of the war on the moral attitude to Thucydides. 'To put the matter in one word, we have learned to become more tolerant' (Churchill archives 1/6/19: 8). In effect, Powell writes:

> To appreciate the gulf which separates pre- and post-war in this respect, one should turn, for example, from the priggish superiority of Arnold's appendices, or the theoretical superiority of such pre-war books as 'Thucydides Mythistoricus' to the urgent sense of kinship which animates a Thibaudet or an Abbott.
>
> Churchill archives 1/6/19: 8

Powell's argument that the war led scholars to become more tolerant of Thucydides is an early way of thinking about the 'turn' to the Greek historian in the sense that it is at this moment that new readings of the text, focused on political equivalences, began to emerge. Thibaudet and Abbott are both writers spiritually united by the equivalence they draw between the ancient and modern wars. However, crucially they also point to the change that the Great War wrought on ideas about the moral attitude of Thucydides himself, which in turn leads to a reconsideration of the value of his pessimistic thought for post-war Europe. Becoming tolerant of Thucydides does not entail simply finding parallels from his *History* but taking seriously his thought and attempting to find its value for the contemporary moment. For Powell, this toleration manifests itself in different ways by different commentators. Schwartz comments that during the Melian dialogue Athens is right to think in terms of cold politics rather than vague hope. Thibaudet points to the 'truth' that an insular sea power is always invulnerable to a land power. There is even, in Powell's own interpretation, an indication that Thucydides describes a bipolar world. All these interpretations remove moral considerations from the text. For Powell, the Great War had taught commentators to 'tolerate' Thucydides' clear-eyed description of politics with no room for morality in the conduct of international affairs.⁴ At the same time, however, the focus on Thucydides' personal reaction to the war, the man broken by the destruction of the empire in Schwartz's opinion, leaves the door open to the idea that Thucydides himself possessed a deeply moral view of the world. What role then, Powell asks, does morality play in our response to Thucydides? We shall return to this question later in the chapter.

Perhaps the most pressing problem Powell identifies is that of the stability or the permanence of the move to better tolerate Thucydides. Throughout this book, I have tried to identify those places where readings of Thucydides have been forgotten today and where they have had an afterlife in post-Second World War scholarship. Powell's paper reminds us that in the 1930s any gains made in understanding the *History* were extremely fragile because of the rise of fascism and Nazism and the impending Second World War. Powell gave the paper not to laud the achievements of the classical scholars he referenced, but because he felt that the unprecedented seventeen years of Thucydidean scholarship he had identified was coming to an end under the pressures exerted by the rise of Nazism. In the Anglo-Saxon world, these pressures were manifesting themselves as pacifism. At a previous AGM, Powell noted, 'a celebrated English scholar' had likened Thucydides to Aristophanes and Euripides as an exponent of pacifist ideals. This scholar was almost certainly Gilbert Murray.⁵ Worse still, Charles Cochrane had released his book *Thucydides and the Science of History* in 1929, which completely ignored the unchanging human nature and bipolarity of Greece evident in Thucydides, arguing instead that the *History* represented one of the most devastating indictments of war ever written (Churchill archives 1/6/19: 11–12).⁶ Murray and Cochrane, rather than praise the detachment of Thucydides' amoral depiction of events, had misguidedly attempted to find in the *History* a moral criticism of war. In Germany, affairs were even worse under the rise of Nazism. The rot had begun as early as Felix Wassermann's 1931 *Neus Thukidesbild*, where it is claimed that the funeral speech argued for the absolute subordination of the individual to the state (*Einfügung*), which required an absolute leader (*Führer*) (Churchill archives 1/6/19: 14). Powell then identifies Werner Jaeger's *Paideia*⁷ and the dissertation of Dietzfelbinger as works influenced by National Socialist ideology before claiming that today Germany is turning out 'pseudo-philosophy' under the guise of Classics to justify its regime (Churchill archives 1/6/19: 14–15). For example, in 1934 Heinrich Weinstock published a work titled *Polis, der greichische Beitrag zu einer deutschen Bildung heute, an Thukydides erläut* (which Powell translates as *The Greek Contribution to German Education To-day, Illustrated from Thucydides*), in which he argued that the old humanism of the nineteenth century was much too involved with individualism and liberalism. It is now time to invent a new, third, humanism worthy of the new Reich. Hitler had shown that citizens need to give themselves completely to the state, so it is time for Germany to turn again to the example of the Greek people whose every activity is, supposedly, directed towards the *polis* or the state (Churchill archives 1/6/19: 12–14). The rise of Nazism, I believe, and its effect on scholarship genuinely shocked Powell: '[I]n present-day Germany one of the chief monuments of that liberation of the human mind which is the deepest significance of Greek civilisation for us, is being pressed into service as an additional justification for taking men's freedom away' (Churchill archives 1/6/19: 16). Despite Powell's emphasis on philological and classical readings of the text, he was aware of the political stakes involved in reading Thucydides in the years before the outbreak of the Second World War.

Powell felt that the National Socialist inspired readings of Thucydides are to be resisted. They represent a terrible doctrine politically and they do great violence to the text through the imposition of a morality foreign to Thucydides' sensibilities. However, one could argue that all readings of Thucydides through a contemporary political lens do violence to the text and obscure any truths that the *History* offers. Stahl, for example, argues that Schwartz's biographical approach to Thucydides left scholarship with a fundamental problem (2003: 18–21), namely, that it is all too easy to see in the different layers of Thucydides' text, that is to say Thucydides' writing at different stages of his life, a patriotic defender of national liberty or a clear-eyed political realist – depending on the reader's view of the world. Powell, I believe, was aware of this problem posed by the *Thukydidesfrage*. He points not only to the value of the scholarship produced in the years following the Great War, but also of the need to reformulate it to understand Thucydides' political and moral thought on a sounder philological and theoretical basis in order to resist pacifist readings in Britain and America and fascist readings on the continent. Let us now turn to consider how he went about this task and question how successful he was in this endeavour.

The moral and political principles of Thucydides

Powell's paper would be little more than a curiosity in the history of scholarship were it not for the fact that he also wrote a fellowship dissertation on Thucydides: *The Moral and Political Principles of Thucydides and their Influence on Later Antiquity*.[8] In this work, which was never published, Powell presents his own vision of Thucydides as a 'Realpolitiker', that is to say a writer of tremendous artistic ability who presented history with no moral or ethical bias. For Powell, efforts to read morality into the *History* are, at best, misguided, at worst, deliberately misleading. Instead, Powell claims that Thucydides takes as his subject the history of the Athenian Empire. Human nature is a constant driven by three passions: fear, honour and, most of all, *pleonexia*, or the lust for power and wealth. The way individual city-states act is fundamentally conditioned by their relative power and wealth. Athens looks to augment what she has, while smaller states like Melos aim to remain independent of their larger neighbours. For Powell, Thucydides does not describe tragic history nor political cycles as he does for Cornford and Toynbee. Indeed, unlike in the reading of Toynbee, discussed in the previous chapter, the role of change in the *History* is reduced to the bare minimum. States might gain or lose power relative to their peers, but human nature is depicted as remaining constant.

The Classical Association paper had sketched how Powell felt the war had affected Thucydidean studies. In this argument, the *History* is a passive ancient text in which understanding depends on the vagaries of politics and their effect upon scholarly endeavour. For that reason, the rise of pacifism in Britain and Nazism in Germany posed an existential threat to the academic understanding of the *History*. What Powell did not consider in that lecture was what Thucydides could say to the interwar period. He alludes to the possible parallels that could be drawn between the Great War and the Peloponnesian War, but it is only in his fellowship dissertation that Powell begins to explain his own vision of Thucydides' political thought and its utility and applicability to the contemporary world as the storm clouds of Nazism and fascism began to gather on the horizon.

Powell is, it should be understood, a contentious figure in British politics and society. His post-Second World War career as a politician was controversial to say the least and has left a terrible legacy in political discourse that still colours, one might even say poisons, many debates today (on this legacy, see Heffer 1998; and particularly Schoefield 2013). However, I do not intend this chapter to be an intervention in debates over Powell's politics and legacy.[9] Instead, it focuses on his pre-1939 writings on Thucydides, many of which are unpublished and exist only in the archives of Trinity College and Churchill College, Cambridge. These papers, which include the lecture outlined above, teaching notes and essays paint a picture of a man deeply engaged with the philological study of Thucydides and struck by the great leaps forward in scholarship made since 1914 and the threat of pacifism and Nazism to the future of Thucydidean studies. For Powell, Thucydides was above all a Realpolitiker, which made him a uniquely appropriate ancient text in the interwar world, who portrayed not only the vicissitudes of interstate politics but also the psychological underpinnings of the actions of both man and *polis*, which lead to war, expansion and imperialism. On these terms, Powell's Thucydides is perhaps closest to the 'classical realist' interpretation of the Greek historian later offered by Morgenthau (1948) and Halle (1955), and, in a modified form, by Crane (1998) and Lebow (2003). Yet because Powell's material remained largely unread in the archives there can have been no direct contact between his depiction of Thucydides and that of later realist scholarship. In what follows, I will argue that in fact Powell's Realpolitik Thucydides is essentially a reaction to post-Great War German scholarship and, as we shall see later in this chapter, to a reading of Bury, Murray, Jebb, Thibaudet, Abbott and, most of all, Cornford.

My discussion of Powell as engaged in the moral and political aspects of the text will, I hope, add nuance to his reputation as a rather straight-laced philologist focused on the manuscript tradition (see, for example, Powell 1933; 1936a; 1936b; 1938a; 1939b) and editor of the *Oxford Classical Texts* edition of Thucydides.[10] More significantly, however, I hope to suggest in this chapter that Powell's Realpolitik Thucydides marks an important milestone in the Thucydidean turn. So far we have seen that Zimmern, Abbott and Toynbee were working in the wake of *Mythistoricus* in so far as they were engaged with understanding Thucydides' ideas of change, the impersonal forces of history, and the role of psychology in events. Powell continues to probe these same issues but marries them to an abiding concern about the absence of morality in the text. The role of morality, or the lack of, in politics is fundamental to Thucydides' worldview in Powell's estimation. It is also one of the most difficult issues to pin down precisely in the *History*. Thucydides presents a clear-eyed vision of politics and the ways in which wars break out, invasions are launched and rebellious allies punished with little or no compunction. Recall that even Diodotus' speech argues to spare Mytilene but only for reasons of self-interest.[11] At the same time, speakers from city-states appeal to justice, consanguinity and past good deeds and alliances in various speeches (Orwin 1994; Fragoulaki 2013). Thucydides rarely speaks of moral issues in his own voice, but when he does, he paints a bleak vision. The stasis on Corcyra intensifies violence and leads to the breakdown of traditional social bonds: fathers and sons kill each other, reasonable voices become treasonous and even language loses its meaning (3.82). Unsurprisingly, these issues have been given extensive treatment by contemporary scholars. Many realist scholars see Thucydides as describing a fundamentally amoral world in which the pursuit of power is the only thing that matters. Often they take the Athenian portions of the Melian dialogue as Thucydides speaking in his own voice describing an amoral world of power politics (e.g. Garst 1989; Bagby 1995). Set against these arguments, a number of studies have emerged in recent years that point to Thucydides' own moral voice. Crane (1998) argues that Thucydides' various historical actors each offer unique visions of realism that conflict in the text (cf. Williams 1998). Orwin (1994) points to Thucydides' humanity and conception of justice, and Fragoulaki (2013, 2016) to the powerful role that kinship plays in the relationship between Thucydides' actors. Thoughtful scholars of International Relations have attempted to combine the realist view of Thucydides' history as concerned primarily with power politics with an account of the role of morality and ethics in the text (e.g. Lebow 2003; Hawthorne 2014).

However, before we consider in detail Powell's vision of morality in Thucydides, we first need to consider briefly its genesis. The dissertation was born of poverty. Powell took it upon himself to apply for as many different prizes as he could while studying as an undergraduate because he was the child of working-class parents and needed money to augment his scholarship to Trinity College, eventually earning some £300 a year, more than enough to live on comfortably (Heffer 1998: 24–5). The essay on *The Moral and Political Principles* began life in 1933 as just such an essay when it was submitted to, and won, the Cromer Prize in Greek. In this form, it was later submitted to the British Academy. The manuscript of this earlier iteration has not survived. The typescript, which is currently in the archives of Churchill College, is a reworked version that was submitted to Trinity in order to gain a fellowship in 1936, that Powell was duly awarded. It is around 140 pages long and features frequent handwritten Greek quotations and corrections, presumably by Powell himself, suggesting that it is a working draft rather than the final version submitted to the other fellows. The essay is in three parts: 'Part I: The Purpose of Thucydides'; 'Part II: Thucydides' Principles of Morality'; and 'Part III: The Influence of Thucydides' Principles in Later Antiquity'. Parts I and II were substantially rewritten in 1936. The next section of this chapter will consider in depth precisely how Powell presents Thucydides as a Realpolitiker in the essay. First, however, I wish to turn to a theme that runs throughout the entire work: the contemporary applicability of Thucydides' work and the parallels that it is possible to draw between ancient and modern politics.

In Powell's analysis of the *History*, and in opposition to the arguments of Abbott, Thucydides does not write for the practical man. Modern scholars do not agree on the identity of Thucydides' intended audience. Kallet (2006: 336) agrees with Powell that Thucydides does not write for the practical politician, but Wendt (2016) has pointed to the rich tradition of reading the *History* as a statesman's manual. More recently, Allison's notion of the Thucydides trap is specifically intended for policymakers in the US and China (Allison 2017b). For Powell, Thucydides' intended readers are men who contemplate human affairs from a detached standpoint, whose only wish is to acquire knowledge as an end in itself. Thucydides 'writes only for such as himself, inspired with a scientific, not utilitarian, desire to understand by rational means and from a study of the most accurate records those principles which govern man's behaviour in history' (Churchill archives 1/6/24: 23). In other words, Powell saw Thucydides not as writing a handbook or practical manual for men of affairs but as a political historian, one might even say a political philosopher, who invites readers to meditate long and hard on events and their significance. Those intended readers should be inspired with a 'scientific' desire to understand events. Powell is perilously close to imagining that Thucydides chose to speak directly only to scholars such as himself, rather than the politicians, military men and merchants who actually drive events. This view of the intended reader of the text is in accord with 1.22, where Thucydides suggests that only the 'intelligent' reader, or simply those who wish to know, will understand the full import of the *History*. In other words, Thucydides flatters his discerning readers and Powell appears to have bought wholeheartedly into this flattery.

Modern scholars have tended to focus the debate on the meaning of 1.22.4. 'It may be that the lack of a romantic element in my history will make it less of a pleasure to the ear: but I shall be content if it is judged useful by those who want to have a clear understanding of what happened – and, such is the human condition, will happen again at some time in the same or a similar pattern' (trans. Hammond 2009: 12). Scanlon (2002) argues that this passage's claim is based upon the observation of human action leading to 'general paradigms', which are then offered to future readers. Kallet (2006) claims that Thucydides' bleak view of human nature does not lend itself to utility in the sense that the knowledge he offers may help improve conditions in the future. Stahl (2003) offers a similar pessimistic view. Powell's Realpolitik Thucydides is largely in sympathy with Kallet and Stahl. And yet Powell sees problems in Thucydides that appear to limit the political utility of the text that, while they appear conventional today, were still new in the 1930s and go far beyond discussions of 1.22. First, Powell maintains that Thucydides has no theory of history or degeneration like Polybius' cycles (Churchill archives 1/6/24: 25). That is to say, his *History* does not offer a grand historical law of change or decline that can be applied to other time periods and cultures, as Toynbee had attempted to do. Nor does Thucydides propose a system of evolution or Darwinism. Powell takes particular aim here at Cochrane because the latter saw Thucydides as espousing an evolutionary view of historical change.[12] Powell rather snidely claims that the only value of Cochrane's book rests in its efficacy as a warning of how not to study Thucydides: 'modern ideas, many of them of the most indefinite nature, he has selected according to private predilections' (Churchill archives 1/6/24: 101–2). Second, the reason that Thucydides speaks to contemporary readers is because of his accurate and no-holds-barred depiction of human nature. The reader who wishes to understand Thucydides' view of politics, therefore, must grapple with this view of human nature and its connection to Thucydidean necessity in the events of the *History*. Yet even here, there is a problem. Thucydides 'does not have the right to draw from the narrow material to which, for the sake of accuracy, he voluntarily restricts himself, conclusions regarding the whole course of human history' because he chose to write about a small war in a geographically restricted part of the world (Churchill archives 1/6/24: 28). Powell appears here to limit the practical applicability of the text. Yes, Thucydides claimed to have written a book that explained the intricacies of human nature and their relationship to politics, but for Powell the history of a small war written 2500 years ago cannot approach the level of political philosophy that is universally applicable or relevant today.

Powell explains that faced with these difficulties a whole host of interwar scholars had simply read their own politics into the *History*. Powell names imperialist, particularist, patriotic and internationalist opinions as all leaving their mark on interpretations of Thucydides and the Athenian Empire (Churchill archives 1/6/24: 113–15). Schwartz saw Thucydides as returning from banishment to find a generation that had misunderstood the glory and mission of the old empire. Murray sees through the funeral speech Thucydides the patriot (1903), while Abbott (1925: 140–7) detects a condemnation of empire and Grundy is wrong to see Thucydides as a critic of empire (1911). The difficulty with all these opinions is that they reduce Thucydides' thought to a simple support for or condemnation of a particular issue, be that democracy, empire or the Peloponnesian War itself. Such opinions are far too limiting. We have already seen that Powell found Thucydides' thought so rich that it approached the level of political philosophy that could appeal only to scientifically minded men. Thucydides intended to speak to the future with a system of thought that is applicable to political orders and events as they recur in very different material circumstances precisely because of the unity of human nature. Ultimately, for Powell, Thucydides simply '[s]tands as a Realpolitiker aloof from patriotic and imperialist feeling! The forces of human nature, which built an empire, would also, he saw, destroy it; and his part was not that of a champion or an apologist, but of an observer who cared only for realities' (Churchill archives 1/6/24: 116). One could not simply reduce Thucydides' ideas to a label used to support or condemn a particular creed of which the reader either approved or disapproved.

Thucydides the Realpolitiker

Underlying Powell's view of Thucydides' harsh depiction of political life as increasingly tolerated following the war lay a vision of the Greek historian as a Realpolitiker. We have seen throughout this book that various early twentieth-century scholars tried not only to understand the importance of Thucydides' writings and their relevance but also to pigeonhole him. For Cornford, he was a tragedian; for Zimmern, a psychologist; for Toynbee, a contemporary; for Cochrane, a scientist; and for Abbott, a realist. Powell's attempt to pigeonhole Thucydides as a Realpolitiker represents an interesting step forward in this debate over the nature of the Greek historian's thought. Before we consider what Powell meant by Realpolitik, however, we should first consider briefly the history of the concept.

Realpolitik is a difficult concept to define precisely. At its core lies the proposition that morality has no place in politics. Realpolitik focuses, almost exclusively, on how a state can secure and sustain power. It is not much concerned with issues of psychology and culture in politics but instead focuses on the effects of bipolarity, empire, military occupation and expansionary warfare. On these terms, Realpolitik is easy to caricature as a simple and heartless vision of politics. The term has become a synonym for power politics or even Machiavellianism. Bew (2016: 65–84) traces the origins of Realpolitik to the writings of the German thinker and politician Ludwig von Rochau (1810–73), who argued that the Enlightenment had showed the world that might does not necessarily make right but also that post-Enlightenment political theorists had failed to grasp that the realities of power politics remained. Rochau's 1853 book, *Grundsätze der Realpolitik angewendet auf die staatlichen Zustände Deutschlands*, is, in Bew's analysis, an attempt to use Realpolitik as a guide to show how to achieve liberal Enlightenment goals in a world defined by the harsh realities of power politics. However, the original meaning of the concept was soon lost. By the 1890s, the term Realpolitik had entered into the English vocabulary where it became increasingly associated with terms such as *Machtpolitik* and *Weltpolitik* (Bew 2016: 85–134). In the early twentieth century, idealist figures such as US

President Woodrow Wilson were already positioning their ideas in apposition to Realpolitik. By the 1930s, the term was increasingly associated with the aggressive territorial policies of Adolf Hitler and the Nazi Party (Bew 2016: 167–86).

Powell frames his definition of Realpolitik in Thucydides around the issue of morality. He explains that many previous scholars had decried Thucydides for suppressing moral judgements, when in fact moral judgement is entirely absent from the *History*.[13] Thucydides' standpoint is Realpolitik because he considers solely *what is*, not *what ought to be*. When morality and sentiment are present in the text, they are only 'a single force among the many whose interplay makes up the grand, un-moral, or indeed super-moral, sweep of history' (Churchill archives 1/6/24: 75). Thucydides' Realpolitik outlook is fundamental to his 'supreme greatness as a historian' (Churchill archives 1/6/24: 75). Powell works out this greatness through a comparison with Plato. He paints Plato's sketch of the four degenerate constitutions in the eighth and ninth books of the Republic as almost ludicrously unreal and schematic, particularly his treatment of the tyrant as a nadir of impotent wickedness (Churchill archives 1/6/24: 75–6). Like many contemporaries, Powell is defining Realpolitik through a comparison with a more idealistic writer. Thucydides describes the world as it is; Plato, as he would like it to be. There is no reference to Nietzsche in those pages, although Powell had studied extensively the German philosopher's work (Heffer 1998: 10, 11, 16, 23–4, 136–7), but there is a clear nod to the former's idea that Thucydides was a cure to Plato's idealism.[14] Because he looks at the reality of the world unflinchingly, he shows courage in the face of reality.

Modern scholars have been quick to question the relationship between Realpolitik thought and Thucydides. Bew denies that it finds its roots in Thucydides (2016: 17), instead pointing to Realpolitik's mid-nineteenth-century origins in Germany. Paul Rahe (1995) anachronistically sees Thucydides as offering a critique of the amorality of Realpolitik, while Alek Chance (2013) argues, similar to Rahe, that in fact 'Thucydides suggests a connection between the aspirations of Realpolitik and the desire of the political community to preserve the freedom to effect justice and not subordinate its will to the dictates of necessity – especially necessities imposed by other political bodies.' All agree that Thucydides presents the harsh reality of politics, but refuse to claim that the Greek historian endorsed Realpolitik as a workable system of politics among nations. Instead, commentators such as Crane (1998) are keen to point out that Thucydides offers a critique of the politics that led to the Peloponnesian War as a deviation from the ancestral nomos of the Greeks. Indeed, while Realpolitik is a term that semi-regularly attaches itself to Thucydides, scholars rarely define it.

Crane (1998) and Garst (1989), for example, ultimately conflate Realpolitik with the varieties of post-war realism that came to dominate the discipline of International Relations. This conflation is unsurprising because, as Brian Rathbun (2018) reminds us, Realpolitik forms the core of much realist thought. The difference lies in the fact that realism, in its various forms, represents a theoretical and methodological way of viewing the world, while Realpolitik is a practical system to conduct international politics. Powell's Thucydides may not have written for statesmen but he described for scholars how certain individuals and states get ahead and how others make mistakes and slip up.

Realpolitik is of primary interest today to political scientists and modern historians. However, Powell believed that the only way to approach Thucydides' Realpolitik was through philology, by which he meant not only a thorough familiarity with the Greek text of the *History* but also the manuscript tradition that lay behind modern editions. This is hardly a surprising view for him to take. We have already seen that he believed the increasing toleration scholars felt for Thucydides was led by advances in German philological readings of the *History*. Moreover, among Powell's papers is an essay titled the *Manuscripts of Thucydides in Cambridge and Venice*, which also formed part of his application for a fellowship and later formed the basis for a number of academic papers (cf. Powell 1933; 1936a; 1936b; 1938a; 1938b). In a collection of notes Powell prepared to lecture undergraduates at Trinity College, Cambridge, on the *Pentekontaetia*, he opined that 'Textual criticism ... is at once a science and a humanity. It is in fact the ideal education and queen of the humane sciences' (Powell Add. Msb. 90: 45). It would be unfair to claim that Powell's depiction of the Realpolitik of Thucydides is uncomplicated or simple or that it is a simple caricature of the *History* as an account of ancient power politics. Rather, Powell based his view of Thucydides the Realpolitiker on a thorough philological analysis of the text, which allowed both a link to the Athenian historian's mind and the world in which he lived. He saw Thucydides as writing a Realpolitik account of events, but the man behind the text was an accomplished literary artist, a keen observer of human nature and a perceptive historian of war and empire. Thucydides' Realpolitik was, then, a product both of his age and of his temperament as a writer and a thinker. Powell describes the fifth century BC, after the Persian Wars, as 'the age of political realities, Realpolitik, whether conscious or unconscious, an age of which moderns can grasp the aims and motives with full sympathy' (Churchill archives 1/6/24: 17). Thucydides is the perfect historian to capture the spirit and politics of this age. Unlike Herodotus, who is characterized as a geographer and ethnographer, Thucydides is a 'political thinker' and writer of political history

(Churchill archives 1/6/24: 11). That is not to say that his work is polemical in any way, but rather that Thucydides simply wished to describe events as they really were, '*er will nur sagen wie es eigenlich gemesen ist*' (Churchill archives 1/6/24: 35), with a degree of accuracy that would satisfy a court of law (Churchill archives 1/6/24: 15). Powell is here, of course, referring to Leopold von Ranke's famous dictum.

The fundamental unit of Thucydides' political analysis, according to Powell, is man. He notes that the Greek word *anthropos* occurs at key times during the text, such as at 1.22, when Thucydides describes the value of his work; at 3.82, the famous *stasis* passage; and at 5.105, in the Melian dialogue. Thucydides, like the philosophers of Asia Minor and the sophists, had realized that man was the measure of all things. The nature of man, in Powell's reading of Thucydides, does not change: *kata to anthropinon* (κατὰ τὸ ἀνθρώπινον) should be translated as 'by reason of human nature' or 'because of the unchanging characteristics of humanity' (Churchill archives 1/6/24: 22–3). Here, Powell is offering a rather eccentric view of Realpolitik, which traditionally focuses on the nation state as the fundamental unit of political analysis, often to the detriment of the study of other actors. Thucydides, of course, is interested in the *polis*, but his claim to the usefulness of his work (1.22) rests on the assertion that human nature is the same or similar in all ages, and that under similar circumstances men will act in similar ways. By reducing the unit of political analysis down to man, Powell believed, Thucydides could establish his work as a *ktema es aiei* (κτῆμα ἐς αἰεὶ).

That is not to say, however, that Thucydides ignored the material realities of life. The genius of Thucydides is to demonstrate how human nature interacts with local circumstances, specifically the division of wealth and power in society. Here Powell opens the door to the role of the state, the *polis*, empire and even irrational forces in Thucydides' thought. Thucydides represents 'nations' as following logically the consequences of their position, which is dictated by the combined effect of the natural forces of human nature and their material circumstances. His Realpolitik analysis focuses on the different psychologies produced by the interplay of human nature and material circumstance. Most important is the analysis of empire. The dominant motif of the *History*, in Powell's estimation, is larger states' thirst for empire and, conversely, smaller states' desire to resist their expansionary neighbours. In this interpretation, Thucydides believed that the most profound of all the forces in human nature is the natural and irrepressible desire of one community or nation to rule another, and the equally strong reaction in favour of independence and self-government (Churchill archives 1/6/24: 76). This force is not just found in Athens but in all states. Thucydides' Hermocrates is an imperialist in the conference at Gela. He wants Sicily for the Syracusans, but is ready to suspend those aims only when the external force of Athenian intervention provides a common enemy that needs to be dealt with first (Churchill archives 1/6/24: 77). The psychologies that drive imperialism are rooted in the passions that take hold of individuals (Churchill archives 1/6/24:79): 'We ourselves know these principles under the names "imperialism" and "separatism" or "particularism"' (Churchill archives 1/6/24: 76).

The final element in Powell's definition of Realpolitik now falls into place: expansionism. Powell, writing in the 1930s, supports Bew's assessment that by that decade Realpolitik had become associated above all with war, expansionism and the pursuit of power. While psychological and environmental elements remain crucial to understanding the actions of men, it is the desire for empire that drives politics forward. Ultimately, in the world described by Thucydides, large states look to expand and smaller states to resist that expansion, often at terrible cost. Powell, as we saw above, was deeply suspicious of the Nazis but he associates this drive for expansion less with Germany and much more with imperial Britain. For that reason, it does not frighten him. Rather, he embraces Thucydides' supposed Realpolitik view of the world as something natural, even inevitable.

The speeches as political thought

Powell's view of Thucydides' attitude to Realpolitik and empire is rooted in his reading of the speeches, which have long presented a seemingly insoluble problem to scholars. In this section, I will explain how Powell believed he had solved the problem of the speeches and how the political thought contained within them might be recovered. At 1.22, Thucydides explains that some of the speeches in the *History* he heard for himself and others had been reported to him by eyewitnesses. However, because of the vagaries of human memory – both Thucydides' own and his sources' – he found it impossible to record what was actually said. Instead, the speeches accord with what Thucydides believed was demanded by the occasion, while maintaining the upshot or opinion (*gnome*, γνώμη) of the original orations. Scholars engaging with the *Thukydidesfrage* had inevitably debated at great length which speech was composed when. Powell thought that German scholars had, by and large, assumed that the speeches could be used to demonstrate the evolution of Thucydides' thought over the course of the war (Churchill archives 1/6/24: 41), while Dionysius of Halicarnasus (Pritchett 1975) and Jebb (1907) had suggested that the speeches should be divided into those which Thucydides had certainly heard (and were therefore more reliable as genuine orations) and those he reproduced based upon second-hand reports. Powell believes both these approaches miss an essential truth about the speeches, namely, that they are all Thucydidean compositions designed to indulge the Athenian historian's love of rhetoric and his skill. Thucydides trained with the sophists and from them he acquired a love of rhetoric. While he could certainly know what was said at each speech from either experience or report, he gave himself free reign to show off his skill, excepting only to preserve the upshot of what was said (Churchill archives 1/6/24: 45). This is an absolutely crucial point because it means that the speeches are all Thucydidean compositions that can be used by the modern scholar to try to understand Thucydides' own historical philosophy (Churchill archives 1/6/24: 35). For Powell, Thucydides' speeches are true because they display his vision of the innermost motives of the speakers, sometimes even things that he may have wished to hide (Churchill archives 1/6/24: 47). In other words, they get to the psychological heart of his subjects, and thereby elicit sympathy (Churchill archives 1/6/24: 49).

Perhaps the summation of Powell's vision of Thucydides the Realpolitiker is found in his treatment of the Melian dialogue. Referring to the dialogue, Powell posits that 'if it is true that Thucydides, however unconsciously, has given in his speeches not dramatic fictions on a slender basis of fact, but his own most genuine interpretation of human actions and historical events, we are justified at last in seeking there above all his moral principles and his philosophy of history' (Churchill archives 1/6/24: 60). Powell notes that most British scholars had seen in the speech a damning indictment of Athenian imperialism. Bury, for example, wrote that:

> the historian has artfully used the dialogue to indicate the overbearing spirit of the Athenians, flown with insolence, on the eve of an enterprise which was destined to bring signal retribution and humble their city to the dust. Different as Thucydides and Herodotus were in their minds and methods, they both had the same, characteristically Greek, feeling for a situation like this ... although *Nemesis* is not acknowledged by Thucydides, she seems to have cast a shadow here.
>
> Churchill archives 1/6/24: 61, quoting Bury 1900: 463

Grundy (1911: 436) sees the dialogue as preparatory notes for a more developed piece and Abbott even goes so far as to doubt the literary and intellectual merits of the dialogue, which he labelled as 'flabby' (Abbott 1925: 192). These views are broadly in accordance with scholarship as it has developed over the past forty years or so, which has drawn attention to the dialogue as demonstrating the degeneracy of the Athenian Empire (for example Andrewes 1960; Bosworth 1993; Taylor 2010). At the same time, Macleod (1974), Parry (1981), Orwin (1994) and Greenwood (2008) have drawn attention to the dramatic qualities of the text. However, Powell argues that fresh insight had been provided by Schwartz, who saw that the dialogue belongs to the same 'stratum' of speeches as those written for Pericles after the fall of Athens, when Thucydides had become disillusioned with the imperial project, at least as it had developed under Cleon (Schwartz 1919: 137ff.). Because Schwartz wrote during wartime, he saw the Athenian position as objectionable and logically unanswerable. In other words, the Athenians are wrong to bare their power so nakedly to the Melians. However, the Melians are also wrong to put their faith in vain hopes and resist. Against Schwartz, Powell maintained that an unbiased reading of the dialogue will discover no *hubris*, but only rational points of view put forward by both Athens and Melos.

Powell himself was struck by the literary qualities of the dialogue. He argues that it is the most elaborately worked out part of the entire *History* because speech and counter-speech are polished to a 'nicety'. He even writes that read aloud, and I think we should imagine that Powell tried this with his students, the dialogue has the sound and qualities of a hymn (Churchill archives 1/6/24: 65). This is an aesthetic judgement that also suggests that the Melian dialogue is a summation of Thucydides' political theory.[15] That theory rests on a cold hard analysis of human nature. Powell argues that an unprejudiced reading of the dialogue will reveal neither *hubris* (ὕβρις) nor *asebeia* (impiety, ἀσέβεια) in the Athenian speeches nor unreasoning obstinacy in the Melian. Instead, the reader will find only that both sets of speeches represent opposed but rational points of view, 'eternal as human nature itself, whose examples are before our eyes through all history' (Churchill archives 1/6/24: 63). Athens is powerful and it is human nature to want to dominate one's weaker neighbours in such a position. Melos is weak but proud, so it makes sense for her to want to maintain her independence. Powell is at pains to point out that there is no religious or theological critique of the Athenian position in the dialogue. He quotes 5.105, in untranslated Greek, where the Athenians assert that:

> There is nothing in our claim or our conduct which goes beyond established human practice as shown in men's belief about the divine or their policy among

themselves. We believe it of the gods, and we know it for sure of men, that under some permanent compulsion of nature wherever they can rule, they will. We did not make this law, it was already laid down, and we are not the first to follow it; we inherited it as fact, and we shall pass it on as a fact to remain true for ever; and we follow it in the knowledge that you and anyone else given the same power as us would do the same.

trans. Hammond 2009: 304

Powell acknowledges that these sentences are shocking to readers, and remains so today. However, he argues that there is no impiety or insolence in the Athenian words. The Athenian ambassadors' claim that they act as men believe the gods themselves to act. They did not invent the system of politics under which they live, but are simply the latest in a series of empires, not the first nor the last, 'in the grip of an eternal necessity under which all men do alike' (Churchill archives 1/6/24: 64). This is simply an observation of the reality of the situation, rather than an a priori attempt to remove morality from politics. The Athenians understand that they are bound to act by a force of necessity. Modern writers have attempted to find a moral point of view in the *History*, and in the dialogue in particular, but Powell argues that here Thucydides is neither a pacifist nor an anti-imperialist. That said, Powell maintains that 'no writer can have had a deeper sense of human suffering than Thucydides' (Churchill archives 1/6/24: 110). Thucydides depicts the world as it is, but that does not mean that he did not have sympathy with the fate of the Melians and, indeed, with the Athenians. Powell concludes his analysis of the dialogue with the following question: 'And is it not only when man sees his helplessness in the power of eternal forces that true piety begins?' (Churchill archives 1/6/24: 64).

Powell adopts a similar approach to the Mytilene debate. Again, he positions his reading as a sharp departure from previous moral interpretations of the speeches. He notes that Schadewelt (1929: 32) saw Cleon as the advocate of a perverse political brutality, while Schwartz (1919: 140) had argued that the speeches are Thucydides' formulation of the extreme consequences of *Machtpolitik*, with the aim of discrediting them, including Diodotus' portrayal of Cleon's arguments as politically perverse. In Britain, Adcock (1927: 218) had suggested that the speeches represent a contrast between reason and passion. For Powell, however, an examination of Cleon's speech reveals not a single false statement or exaggeration. Instead, he concludes with Schadewelt (1929: 32) and Pohlenz (1919.129) that both the speeches of the Mytilene debate were written at a similar time and that Cleon's views of the empire are shared not only by

Pericles but also by Alcibiades and Athenian spokesmen elsewhere, even perhaps with Thucydides himself (Churchill archives 1/6/24: 70). For Powell, Cleon's speech represents genuine Thucydidean thought on the harsh reality of empire and is not a view put forward to be pilloried. However, one should not take Cleon's speech in isolation. Rather it must be 'taken together' (Powell's emphasis) with Diodotus' speech (Churchill archives 1/6/24: 71). In doing so, the reader will learn of the hatred and isolation which all imperial states experience. The reader may then choose between the best course of action, either Cleon's coercion or Diodotus' conciliation, but in either case, it is evident that an imperial power will eventually perish at the hands of the forces she has provoked over a period of time. Thucydides does not present these speeches as contrasting moral views of empire. Diodotus' logic is as immoral as Cleon's. Morality is absent from both sides, not as Schwartz says because it was pushed out by political reasoning (Pohlenz 1919: 140), but because in Thucydides' thought, morality is absolutely irrelevant to the principle under discussion.

Powell felt that the essential truths of the Melian dialogue and the Mytilene debate were evident in all the speeches throughout the *History*. However, it is undeniable that he gave these two rhetorical exchanges pride of place in his discussion of Thucydides' political philosophy and devoted the greatest space to the Melian dialogue. Today that would hardly be surprising. A majority of contemporary realist readings of Thucydides focus on these speeches, often equating Thucydides' views with those of the Athenian generals on Melos. However, in the 1930s the focus on these Thucydidean set pieces must have been rather unusual. We have seen that Abbott and Grundy largely dismissed them, while Zimmern spoke of the Melian dialogue only at the very end of the *Greek Commonwealth* and even then as an example of the moral degeneracy of the Athenian Empire (Zimmern 1911: 434–7). Few British commentators at the time wished to spill much scholarly ink on these episodes, perhaps because they were so horrific and unabashed in their description of raw power politics. Powell's extensive focus on these pieces, therefore, is an instance of learning to tolerate Thucydides in the new post-Great War reality.

Political psychology and historical change

In his analysis of Realpolitik in the Melian dialogue, Powell is at pains to argue that both Athens and Melos are acting in a rational manner. They both understand their relative power and act accordingly. Powell simply dismisses those critics who suggest that the Melians might have been better to submit to Athens and live. Their desire for independence is wholly in accordance with a rational idea of their material situation.[16] However, Powell was similarly aware that rationality could disappear from Thucydides' account of politics. This creates a space, in Powell's estimation of Thucydides, filled by the psychological drivers of the actions of states. In what follows I shall turn to Powell's take on the theme of the role of psychology in Thucydides, which this book has so far followed through the interpretation of Cornford, Zimmern, Abbott and Toynbee.

Powell points specifically to the emotions of *deos* (apprehension, fear, δέος), both of Athens regarding her allies' potential to revolt and the allies' fear of Athens' power; *philonekia* (tenacity, φιλονικία); *ophelimos* (advantage, ὠφέλιμος); and *pleonexia* (greed, πλεονεξία) as the primary drivers of Thucydides' actors. Powell also mentions *euergesia* (εὐεργεσία), or the good deeds that bind the benefited and the benefactor. This aspect of human nature is rarely discussed in Thucydides today, but Powell notes that Sparta aided the Aeginetans because of the help they had provided in the Messenian War a generation earlier (2.27; 4.56). Diodotus alludes to the benefit Athens derived from the goodwill of the Mytilenean demos (3.47), and both Corinth and Corcyra play upon this theme in the Corcyrean debate. In acknowledging the role of psychology in Thucydides, Powell acknowledges a rare debt to Cornford (Churchill archives 1/6/24: 96). Cornford had argued that all events in ancient historiography were attributable to psychological causes (1907: 66). These psychological forces play themselves out primarily in the collective mind of the *polis*, which Powell here terms the 'nation' (Powell's emphasis). Individuals are important only in a supporting manner. They come into the text as an embodiment of their *polis*, or perhaps their political party (Cleon, for example, speaks for extreme democrats), and occasionally have roles in shaping minor events, usually through intervention in military affairs (Churchill archives 1/6/24: 106). The great national motives of desire for power, of fear, of honour, of greed, reproduce themselves from the minds of individual men to influence group or collective psychology through the *polis*.

Powell's observation of the primary role psychological factors play in Thucydides leads into a more general discussion of historical change in the *History*. Powell claims that the course of Thucydides' political history followed the principles of *phusis anangkaia* (φύσις ἀνάγκαια), or the necessity of human nature. Most of all, this is true in a 'war period' when the more elementary side of human nature comes into greater prominence (Churchill archives 1/6/24: 97). I noted above that one of the reasons Powell condemned Cochrane's 1929 book was because it espoused the idea that Thucydides saw historical time as proceeding along the lines of biological evolution. Neither could Powell accept that Thucydides thought in terms of historical cycles, like Polybius or Toynbee. Thucydides had no theory of decline. In the archaeology there is only growth as states rise, acquire more land, money and security (Churchill archives 1/6/24: 102). In place of cycles, Powell proposed a view of causation and historical time in the text in which humanity lives in an eternally repeating present. He maintains that in only one sense is it legitimate to speak of a 'causal law' (Powell's emphasis) in Thucydides. Since human nature remains constant, history must necessarily not indeed 'repeat itself', but 'persistently show the same conjunctures and the same antagonisms' (Churchill archives 1/6/24: 98). Here Powell is elaborating on his view of human nature in Thucydides and its relationship to historical time. Power will shift from one actor to another as events change, but human nature remains fundamentally the same and therefore historical events come to resemble each other, even as they recur in different circumstances. Indeed, an unchanging human nature drives these shifts in power.

Neither in the paper on the effect of the war on Thucydidean studies nor in the dissertation does Powell mention Zimmern's essay on political psychology. Nevertheless, Powell's analysis of the role of psychology in Thucydides treads similar ground. In his account of Thucydides' political psychology, Powell privileges fear and greed – as might be expected in a Realpolitik reading. He also notes that a number of other psychologies are at play, which can even lead states to help their neighbours with no expectation of immediate benefit. The inclusion of a discussion of political psychology pushes Powell's Thucydides beyond a simple reading that would focus on the lack of morality in the text to focus on power. In the dissertation we find a rich and nuanced account of political psychology and its relationship to the pursuit of power, or independence, in the Greek interstate system. Here, we might even claim that Powell has pushed his arguments further than Zimmern. The latter simply drew an analogy between the psychologies of ancient and modern states while exhorting modern students to take note of Thucydides' methodology. Zimmern characterizes each state as given over to a particular psychology. Powell goes further than this by suggesting that the different psychologies affect the Greek states at different times as they deal with different neighbours. Sparta feels fear towards Athens but *euergesia* towards Aegina. She would, no doubt, experience different passions in relation to different states at different times. Powell, therefore, is aware that as material circumstances and events change, the motivations of a *polis* might similarly shift.

Thucydides the imperialist

Powell presents the Realpolitik lessons contained within the text as particularly relevant for British readers. For an 'imperial Englishman', he maintains, the motives of *deos* (fear, δέος), *time* (honour, τῑμή), *ophelimos* (advantage, ὠφέλιμος) in forming, and more especially in retaining, an empire 'need no illustration' (Churchill archives 1/6/24: 97–8). Similarly, an imperial Englishman will scorn the virtuous *apragmosune* (love of a quiet life, an isolationist tendency, ἀπραγμοσύνη) and *esuchia* (peace, stillness, ἡσυχία) of the little Englanders who wished to withdraw from the empire in terms similar to those Pericles directed at those Athenians who took no part in public business. Beyond these political psychologies, Powell believed that there were specific parallels between the Athenian and British empires. He explains that the 'natural law' that imperial states should stand together, Britain is learning to her cost today. Powell continues with the rather cryptic thought that Britain is reaping what she sowed in Ireland and India, in Poland and Czechoslovakia. Presumably, Powell is here referring to British 'toleration' of independence movements and contemporary calls from Nazi Germany for *Lebensraum* in Eastern Europe. This is a rather tortured parallel to draw from Thucydides. Athens only ever reacted harshly to her allies in revolt, but she still faced a number of rebellions inspired by the desire for independence.

Powell draws a further comparison between the Peloponnesian War and the Great War. Unlike Zimmern, Powell refuses to give examples of the influence of national character on events because he believed they were 'superfluous'. It would be too easy to compare the French, British and Germans to the Corinthians, Athenians and Spartans, although he does note that 'the French, in particular, could sing England a song not unlike that which the Corinthians sang to their Spartan allies, 1.68–71' (Churchill archives 1/6/24: 97–8). Instead, Powell attempts to draw broader lessons from Thucydides in the form of short sound-bite-like statements, despite his earlier criticism of such interpretations of the *History*. We read that the 'similarity of constitution [which] promotes common action between nations ... will be denied by no one who sees the relations between democratic France and democratic England grow more cordial as one power after another loses its political freedom' (Churchill archives 1/6/24: 97–8). In addition, he argues that geographical proximity promotes antagonism between neighbouring states. So in the Great War, 'Europe was striped like a zebra' by the combatants: Russia (allied), Germany, France (allied), Spain (pro-German), Portugal (allied). Germany could even point 'triumphantly' to

Thucydides' condemnation of the Treaty of Versailles at 4.19 (Churchill archives 1/6/24: 97–8). It is not clear that Powell thought these parallels between ancient and modern politics really attained the level of 'utility'. He claims that the similarities between the Athenian and British outlook on empire and the similarities between the Peloponnesian War and the Great War need 'no explanation', but in the passages cited above rarely does Powell identify specific points in the text in support of his parallels. Moreover, it is not clear whether Powell imagined that these parallels are only to be found in Thucydides, or if they could they be found in Herodotus, or Tacitus, or indeed any other ancient text. Simple parallels do not point to the unique qualities of Thucydides' thought. Powell is, perhaps, on firmer ground when he talks of motives or psychologies. Ultimately, I believe Powell found it difficult to articulate what utility there may be in Thucydides without resorting to claims that his work was not simply a Realpolitik treatise but written with such literary art that it evokes strong feelings of sympathy in readers. Powell concedes, and no doubt genuinely believes, that no writer could have had a deeper sense of human suffering than Thucydides (Churchill archives 1/6/24: 110), explaining that:

> It is impossible to read his description of the plague at Athens closing in that most touching of ironies, that such as escaped alive persuaded themselves it would require much to kill them after surviving that (2.51); or to read the description of the Athenian departure for Sicily (6.30f.) or the final scene in the gully of the Assinarus 7.84; without being convinced that Thucydides, if any one, felt the tragedy of what he saw and heard.
>
> Churchill archives 1/6/24: 110

There is, therefore, an important distinction to be drawn between the lessons provided by the *History* and the personal sympathies and belief of the historian himself, as noted by many writers today such as Connor (2013), Orwin (1994), Crane (1998), Price (2001) and Hawthorne (2014), who each see Thucydides as a man deeply affected by the war and the suffering that he so powerfully chronicles. In the case of Powell, however, we are left with an unexamined paradox. If we accept Powell's claim that Thucydides described the reality of an 'unmoral' (his word) world and that he wrote for thinking men, rather than men of action, then why exactly did he write the *History*? It cannot have been as a guide or statesman's manual to help future leaders avoid the suffering that so clearly affected Thucydides deeply. In Powell's estimation, statesmen were not the intended audience of the *History*. Nor does Powell believe that Thucydides offers any answers to the problem of the immorality of international politics. For sure, Thucydides left us with a realist work of art that describes man as he really is, but he offers us no way out of the quagmire. Ultimately, I believe that Powell was trying to have his cake and eat it. As a philologist, he was alive to the great literary art of the *History* and its power to evoke sympathy in the reader, but he also wished to cast Thucydides as a Realpolitiker, a figure who recognized that morality and custom counted for very little in the dog-eat-dog world of international politics. Thucydides, therefore, provides no answers. Instead, he identifies the problem caused by a tension between the morality and cultural norms that regulate the relations between men and their unenforceability in interstate relations. Powell's Thucydides leaves us scrambling around in the anarchy of international politics with the refrain ringing in our ears that this is as good as it gets, as good as it can be.

Conclusion: The morality of the city and man

We know of very few people who read Powell's dissertation. One of his referees for the position of professor of Greek at Sydney, which Powell was elected to at the remarkably young age of twenty-five, wrote that it was a solid piece of work that appeared to belong to a much more mature mind.[17] After the Second World War, Powell received a letter from an American Rhodes scholar, A. L. Mayfield, requesting the dissertation. I have been able to uncover little information about Mayfield. He claims that he had a paper under review in the *Journal of Hellenic Studies* on 'Thucydides the Sophist', which does not appear to have been published there or anywhere else, although it is mentioned briefly in the *Classical Review* (Anon. 1947). To aid him in his study, Mayfield wrote to Powell asking to see his essay on *Thucydides' Moral and Political Ideals*, which he identifies as the essay that won the Cromer prize in 1933. Powell wrote back to say that the earlier essay no longer existed, but it became the 1936 dissertation. Although Powell cautioned Mayfield that he was now looking to work in politics and had abandoned the study of the Classics, the manuscript was duly sent off, which Mayfield kept for a number of months. Mayfield even lent it to T. A. Sinclar, Professor of Greek at Queen's University Belfast, who was then writing *A History of Greek Political Thought* (first published in 1951, cited in the bibliography as Sinclair 2010). He finally returned it on 7 July 1948 with an extended commentary by way of thanks. The concluding section of this chapter will focus on this commentary because it illuminates and recapitulates many of the tensions inherent in Powell's reading of Thucydides. It also represents the moment that the dissertation disappeared from the scholarly landscape. In the commentary, Mayfield claims that Powell's view of Thucydides represented the closest approximation to his own views. Like Powell, Mayfield maintains that Thucydides is a Realpolitiker. However, he also attempts to explore the limits of Thucydides' Realpolitik by contrasting the lack of morality in Greek interstate politics with the ethical beliefs of individuals in the *History* (Churchill archives 1/6/21: 4).

In Mayfield's estimation, Thucydides writes with two didactic aims in mind. First, he wants to show that there is no essential difference among men, Greek or Barbarian (1.6, 2.6). All men are the same because all men aim to rule the weak. War is therefore inevitable as a continuation of politics by other means and the stronger always win. Following this point, Mayfield argues that Thucydides' second motivation is a desire to show that 'greatness' is assessed in money, ships, men, walls – what we might call the material potential to wage war (Churchill archives 1/6/21: 7). Because all men wish to dominate their lesser rivals, power can be measured in their capacity to wage successful wars. Focusing on these two motivations allows Mayfield to raise Thucydides to the level of a political philosopher. The value of this account lies in its 'specimen value' in conveying these truths and not as simple history. Thucydides meant to show the embers of rivalry, latent from birth in every man, bursting out into this conflagration, the greatest war of all time (Churchill archives 1/6/21: 3). Mayfield presumably had this view of Thucydides before he read the dissertation, but he finds Powell a kindred spirit who elucidates both these motives at great length through his discussion of the 'changelessness of human nature' (Churchill archives 1/6/24: 111).

According to Mayfield, historical change in Thucydides is rooted in these two beliefs. The rise and fall of empires are described as the manifestation of *phusis* (nature). Here we see that for Mayfield, force, expressed through military armaments and wealth, almost always equals Thucydidean necessity (Churchill archives 1/6/21: 6). He has dispensed with Powell's somewhat more nuanced reading of human psychology and emotion to focus almost exclusively on the will of the strong to dominate the weak. In this view of the text, 'According to Thucydides right and wrong are of no account between states, but only inside them' (Churchill archives 1/6/21: 5). Humans, individually, might care about their fellows, but states show no such compunction. Mayfield roots this distinction in his reading of the *History*. He argues that by showing the powerlessness of morals, Thucydides also shows a real concern for human values and made it clear that power is not the only relevant criterion for human endeavour, exemplified in his account of those who attempted to help the plague victims (7.85, 2.53), or Thucydides' assertion of the kinship of all men at 2.6. (Churchill archives 1/6/21: 9–10). However, when it comes to interstate relations, states will do whatever it takes to get ahead. Both Corcyra and Epidamnus even call in barbarian aid during their disputes, showing that the bonds of race and kinship are subordinate to Realpolitik (Churchill archives 1/6/21: 9–10).

The strong distinction drawn between the amorality of the state and the morality of individuals is often typified in the speeches, which Mayfield argues show moral egoism tempered by the compromises individualism has to make for unified action (Churchill archives 1/6/21: 11). Thucydides' uniqueness lies in his attempt to blend orthodox morals with the anarchist antinomianism of the sophists. Citizens are called upon to be unselfish in support of their city's self-interest: 'Empires are amoral: all men as a matter of fact seek them: but the only practicable way of doing so is to unite and morals follow from this' (Churchill archives 1/6/21: 8). Thucydides assents to the amoral egoism of states but not of individuals. Therefore, Mayfield cannot agree with Powell that Athenian appeals to justice in defence of their empire are ultimately hollow (Churchill archives 1/6/24 60, 86/7, cf. 1.75, 6.83). Mayfield reveals himself here to be not wholly convinced by Powell's Realpolitik Thucydides. The Athenian historian certainly removed much morality from his description of international politics but, ultimately, could not believe that Athenian appeals to justice were groundless. They may, of course, remain self-serving.

I have summarized Mayfield's commentary both because it is an interesting text in its own right and because it summarizes and responds to Powell's main arguments. The young man wishing to impress the elder is eager to show that he has read the dissertation carefully and taken on board its main arguments. Therefore, we find that Mayfield emphasizes the main tensions identified by Powell between historical change and the uniformity of human nature and the role justice plays in governing relations between individuals within the state and the immoral nature of interstate politics.

It is regrettable that Powell never thought to publish his dissertation, but the manuscript would doubtless have required significant revision and perhaps expansion if it were to have been taken up by a university press. However, the arguments contained therein are novel for their time and would, I believe, have stimulated a vigorous debate among Thucydidean scholars on the value of the Realpolitik readings and their relationship to contemporary politics. The fact that Powell never published the dissertation and that it was read by so few people means, of course, that it cannot have exerted any influence at all on the wider British Thucydidean turn or the post-Second World War emergence of

Thucydides among realist scholars of International Relations. However, I have attempted in this chapter to emphasize parallels and differences between Powell's interpretation and contemporary writings of Thucydides. This is because Powell's dissertation marks an important moment in the reception history of the text. As he would term it, it is a remarkable instance of someone becoming more tolerant of Thucydides. His dissertation is a witness to a growing acceptance in the 1920s and 1930s of Thucydides' dark depiction of human nature and the lack of morality in interstate politics. As Powell observed, this acceptance was often accompanied by an increasing sensitivity to Thucydides' literary qualities and recognition of the sympathy that he evoked in readers. In a stroke of his pen, Powell united two themes that define Thucydides' text today and still cause considerable scholarly consternation: his political realism and his artistic merit.

7

Epilogue: American Thucydides(s)

In March 1943, the Second World War was raging around the world. That month the Polish government in exile announced to the Allies the existence of the Auschwitz murder camp. At the same time, US and Australian forces sank twelve Japanese ships in a battle in the Bismarck Sea and in the heaviest British air raid of the war so far, the RAF dropped 1,000 tons of high explosives on Berlin in a single night. It was also in that month that Louis Lord, an American professor of Classics and Latin, presented a series of papers in Oberlin College, Ohio, to assembled students and academics on *Thucydides and the World War*. Lord's papers draw out at great length the parallels between the Peloponnesian War as presented by Thucydides and the carnage of the Second World War. Lord explains to his audience the supposed similarities between Sparta and Britain, as states slow to go to war, and Athens and Germany as states keen to fight for empire and expansion; to the equivalence between Athens and Britain as liberal polities; and to the sad fate of Melos and Belgium, caught in the crossfire between their larger neighbours.

Lord's book, I will argue in this epilogue, is important because it points to the growing importance of Thucydides in America in the first half of the twentieth century but also the limits to scholarship on the other side of the Atlantic in the 1930s and 1940s. Unlike Cornford, Zimmern or Powell, Lord is content simply to draw parallels between Thucydides and the modern world without first rooting them in an analysis of the Greek historian's methodological and historical system. There is, in other words, no attempt to uncover Thucydides' political thought beyond the assertion that he was critical of war and expansionism. For this reason, I claim that Lord's speech marks a transitional moment when the British interest in Thucydides' political vision begins to emerge as a topic of academic interest in the US. Harvard University Press published Lord's lectures on Thucydides in 1945. In this book, Lord offered a series of papers offering rather conventional views of Thucydides' style, speeches and historical project. Despite the uninspired quality of the volume, I nonetheless believe it to be a fitting place to end this study of the Thucydidean turn for two reasons.

First, it represents the summation of a growing tradition in American academia to use Thucydides to draw parallels between the ancient and modern worlds in the first half of the twentieth century. Often these parallels were no more than window dressing to give the author's arguments a veneer of classical learning. These parallels and their relationship to Lord's Thucydides will be considered in the first section of this chapter, which charts the end of the turn in Britain and the diminishing role of Thucydides as a political philosopher and International Relations scholar in the early 1940s.

Second, this epilogue will explore the subsequent place of British interpretations of Thucydides that we have been following in this book in American scholarship from the 1950s and 1960s, when Thucydides once again emerged as a political philosopher and theorist of note and the father of American International Relations. There are a number of continuities. American scholars continue the interest of Cornford, Zimmern and Toynbee in the role of political psychology and historical change. Even more prominently, the interest of Abbott in doctrinal realism and, in certain ways, Powell's Realpolitik (re)emerges in the American 'realist' Thucydides, a paradigm that came to dominate interpretations of the *History* for much of the second half of the twentieth century.

However, there are also significant discontinuities. American scholars built on their own indigenous traditions of interpretation of Thucydides as well as the work of Cornford, Abbott et al. to create new and important interpretations. In particular, Leo Strauss began a new tradition of reading that led to an interest in the positive role of justice and custom in Thucydides (cf. Orwin 1994). This interest in justice has even established itself among scholars opposed to the Straussian interpretation such as Lebow (2001, 2003). I argued in Chapter 1 that the various labels that British scholars of the turn applied to Thucydides have survived and prospered throughout the remainder of the twentieth century. At the same time, their essays and books have met with a mixed response. While Cornford and Abbott were read and dissected by many scholars in the US, the work of Zimmern and Toynbee was soon forgotten, while, as we have seen, Powell's work lay unread in an archive in Cambridge. The relationship of the British turn to Thucydides, therefore, is not a story of direct influence. Instead, the British turn created a number of research themes – such as the role of psychology, historical change, and realism in the text – that are continued in the US but creatively reinterpreted and augmented.

Wars ancient and modern: Thucydides in America

Throughout the first half of the twentieth century, a number of American scholars working in International Law and Political Science cited Thucydides in their academic papers. For example, in 1912 a certain David J. Foster cited Thucydides as an authority on international arbitration to an audience in the Hall of the Americas in Washington, DC (Foster 1912). Foster was followed by William Lingelbach in 1930 who cited Thucydides in a discussion of the economic causes of war in a paper published in the *Annals of the American Academy of Political and Social Science* (Lingelbach 1930). While John Gilbert Heinberg cited the speech given by Sthenelaidas as part of a history of the majority principle in the the *American Political Science Review* (Heinberg 1926). These references to Thucydides shared a certain casual air. Thucydides was not yet held up as a great political theorist of interstate relations, let alone the originator of doctrinal realism, but his name, and references to the *History*, cropped up in discussions of diverse topics and as historical evidence to add texture to the overall argument. In America at this time, the contemporary relevance of Thucydides' thought was rarely discussed or theorized. Indeed, the only writer that I know of to have considered Thucydides' relevance was A. E. K. Boak in a 1921 paper in which he denied the existence of any parallel between the Athenian historian's depiction of international order in ancient Greece and the League of Nations (Boak 1921).

In the late 1930s and 1940s, scholars working in both the social sciences and Classics became more open to using Thucydides to draw comparisons between the ancient and modern worlds. The reason for this development is not hard to discern – namely, the rise of Nazism, the Japanese attack on Pearl Harbor and the entrance of America into the Second World War. As early as 1937, Felix Morley, a Pulitzer Prize-winning journalist in the US, published a paper on how the US could assist in maintaining world peace in an age of increasing uncertainty. The paper opens with a reference to Thucydides and the Peloponnesian War, inviting readers to consider how policymakers might overcome the lust for power and resort to expediency in international politics (Morley 1937). Has, Morley wondered, anything changed in the international arena since Thucydides' day? During the years of the war, scholars began to draw explicit parallels between Thucydides' depiction of Athens and Sparta and the contemporary positions of Britain and Germany and the complexities of a conflict fought between a sea power and a land power. We also see Thucydides used as a source of quotations. The American admiral W. L. Rodgers (1942: 39) concluded his piece on the *Guarantees of Peace* with lines from the funeral speech: 'Remember that prosperity can only be for the free, that freedom is the sure possession of those alone who have the courage to defend it.'

This material hardly represents a high number of engagements with Thucydides in American Political Science and International Law, but it does remind us that his name could emerge with surprising frequency and, by the time of the Second World War, in contexts that drew specific parallels between the ancient and modern worlds. Lord's speech and book on *Thucydides and the World War* is, when viewed in light of this literature, hardly a surprising intervention in American Thucydidean scholarship. We might imagine that many listeners in the Oberlin auditorium and readers of the book were alive and receptive to the contemporary value of Thucydidean parallels. Lord attempts to argue that Thucydides meant for men of consequence in the future to read his work and that history repeats itself. He further argues that the Great War and the Second World War are really one single conflict, just as Thucydides had argued that the peace of Nicias was not a real peace and that, in fact, the Peloponnesian War was one single twenty-seven-year conflict (Lord 1945: 235). Moreover, Lord maintains that both conflicts were 'world' wars because they eventually engulfed the participants' entire geographical horizon (Lord 1945: 225ff.; cf. Th. 1.1). Athens plays the part of Germany in that she leads a coalition of Greek states forced to follow her, while Sparta represents Britain in that she leads a much looser confederacy determined to defend the liberty of smaller states. At the same time, Lord maintains that internally Athens more closely resembles the UK and US, and Sparta Prussian militarism. He also recognizes that the role of land and 'continental' powers has been flipped in his scheme. He then offers a number of different parallels between the ancient and modern conflict, such as the idea that the modern coalition (the Allies), like the ancient Peloponnesian League, is fighting for liberty and that the two wars are equivalent because they involved the 'whole world' (1945: 228). Thucydides 3.82 'is a picture of what will happen in Europe when the dragon's teeth sowed by the Nazis produce their awful brood' (1945: 246). Lord is at pains to point out that these parallels extend directly from Thucydides' work rather than the history of the Peloponnesian War, but there is little here that relies upon Thucydides' supposed intelligence or political philosophy. Ultimately, there is no deep engagement with Thucydides' thought in Lord's analysis beyond a recognition that events are repeating themselves. Lord sums up the insights he has garnered from Thucydides, in the following words predicting the future of the Second World War:

To use, then, the experience of history to arrive at political knowledge of what this war will bring: the employment of vast numbers of voters by the government as a result of the war effort constitutes a real danger to our democratic institutions; it was fatal for Athens. There will be no freedom for small states except in collective security. As the war goes on, even greater crimes against humanity will be perpetrated by the central powers. But a predatory empire has in its nature the seeds of destruction, and when that destruction is imminent, nations now neutral will join the allies. Victory will go to the side with the greater resources. A complete victory, unconditional surrender, will be necessary to a lasting peace. The soldiers of the democracies will show greater stamina, better morale. The collapse of the central powers will be sudden. There will be no long fight to the death, for the bully is not a good loser. Magnanimity will be shown in the peace terms and will be extended to the defeated by America, the British Commonwealth, China or Russia, but not by the lesser nations.

Lord 1945: 248

Lord suggests that the US is too isolated and strong a power to reflect seriously on the sufferings of war. The Americans do not, yet, need Thucydides in the same way as the British. That is not to say that US scholars suddenly forgot the British readers surveyed in this book. From the bibliography to *Thucydides and the World War* it is clear that Lord was familiar with many of the British scholars working on Thucydides in the first half of the twentieth century, as well as the more significant works of German scholarship. Regarding the latter, it is not surprising to find that during a time of war at least Lord shows a certain degree of hostility to German Classical Studies, although he justifies this through a rather unfair summary of that body of scholarship's supposed deficiencies:

In the Bibliography I have listed only a few of the German works on Thucydides nor can I recommend even these. I strongly distrust the soundness of conclusions as to style, method and date of composition arrived at by such critical methods. Scholars who approach literary works without a sense of humor or proportion, who have no knowledge of the psychology of non-Teutonic peoples, are likely to arrive at conclusions that are ridiculously unsound. Even as distinguished a historian as Eduard Meyer explained the phrase 'red-blooded Americans' as a description of those Americans who have in their veins [the] blood of the American Indians. The dreary decades of Homeric criticism have borne such dry fruits! Just so, all the elaborate arguments for the fragmentary composition of the history of Thucydides put forth by Schwartz, Pohlenz and Schadewaldt have been refuted at vast labor by Grosskinski and Partner and finally dismissed by Finley. After sixty years of German-inspired argument we are just where we started.

1945: unnumbered preface

In the bibliography itself, however, Lord offers short annotations where he elaborates on his dislike of German work. He claims that Schwartz's work is an example of how Thucydidean scholarship should not be conducted, because Thucydides should not be placed on the 'stand' as a witness where every statement can be taken not for what it means but what it can, through distortion, be made to imply (1945: 273). Interestingly, Lord endorses Meyer's 1913 *Thucydides und die Entstehung der Wissenschaftlichen Geschichtsschreibung* for its breadth of knowledge and store of information that is truly 'appalling'. He laconically and begrudgingly concludes that Meyer was a 'great scholar' (1945: 273).

Turning to Lord's reception of British scholars, we find a mixed bag. Grundy (1911) is praised for his topographical knowledge. Zimmern's *Thucydides the Imperialist* (1928) is simply 'suggestive' and *The Greek Commonwealth* (1911) is 'a book of real genius' for its discussion of Greek civilization in light of Pericles' funeral speech (1945: 274). Cornford's *Mythistoricus*, however, is described as 'probably the worst book on Thucydides in English', and J. B. Bury's essay on Thucydides is not one of his best efforts: 'It gives the impression of being written under contract to fill a lecture appointment' (1945: 274). The works that Lord found truly illuminating, however, are those produced by American scholars, suggesting that a distinct 'American' Thucydides is already beginning to emerge. Paul Shorey's essay on the *Implicit Ethics and Psychology in Thucydides* (1897) is a 'brilliant piece of work, remarkable for its insight and analysis' (1945: 275). Lord's most favoured scholar working on Thucydides, however, is J. H. Finley, who had published extensively on Thucydides in the 1930s and was a professor at Harvard. Finley had made his name arguing against European Thucydidean shibboleths. He disagreed with those German scholars who believed that different sections of the *History* were written at different times, arguing that Thucydides was a unitarian (Finley 1967). In opposition to Cornford, Finley saw Thucydides' primary ancient influence as Euripides rather than Aeschylus (Finley 1967). Lord refers to Finley's 1942 book, titled simply *Thucydides*, in the following terms:

> An excellent book, clear and sane. I find it hard to forgive Professor Finley for saying better than I possibly could so many things I should like to have said. I am especially grateful to him for his essay on 'The Unity of Thucydides' History,' Harvard Studies in Classical Philology, Supplementary Volume I (1940), pp. 255–298. This has, I hope, put an end to the fruitless endeavor to demonstrate the patchwork composition of the History.
>
> 1945: 274

Despite Lord's evident admiration for Finley, his book marks a departure from the interpretations of Cornford, Abbott, Zimmern, Toynbee and Powell. Lord is clearly content to think of Thucydides as a relevant political thinker and he has read much, but by no means all, of the literature that had explored how Thucydides' philosophy, historical system or methodology might be brought to bear on the present day. Lord, however, did not care to rely on such large-scale engagements with Thucydides' intellectual project in his discussion of the *History*'s relevance to a world torn apart by war and aggression. Instead, he was content to draw historical parallels between specific aspects of Thucydides' presentation of the Peloponnesian War and the contemporary experience of total war. Seen from this perspective, Lord's Thucydides has more in common with those early modern scholars who used the text as support for their position on the rights and wrongs of entering into war (Hoekstra 2012) or the eighteenth-century British and French readers who used Thucydides to create sometimes elaborate parallels between the Athenian Empire and European colonial systems, ancient and modern sea powers (Earley 2015, 2016; Payen 2015) and the Corcyrean *stasis* and the French and American revolutions (mentioned in Chapter 1). Nevertheless, Lord is a liminal figure who bridges earlier British and European interpretations to the post-Second World War US International Relations tradition of reading Thucydides.

Just as Lord was delivering his lectures to the audience at Oberlin and preparing his publication for Harvard University Press, the turn was coming to an end among British Classists. Two works mark the end of the tradition outlined in this book. First, there is the second volume of Grundy's *Thucydides and the History of His Age*, published in 1947. Readers may recall that we first encountered Grundy in Chapter 3. In 1911, he had published the first volume of this work, which provided a very detailed account of the Peloponnesian War and Thucydides' depiction of it that dealt with a number of topics of purely antiquarian interest. Grundy's book gave a warm reception to Cornford's ideas of the 'true' economic and political causes of the war. The second volume represents a much slimmer and more highly interpretative effort. It focuses on understanding Thucydides' philosophy of history and life. Grundy even felt compelled to open the volume with a poem, which Morley notes is a unique way to engage with Thucydides (2013: ixff.). In his chapter on Thucydides' philosophy of history (1947: 28–81), Grundy offers a series of translations from the *History*, which are then used to make simple parallels with the modern world or uncomplicated universal observations on politics. For example, Grundy translates 1.42 as 'To abstain from wronging others who are your equals affords a surer basis for power than a dangerous pursuit of gain incited by an apparent temporary advantage', which is presented as 'a truth which Germany would have done well to realise before the first [sic.] World War and, to a certain extent, before the last war' (1947: 53). Turning to a more general example, Grundy offers the following translations of three passages of Thucydides:

> (II. 61.) For the judgement of mankind is relentless to the weakness that falls short of a recognised renown, as it is jealous of the arrogance that aspires higher than its due.
> (II. 64.) Besides the hand of heaven must be borne with resignation, that of the enemy with fortitude.
> (II. 64) Decay is a law of nature.

Grundy takes these passages as a commonplace in Thucydides' day, which idealists have to be reminded of following the Second World War because they might easily forget that such laws may also be at work in democratic institutions, even following their victory in the great struggle. A second simple reading of the parallels that can be drawn between Thucydides and the modern world is offered by the Briton Thomas Callander (1877–1959). He was Professor of Greek at the Queen's University Kingston, Canada, but was a native of Scotland and had been educated at Trinity College, Oxford. In 1961, Callander's friends published a book from a manuscript found among his papers on *The Athenian Empire and the British*, which had probably been written in the late 1940s and 1950s. Callander declares in the short preface that he had been a lifelong Tory, who later became a harsh critic of imperial politics having experienced the horrors of the world wars and the increasing haughtiness of the British towards their imperial possessions. The first chapter provides a critical account of the Athenian Empire and Greek history. Callander saw the desire for empire as the result of *pleonexia*. His main sources are Plato and Thucydides. He presents the Peloponnesian War as the Great Hellenic war and Thucydides as its 'realist' chronicler. Plato, in a now familiar pattern, is the 'idealist' who offers a solution to the problem of greed and empire in international relations. The remainder of the book is devoted to a spirited attack on British statesmen and imperialism written by a man clearly disillusioned with the imperial project. Callander uses Thucydides to frame the problem of greed, which he presents as common to all empires. The Athenian historian's thought on the topic is simply assumed to be universally valid. The vast differences in time, scale and law between the two empires (Athenian and British) barely gets a mention. These late works by Grundy and Callander represent the last British works to specifically use Thucydides in a manner shaped by the Great War to critique contemporary politics. They point to the fact that Lord's reduction of Thucydides to a source of historical parallels was representative of a transatlantic phenomenon. At the same time, they also mark the moment at which the focus of any study of the political reception of Thucydides should shift to the US. In Britain after the Second World War Thucydides rarely emerged as a staple of International Relations and Political Science reading lists.[1]

Thucydidean turn(s)

The 1940s and 1950s, therefore, represent the moment at which American scholars begin to consider in detail their own interpretation of Thucydides' political thought and what to do with the British scholarship that they had inherited. During the 1930s and 1940s, the US welcomed many emigre German and European scholars fleeing the Nazi regime. They bought with them European traditions of scholarship and points of view that would lead to the re-emergence of Thucydides as a thinker and philosopher worthy of study in first Political Science and then International Relations. Initially, at least, post-Second World War Thucydidean studies were centred on the University of Chicago. It was there, in 1937, that David Grene, an Irishman who had just taken his MA in Classics at Trinity College Dublin, took up his first academic appointment. Grene would go on to co-found the famous Committee for Social Thought at Chicago and become a noted translator of Greek literature. It is his 1950 work, *Man in his Pride: A Study in the Political Thought of Thucydides and Plato*, that most interests us here. The initial goal of this work is to interrogate Thucydides and Plato as witnesses to the state and nature of politics at the end of the fifth century BC, an age that Grene felt was next to his own because of the declining role of religion and an increasing focus on man in public and academic discourse. Grene, however, does not simply draw parallels but interrogates both Thucydides and Plato's writings to understand their methods in passing judgement over political events. He even goes so far as to suggest that it is from the space between the intellectual projects of Thucydides and Plato that all Western political thought descends. Referring to Thucydides in particular, Grene explores how necessity forced Athens to exclude moral considerations in her interstate dealings, a necessity that may prove common to all imperial powers. He shared with Cornford an interest in necessity and change, and with Abbott an interest in Thucydides' literary and political realism. In this short book, therefore, Grene attempts to think hard about the value of Thucydides' intellectual system today and elevate him to a foundational place in the history of Western political thought.

Chicago, however, did not produce a unified school of Thucydidean studies. Instead, we find Grene's colleague Leo Strauss offering a radically distinct vision of the Greek historian.[2] Strauss was born and educated in Germany but was forced to flee by the rise of the Nazis, first to Paris, then London, followed by the New School in New York and finally Chicago, where he took up his first academic position in political philosophy. Liisi Keedus (2016) has recently and helpfully recapitulated Strauss's scholarly and philosophical approach. The account that follows is largely based on her work.[3] Strauss's academic programme focused on rescuing great thinkers of the past, including Aristotle, Plato, Maimonides and Hobbes, from what he felt were the dangers of historicism, which he took to be the belief that the thought of great philosophers could only be understood within their original context and that that context could only be accurately reconstructed through the historical arts. Strauss argued, contrary to historicist readings, that each thinker had had to guard carefully what they wished to say to avoid offending the political and religious taboos of their time. The modern scholar, therefore, needed to read carefully each philosopher to understand the different layers of the text in order to disentangle what they intended to be superficial and their more hidden thoughts, which carried much more value and import (Keedus 2016). Turning to Strauss's reading of Thucydides in his 1961 book, *The City and Man*, and his recently discovered 1971–2 lectures on the gods in Thucydides, we find great emphasis on recovering not simply the Athenian historian's views of democracy and empire but also the more obscure layers of the text and his deeper philosophical speculations. Strauss implored his students to pay close attention to the words that Thucydides used and their position in the text. So, for example, in his lectures he drew his students' attention to the first words of the Corcyrean and Corinthian speeches in book 1. The Corcyreans begin with *dikaion*, justice (δίκαιον), while the Corinthians begin with *anangke*, necessity (ἀνάγκη). From this observation, Strauss argued that Thucydides was subtly hinting to readers one of the antitheses that would be explored throughout his entire history: the complex relationship between justice and necessity in human affairs. Indeed, Keedus has argued that for Strauss, all of Thucydides political thought is only recoverable through the study of antagonisms, conflicts, ambiguities, tensions and contradictions (Keedus 2016: 81). There is much debate about the value of the 'Straussian' approach to ancient texts, although through the supervision of doctoral students and their spread throughout North American universities it is clear that Strauss exerts a great deal of influence on Thucydidean studies even today.

Strauss's reading, I would argue, also continues, or restarts, the turn to Thucydides on American soil. He even introduces a new label, after his death: Straussian. In the essay on Thucydides in *The City and Man*, Strauss mentions very little previous scholarship, preferring instead to give the impression that he is working directly and exclusively from the ancient sources in front of him. We may surmise that he had almost certainly read the work of Cornford, Schwartz, Abbott and Cochrane, but he does not position his reading in relation to theirs. He also doubtless knew of the *Thukydidesfrage* and German scholarship on the *History* more generally. Instead, his intellectual project is to convey to readers the urgent need to recover the ancient political thought of Aristotle, Plato and Thucydides in the modern world. In each of his essays on these three authors, he accordingly suggests ways of recovering their thought and understanding their intellectual system. And yet Strauss's focus on how the reader should recover Thucydides' political thought and his analysis of themes such as justice and necessity in the text suggest congruencies with earlier British scholarship. Strauss was working in a world in which Thucydidean studies had shifted significantly. No longer, as in the in the late nineteenth century, were analyses of Thucydides limited to philological or historiographical topics. The recovery of the Athenian historian's political thought could now take centre stage in academic monographs and university lectures. Moreover, Strauss's vision of Thucydides' political thought is rooted in the discussion of necessity in the text, a theme introduced by Cornford and which was taken up in different ways by Abbott, Zimmern, Toynbee and Powell. Strauss's Thucydides is not obviously a direct reaction to these scholars' interpretations, but he is working in their wake.

Following the work of Grene and Strauss, we might point to a number of other scholars who can also be said to have turned to Thucydides as the Cold War changed and developed and gave new salience to the bipolarity of Athens and Sparta (Lebow and Strauss 1991). Edward Keene (2015) has recently explored the early reception of Thucydides in this period. He points out that while the original edition of Hans Morganthau's 1948 study, *Politics Among Nations*, did not contain any references to Thucydides, the Athenian historian became increasingly prominent in later editions. Morganthau's work gave growing prominence to the realist reading of Thucydides among American International Relations scholars. By the end of the 1960s the Classicist Donald Kagan was already interpreting Thucydides through a (neo)conservative lens and using the Athenian historian to support his own political views, not simply to draw parallels between the ancient and modern worlds but to explore what he took to be the perennial problems of democratic hegemony and empire

(Kagan 1969, 1971, 1981, 1987). By the 1970s and 1980s it was not uncommon to find Thucydides hailed as the founder of International Relations, particularly in its realist iteration. Indeed, realist interpretations were becoming so common that they had become a 'cottage industry' ripe for gentle ridicule (Bagby 1994; Welch 2003). Finally, the end of the Cold War and emergence of an American 'Empire' in the 1990s and 2000s has only heightened interest in Thucydides, notably among scholars looking to critique realist paradigms in an age of increasing cynicism following the failure of military adventures abroad (Crane 1998; Luginbill 1999; Lebow 2003).

This book has highlighted where and when prominent American scholars cited the British writers of the turn, particularly Cornford and Abbott. The themes of political psychology and historical change have continued to provide a common ground for interpretations of Thucydides from many different and disciplinary angles. However, it is undeniable that much has been forgotten. In the case of Powell, the cause of his lack of subsequent influence is immediately apparent. His interpretation of Thucydides lay unread among his own papers until they were bequeathed to Churchill College, Cambridge. The post-Second World War reception of Zimmern and Toynbee's readings are a little more complex, but I believe intelligible. Both men occupied key positions in the discipline of International Relations in the immediate post-war years and continued to write and exert a certain measure of influence over the scholarly landscape. However, both men were now characterized as 'idealists', an intellectual system and political ideology that had clearly failed in that international organizations had proved powerless to arrest the rise of the Nazis in Germany and the outbreak of the Second World War. I have argued in this book that Zimmern's Thucydides was a political psychologist and Toynbee's a contemporary, both labels that have continued in use until today, but as the writings of both men began to be forgotten there was no reason to trawl through their work looking for analyses of the *History*. At the same time, Cornford's interpretation of Thucydides as a tragedian and Abbott's presentation of his realism continued to elicit interest among successive generations of scholars. The British turn to Thucydides bequeathed to the world many of the labels still applied to the Athenian historian today. However, not every British scholar's interpretation, as this book has shown, enjoyed a long afterlife.

With that claim in mind, in the final section of this epilogue, I will leave the reader with my thoughts on why the readings of Cornford, Abbott, Zimmern, Toynbee and Powell are not just important but crucial to our understanding of Thucydides today.

The value of the (British) Thucydidean turn

The rediscovery of the value of Thucydides in Chicago and then among realist scholars working in the 1950s, 1960s and 1970s is clearly the direct antecedent of the unprecedented place Thucydides occupies in both teaching and research in Political Science and International Relations in the US today. In Britain and Europe, Thucydides is not nearly as important in the Social Sciences. There the study of the *History* is confined almost exclusively to departments of Classics and Ancient History. This observation leads to two problems with which I would like to conclude this book. First, I would like to discuss what is special about the British turn, and second, I would like to point to its continuing relevance today.

I have argued in Chapter 1 and in this epilogue that the British turn to Thucydides marks a major turning point in the reception of the Athenian historian. Scholars had been reading the *History* for centuries for political insight and historiographical guidance, but it is mostly in Britain between 1900 and 1939 that the recovery of Thucydides' political philosophy, in a form relevant to the contemporary political situation, emerges as a topic of legitimate academic study. This turn occurs mainly in departments of Classics, certainly, but also in the new fields of International Relations as understood by Zimmern and Toynbee. Another feature worthy of note is that in Britain Thucydides did not become exclusively associated with one particular school of thought, such as realism or Straussianism. Rather, as I pointed out in Chapter 1, it is at this moment, almost at once, that a number of different labels begin to be applied to Thucydides: he became a *Mythistoricus*, a realist, a political psychologist, a contemporary, a scientist and a Realpolitiker. None of these labels came to dominate the field and I have tried to argue throughout this book that the British turn to Thucydides is united by the diversity of interpretations that it produced. There is a significant amount of cross-fertilization of ideas and tension between these different labels, which has fed into subsequent scholarship. After Cornford, Zimmern and Powell, there was no going back to claiming that Thucydides was just an ancient historian or just an historical scientist. A debate had been opened not only about what Thucydides had said, and what his personal values were, but also about how we should read him and how we should connect his historical thought to his philosophical thought. British scholars realized that it was not enough simply to say that Thucydides supported X or condemned Y. Rather, a quest began in the early twentieth century to understand how Thucydides viewed the world and what system he used to portray it. In wrestling with these questions, scholars were not just asking in what ways Thucydides is relevant today, but, potentially, in what ways might his thought prove universally relevant for all time. In other words, Thucydides began to be elevated to the level of a political philosopher. We might disagree with the ways Cornford, Abbott, Zimmern, Toynbee and Powell represented Thucydides' political philosophy, but we must also acknowledge that they opened new interpretative paths in Thucydidean scholarship down which many scholars still walk today.

I will now turn to my second problem: what relevance does the story of the turn hold for today's scholars? Our approach to Thucydides today is both a product of the society in which we live but also previous readings, which have accrued over the centuries. We do not need to have read Cornford, Abbott or Zimmern to be influenced by them because their work has been used and repackaged by scholars who came after them. Understanding the history of scholarship, therefore, is not an exercise that allows one to escape the past. That would be impossible. It is, however, an exercise in understanding the roots of our own interpretations so that we might better comprehend how our debates and approach to the text have been conditioned by earlier readings. In the history of scholarship, the emergence of Thucydides as an influential political thinker in the first half of the twentieth century has been astonishingly neglected by the vast majority of modern scholars. In the years before, during and after the Great War, Thucydides' *History* was quarried for the many insights that it could offer contemporary politics. It was also used as part of the justification for the academic and cultural relevance of the Greek and Latin Classics at a time of great political upheaval. It was academic classicists and classically trained commentators who were instrumental in this turn to Thucydides' contemporary relevance. I hope I have convinced readers that the quest for Thucydides' political philosophy, therefore, is not an approach that has been confined to Political Science and International Relations, but in fact finds its ultimate roots in the discipline of Classics and the way that this discipline was shaped, in Britain, by the experience of the Boer Wars and the Great War. This claim will, I hope, encourage social scientists to think more critically about their own traditions of reading Thucydides and encourage classicists to enter into greater dialogue with their social science colleagues to re-evaluate the philosophical intricacies of Thucydides.

Finally, the Great War itself has been a constant companion throughout this text. I believe that many scholars are aware of the ways in which changes in society, political events and culture defined and redefined the readings of ancient texts. American realist readings of Thucydides are clear reactions to the Cold War, and Allison's Thucydides' trap is evidently a reflection of American anxiety over the partial loss of her global hegemony to a rising China. The Great War shattered Europe and almost destroyed the British Empire. It inevitably profoundly affected the way that Thucydides was read and interpreted. What is truly remarkable is the variety of responses that the war elicited in readers of Thucydides. We have seen that one single (admittedly momentous) event led Abbott to discuss at length Thucydides' realism; Zimmern to hold up Thucydides' political psychology as crucial in the search for new political orders to ensure peace; Toynbee to meditate deeply on Thucydides' contemporaneity and his place in the history of civilization; and Powell to look with fresh eyes at the role of morality in the *History*. These readings are important because they represent voices from a partially forgotten world that present to us a Thucydides that is at once familiar and different. Each generation, each reader even, invents his or her own Thucydides. Reading previous interpretations reminds us that we are never going to have the final word on a text as profound and rich as Thucydides' *History of the Peloponnesian War*.

Notes

Preface

1. We should also add here the important work by Murari Pires (2007) on Thucydides in the renaissance, Iglesias-Zoido (2011) on the reception of Thucydides' speeches, and a comprehensive account of Thucydides' reception by Meister (2013).
2. Throughout this book, I have capitalized academic disciplines, e.g. Classics or International Relations, but I have left the subject matter of those disciplines in miniscule, i.e. references to classical literature or international relations as a synonym for interstate politics.
3. I have been particularly inspired by Charles Martindale's (1993, 2013) idea of the transhistorical in reception studies. When we read a classical text, we are not just reading an ancient author but all the centuries of interpretation that have accrued in the intervening span of history. It has been my practice, in this book, to situate readings of Thucydides in the scholarly and intellectual milieu, but also to link, say, Cornford's interpretation to more recent discussions. That is to say, I believe, following Martindale, that there are chains of readers of a classical text, of which this book is just another receiver: I read Cornford reading Thucydides. 'Reception on this model (which derives from the work of the Constance School, led by Hans Robert Jauss and Wolfgang Iser) makes it more difficult to fall into one of two opposed illusions common in literary interpretation, which we may call vulgar historicism (the view that we can know the past as it really was, untainted by what came after) and an equally vulgar presentism (the view that everything is wholly adapted to what we think in the present). With both historicism and presentism there are, so to say, only two points involved ("now" and "then", differently privileged)' (Martindale 2013: 170).
4. Cf. also the papers by Crane (2015) and Hawthorn (2012; 2015) outlining the value of reception studies to political scientists interested in Thucydides.

Chapter 1

1. Thucydides is certainly cited by all kinds of politicians, cf. Sawyer (2015).
2. The various situations are outlined on the Thucydides Trap website, https://www.belfercenter.org/thucydides-trap/case-file.

3 Cf. Morley (2013), who speaks of the variety of interpretations that have been offered over the past few centuries, pointing to the number of different interpretive assumptions that have been made in that time. The account that I offer is broadly in sympathy with Morley, but I aim to emphasize how 'labels' themselves relate to underlying interpretations.
4 Thucydides, or course, was incredibly influential as an historical and rhetorical model in the ancient world. His ancient reception has received considerable attention in recent years. I have found most helpful the studies by Canfora (2006) and Burns (2010).
5 Of course, Herodotus was often seen as the 'anti-Thucydides' in that he did not adhere to the strict historiographical programme, factual accuracy and political focus of Thucydides; see Morley (2016b).
6 On the influence of Thucydides on Nietzsche, see Zumbrunnen 2002; Morley 2004: 28–9; Zumbrunnen 2010: 19–20; Jenkins 2011; Polansky 2015.
7 Université de Paris 1, Victor Cousin, *Notes sur Thucydide: matériaux inédits pour une thèse de doctorat (1812–1813)*, MSVC 48.
8 At the heart of this debate lies the question of how to teach Thucydides as well as how to read him (cf. Orwin 2015a).
9 We should note that one very fruitful area of collaboration has been in the study of Thucydides' reception, legacy and influence where Classicists and social scientists have recently worked easily and profitably together. Thauer and Wendt's volumes have brought together with great success Classicists and social scientists, as have the edited volumes by Harloe and Morley (2012) and Lee and Morley (2015). Cf. also Monoson and Loriaux, who argue that the questions asked of Thucydides in International Relations and Political Science had been steadily diverging and propose a discussion of Thucydides' critique of Periclean policy as an area of common ground between the two disciplines (Monoson and Loriaux 1998).

Chapter 2

1 The first is Jane Ellen Harrison's *Primitive Athens as Described by Thucydides*, published the year before.
2 It should be noted that the last two of these works focus on the 'scientific' tradition in the reception of Thucydides. The idea of Thucydides as a 'scientific' historian is, perhaps, less fashionable today than it has been in the past.
3 Cf. Oost (1975), Marinatos (1981) and Jordan (1986) on the connected, but different, roles of religion in Thucydides' thought.
4 Dunlap (2015: 155) encapsulates Cornford's thought under the rubric 'cultural evolution'. I will argue below that Cornford was far from sure that this evolution was moving forward in a linear motion.

5 On the role of necessity in Thucydides, see Ostwald (1988), Fisher and Hoekstra (2017) and the excellent recent study by Jaffe (2017a).
6 I have taken the following account of Cornford's life from Kellog Wood (1990), Guthrie (1967) and the 2004 *ODNB* entry by Hackforth and revised by Gill.
7 Smail (2004) notes that 'Verrall was an inspiring teacher, both as lecturer and as supervisor, with a particularly fine reading voice. He was one of the first classical scholars regularly to use modern literature in his exposition of ancient poetry, and to investigate Greek plays as examples of drama rather than simply as texts requiring emendation.' However, 'Although Verrall's lectures achieved great popularity, his published works (which were chiefly on Greek tragedy, especially Euripides) received only a mixed reception from other scholars and are no longer highly regarded. His interpretations of individual plays tended to be over-ingenious, and he was too ready to discount straightforward explanations in his search for what he believed to be hitherto undetected truth.'
8 Euripides is only mentioned once in *Mythistoricus* (1907: 243) and this in the context of Cornford questioning the limits of his rationality: 'And yet, when we read the *Hippolytus*, and still more when we see it played, the feeling grows upon us that reason falls back like a broken wave. A brooding power, relentless, inscrutable, waits and watches and smites. There she stands, all through the action, the white, implacable Aphrodite. Is she no more than a marble image, the work of men's hands? Is there no significance in that secret smile, no force being the beautiful mask, no will looking out of the fixed, watching eyes? ... It must be that poetry has forced on reason some strange compromise. We cannot detect the formula of that agreement; but we know that somehow a compact has been made. Had the poet, in one of the long days musing in his seaward cave on Salamis, seen a last vision of the goddess, rising in wrathful form?'
9 Cornford (Cornford and Verrall 1913: xxxix) quotes a 'recent' Trinity student in his *memoir* on Verrall describing the latter's teaching technique: 'I don't think we believed very much what he said; he always said he was as likely to be wrong as right. But he made all Classics so gloriously new and living. He made us criticise by standards of common sense, and presume that the tragedians were not fools, and that they did mean something. They were not to be taken as antiques privileged to use conventions that would be nonsense in anyone else ...' Cf. Horlsey (2008), who claims that Cornford too 'almost seems to have been carried away with a too-clever idea'.
10 Cornford would nevertheless still speak fondly of Jackson in later life; see Cornford (1931: 6–7).
11 Consider the following publications from 1912, which all point to the group's interest in complicating simple accounts of the progress in Greek thought: Cornford (2018), *From Religion to Philosophy. A Study in the Origins of Western Speculation*; Murray (2012), *Four Stages of Greek Religion* (in the 2nd 1925 edition the title became five stages); Harrison (2010), *Themis: A Study of the Social Origins of Greek Religion*.

12 Cornford (1907: 69): 'The chief point in which we differ from Professor Gomperz arises over his last statement, that Thucydides endeavoured to describe the course of human affairs as though it were a process of nature informed by inexorable causality. This is precisely what we have seen reason to deny. Human affairs have, for Thucydides, not even an analogy with processes of nature; much less are they identified with one of the processes of nature; much less, again, is their course informed by inexorable causality.'

13 The concept of 'foreshadowing' is incredibly important in contemporary narratological studies of Thucydides. See in particular Rood (1998) and more recently Liotsakis (2017).

14 See Cornford (1907: 237): 'In the course of this study the conviction has been growing upon us that the comparisons commonly made between Thucydides and Herodotus are based on false assumptions and misleading. It is usual to speak of Herodotus as primitive, and religious to the point of superstition; of Thucydides as advanced and sceptical to the point of irreligiousness. Herodotus is treated as a naïve and artless child; Thucydides as a disillusioned satirist and sometimes as a cynic. These representations seem to us to be founded simply on the external fact that Herodotus was by a generation the older of the two, and on the false assumption that, because their books are both called histories, Thucydides must have started where Herodotus left off, and developed the tradition he originated. Our own view is almost exactly the reverse. If either of the two men is to be called religious, it is Thucydides; if either is sceptical, it is Herodotus. Naivety and artlessness are not terms we should choose to apply to either; something closely akin to cynicism and flippancy is common enough in Herodotus; there is not a trace of either in Thucydides.'

15 Quoted in Hesk (2015: 220).

16 Although Cornford (1907: 6) acknowledges that over time the war became a struggle between oligarchs and democrats, animosity between the two parties does not explain its origins.

17 Cornford (1907: 35–6) sums up the nautical concern of this party in the following words (a passage in which the first line also hints at the possible roots of the book as a lecture course): 'Consider, now, the feelings of the merchants, down in the Piraeus, with the great stream of traffic between Sicily and Italy in the west and Asia Minor and the seas and islands to the east, flowing both ways across the isthmus, under their very eyes. The Piraeus had captured the bulk of the eastern trade formerly carried on by Euboea, Aegina, Megara. The only great field for further expansion was in the west, and Corinth held the gateway. Every vase that the Athenian potteries exported to Italy, every cheese that came from Syracuse to the port of Athens, had to pay toll to the keepers of the isthmus. Attica was cut off from the western seas by Boeotia, the Megarid, Corinth. The weak point in this chain was Megara, which

possessed, moreover, a port on each sea – Pegae on the west, Nisaea on the east – with a road over the pass joining them. What would become of the riches of Corinth, when the Piraeus had established an alternative channel for the trade across the isthmus? And so we read that, in 461, Athens obtained the alliance of Megara, which had quarrelled with Corinth. Thus the Athenians gained *both Megara and Pegae, and built long walls from Megara to Nisaea, and garrisoned them. And from this above all arose the intense hatred of Corinth for Athens*.' The sentence in italics is supported by a footnote reference to Th. 1.103.

18 These are helpfully listed by Chambers (1991: 65) as Diodorus (following Ephorus) 12.39; Aristophanes, *Archanians* 524–39, *Peace* 605–11, 615–18; Plutarch, *Pericles* 29–31; Andocides 3.8; Aeschines 2.175.

19 In the preface to the book, Cornford (1907: viii) justifies his use of the term *Mythicus* in the following way: 'It is the intrusion of this artistic tendency – for a thing so unpremeditated can hardly be called a design – that justifies the epithet Mythistoricus. By Mythistoria I mean history cast in a mould of conception, whether artistic or philosophic, which, long before the work was even contemplated, was already inwrought into the structure of the author's mind.'

20 Stray (1998) notes that the kind of wholesale reform Cornford was advocating did not come about until after the intervention of a Royal Commission in 1922.

21 'Thucydides was one of those prophets and kings of thought who have desired to see the day of all-conquering Knowledge, and have not seen it. The deepest instinct of the human mind is to shape the chaotic world and the illimitable stream of events into some intelligible form which it can hold before itself and take in at one survey. From this instinct all mythology takes its rise, and all the religious and philosophical systems which grow out of mythology without a break. The man whose reason has thrown over myth and abjured religion, and who yet is born too soon to find any resting-place for his thought provided by science and philosophy, may set himself to live on isolated facts without a theory; but the time will come when his resistance will break down. All the artistic and imaginative elements in his nature will pull against his reason, and, if once he begins to produce, their triumph is assured. In spite of all his good resolutions, the work will grow under his hands into some satisfying shape, informed by reflection and governed by art' (1907: 249).

22 For a contemporary critical review of Cornford's thought more generally, see J. S. (1913).

23 For example, Cochrane wrote the following words to his fellow Canadian academic William Hutton: 'If I am right in connecting [Thucydides] with the Hippocratics, then his real achievement was the discovery of a method which may for our purpose be called scientific. This means that it is no more than a method or as I say somewhere a way of looking at the world ... But absolutes are not to be grasped by such processes of reasoning, they are, as you I think admit, intuitive and all the realm

of absolutes belongs to "religion and philosophy" (and poetry & myth). I did not mean to set [Thucydides] on a pedestal further than in crediting him with the application of this idea to the study of society and the net result is to show the very definite limitation of the scope of science and widen immensely the field which belongs to faith. I have been greatly troubled for example by a good deal of modern science, and I think the source of the confusion in my mind and in the mind of many others is that what is merely a way of looking at the world is by many scientists taken to be *the* way of looking at the world, all others being ruled out' (quoted by Beer in Cochrane 2017: 6).

Chapter 3

1. Although his contribution to Hellenic studies is occasionally reassessed. See, for example, Millet (2007).
2. Hedley Bull offers the following succinct definition of idealism: 'The distinctive characteristic of these writers was their belief in progress: the belief, in particular, that the system of international relations that had given rise to the First World War was capable of being transformed into a fundamentally more peaceful and just world order; that under the impact of the awakening of democracy, the growth of "the international mind", the development of the League of Nations, the good works of men of peace or the enlightenment spread by their own teaching, it was in fact being transformed; and that their responsibility as students of international relations was to assist this march of progress to overcome the ignorance, the prejudices, the ill-will, and the sinister interests that stood in its way' (Bull 1972: 34–5). See also Bull (1969) on the history of International Relations thought at this time.
3. For the background to Victorian and Edwardian imperial engagements with the Classics, see the essays in Bradley (2010) and the excellent study of Hagerman (2013). Rome was generally a more significant model than Greece (Butler 2012). However, most of Zimmern's thought on empire focused on Greek history and Athens in particular.
4. Zimmern was hardly the only pro-Periclean and pro-Hellenic scholar working in Oxford in the early twentieth century. Gilbert Murray, who had a reputation for mentoring young scholars such as H. A. L. Fisher, J. A. K. Thomson and Arnold Toynbee (the subject of Chapter 5), believed fervently that the study of Greek language, literature and philosophy could help stimulate freedom, truth and progress (Stapleton 2007: 264). Indeed, Murray was critical of many Oxbridge alumni for merely learning grammar and facts without achieving any measure of understanding of the Hellenic spirit. Instead, he believed that an education in Greek should be open to all people receptive to the value of a liberal education. To that end, he campaigned

for the ending of compulsory Greek at Oxford and the expansion of the subject in Britain's schools. Murray also taught classes in the University Extension movement and the Workers' Educational Association and was a key figure in the establishment of the Home University Library, which aimed to make available to all the latest academic thinking on the arts and sciences. In short, Murray believed that a liberal education in the Greek Classics might help make young people and working men into better citizens. Zimmern shared this belief. He too had given extramural lectures at Oxford and had worked at the Board of Education from 1913 to 1916 (Morefield 2014: 34–5). For both Murray and Zimmern, Periclean Athens represented the summit of human cultural and intellectual achievement, which had tried, and briefly began to succeed, in dragging humanity towards progress through education and the appreciation of knowledge, the arts and literature (Stapleton 2007: 266). It was therefore a crucial topic in lectures both within the university and among interested working men.

5   As Stapleton observes (Stapleton 2007: 277), Zimmern paid homage to Wallas in a footnote for attempting 'to do for modern politics what Socrates did for Greek, to explain to our political craftsmen the nature and use of their tools'.

6   This anxiety finds its roots in the early nineteenth century (Koditschek 2011), but is heightened at the turn of the twentieth century by the Boer Wars and growing voices for independence in Britain's white settler colonies.

7   After the Great War, Gilbert Murray would publish a book titled *Aristophanes and the War Party: A Study in the Contemporary Criticism of the Peloponnesian War* (1919). As the title suggests, this book was an attempt to understand the rise of a 'war party' or a hawkish faction in Athenian politics in the years before and during the Peloponnesian War. The main difference between Murray and Zimmern's account is the role played by political or mass psychology. Zimmern believed that the war fever was the culmination of a vast social and economic revolution, which produced Cleon. Murray thought, based on his reading of Aristophanes and Thucydides, that the war party and the war fever were the products of Cleon's rise to political prominence.

8   Cf. the recent views of Kopp (2016, 2017) that in fact Thucydides subverts readers' expectations of the efficacy of sea power by intentionally contrasting Pericles' rhetoric with the reality of warfare at sea.

9   This essay is cited in the bibliography as Zimmern (1928) because it was only later published as part of a volume of collected papers titled *Solon and Croesus*. An original typescript survives in the Bodleian Library in Oxford. It is not known whether this typescript was produced in 1905 or 1928; however, it contains many handwritten emendations. These emendations overwrite original thoughts, which did not find their way into the printed version. As I argue below, these original thoughts are often illuminating.

10 Cf. (Zimmern 1928: 103): 'It will serve to remind you of all that Thucydides has left out – of the sad-hearted crowds walking slowly back to Athens in the dusk, of the empty, joyless, anxious, impoverished life at home, of the widows and the orphans and the prisoners and the butcheries to be, of the slaves to whom these triremes recalled scenes of shame at Melos or Scione or Potidaea, of the innumerable human tragedies which this one day's working has irrevocably knit.' Zimmern rewrote this passage three times; see MS. 136: 96–7.

11 Zimmern (1914), quoted in Morley (2018b: 419): 'While the book has been passing through the press war has broken out, bringing Great Britain face to face, for the first time since she has become a Democracy, with the full ultimate meaning of the civic responsibilities, both of thought and action, with which in the narrower field of the city-state, the fifth-century Athenians were so familiar. Greek ideas and Greek inspiration can help us today, not only in facing the duties of the moment, but in the work of deepening and extending the range and meaning of Democracy and Citizenship, Liberty and Law, which would seem to be the chief political task before mankind in the new epoch of history on which we have suddenly entered.'

12 'When we refuse formally to reopen an issue on which action is in fact being taken daily, because it is a party question and a Coalition government is in power, when we leave to the healing mercies of time a problem with regard to which inaction itself constitutes a policy, when we deliberately invent party labels or election cries designed to confuse the mind of the voter and to distract him from the real issue, when our politicians have become professionals in the art of what Thucydides described as "the use of fair phrases to arrive at guilty ends" and a British Premier, more euphemistically, as "political strategy", we might do worse than sit down to read, mark, learn, digest, and apply to our modern situations, the immortal speeches or essays in which Thucydides lays bare for us the heart of the political life of his day, and to let them act as a purge of some of our own too sugary diet' (Zimmern 1921: 336).

13 Zimmern (1921: 337) describes Plato's psychological approach in the following words: 'The Republic opens with several books of psychological analysis, no doubt at times a little fantastic in its attempts at premature classification, but full of life and reality, and not only Greek reality but human reality.'

14 'As for Thucydides, his knowledge of men, the fruit of patient experience deepened by disappointment, is felt behind every line of his book, as one describes it in the features of his undegenerate descendant Venizelos' (Zimmern 1921: 337).

15 Zimmern (1921: 341) notes that modern scholars may scoff at the idea of Thucydides as a scientific historian. He counters that if one turns to the opening chapters of the *History* then one finds that Thucydides is a sociologist, who describes the 'evolution' of early Greek society, an anthropologist and a geographer.

16 Cf. 'After all, international politics is only contemporary history, and the master of history, Thucydides, devoted himself to that branch of the subject' (Zimmern 1929: 7–8).
17 Zimmern (1929: 4): 'George Louis Beer was no philosopher of the ivory tower. He was a "man of the world." He lived in the world, and his thoughts were derived from close observation of the world. But, when he was thus *free* from the taint of monasticism, he was equally fortunate in his avoidance of its more fashionable opposite – the temptation to subordinate truth to propaganda.'

Chapter 4

1 Indeed, as Rood has pointed out, Abbott himself was glad to succumb to the power of the Thucydidean mode of history writing (Rood 2006: 227), arguing that even the Greek historian's omissions 'constitute a guarantee of good faith' (Abbott 1925: 36).
2 On this point cf. Crane (1998: 38) who identifies four types of realism in Thucydides (as opposed to in his reception), namely political, literary, artistic and scientific. Crane concedes that this list is hardly exhaustive but maintains that each of these types of realism is at work in Thucydides. I have followed Morley in this chapter because I believe that when studying the reception of Thucydides, his paper more clearly articulates the developing relationship between empirical and doctrinal realism in a way that is more useful in the study of the Thucydidean turn.
3 This view is supported by Donnelly (2000: 6) who notes that realism in International Relations is not a theory defined by an explicit set of assumptions and propositions, but rather is a 'general orientation'. Similarly, Abbott's realism is doctrinal in the sense that it represents an attempt to claim the existence of a political system in Thucydides. That system is presented as flexible and can, sometimes, become vague and even confused.
4 Annette Freyberg-Inan quotes Abbott, alongside Lamb, in her account of the history of realism in International Relations. She cites Abbott in support of the claim that in Thucydides the state comes before the individual, meaning that civic virtue claims pre-eminence as a motivation of the individual's actions. 'The motives to achieve this virtue must be distinguished from the motives acknowledged in realism' (Freyberg-Inan 2004: 30). Cf. Welch (2003: 303) who quotes Abbott (1925: 41–2) to support the claim that Thucydides' writing is magisterial and authoritative. Note also that Nietzsche had already praised Thucydides' realism at the turn of the century. I argued in the Introduction that Nietzsche saw Thucydides as a doctrinal or political realist.
5 Cf. a letter sent by T. S. Eliot (2012: 174) to Thorpe, which explains the evolution of the piece from a review of Abbott's book to a full-fledged article on Thucydides.

6 An independent city-state located on an island in the Aegean. The Melians were descended from colonists of Sparta but their island was located in an area in the control of the Athenians. They attempted to remain independent but were brutally subjugated by Athens in 416 BC.
7 Cf. Stray (2018: 368–9). Murray also points to the limits of such parallels (1911: 11): 'Of course such parallels must only be allowed to amuse our reflections, not to distort our judgements. It would be easy to note a thousand points of difference between the two great contests. But I must notice in closing one last similarity between the atmospheres of the two wars which is profoundly pathetic, if not actually disquieting. The more the cities of Greece were ruined by the havoc of war, the more the lives of men and women were poisoned by the fear and hate and suspicion which it engendered, the more was Athens haunted by shining dreams of the future reconstruction of human life. Not only in the speculations of philosophers like Protagoras and Plato, or town-planners like Hippodamus, but in comedy after comedy of Aristophanes and his compeers – the names are too many to mention – we find plans for a new life; a great dream-city in which the desolate and oppressed come by their own again, where rich and poor, man and woman, Athenian and Spartan are all equal and all at peace, where there are no false accusers and – sometimes – where men have wings. This Utopia begins as a world-city full of glory and generous hope; it ends, in Plato's Laws, as one little hard-living asylum of the righteous on a remote Cretan hill-top, from which all infection of the outer world is rigorously excluded, where no religious heretics may live, where every man is a spiritual soldier, and even every woman must be ready to "fight for her young, as birds do." The great hope had dwindled to be very like despair; and even in that form it was not fulfilled.'
8 MacKenzie (1930: 17) later recalls that he first read Thucydides on the way to Gallipoli 'until I found the well of the *scirocco* too much for my powers of construing'. Later in the same work (1930: 223) he admits that he was understandably not the most attentive of readers while on campaign: 'As a matter of fact, I found all reading out there rather a bore except *Blackwood's Magazine*, with a page or two of Homer or Virgil or Thucydides before going to sleep, Homer and Thucydides, alas, with the help of a crib, though I could still construe Virgil without much difficulty.'
9 Hutton had published a similar essay on Herodotus (1910, 1911) before the war. However, even a cursory glance will demonstrate how the outbreak of the war led Hutton to place contemporary politics centre stage in his study of Thucydides.
10 Hutton draws an explicit parallel between the two conflicts in the following passage: 'Thucydides has told us that he wrote for all time and this work would never be out of date (1.22). If anyone wants to test that soaring ambition let him do what I was able to do recently. Let him sit down quietly and listen to two young students of

Greek reading alternately from Thucydides the dialogue at the end of Book V, called the Melian debate. One reader represents the unhappy and weak neutral – Melos: the other, the callous, cynical, militaristic and aggressive Athens. The readers translated almost literally: change nothing but the names: put Belgium for Melos: and Germany for Athens: and Great Britain for Sparta. For nothing else needed to be changed: and we heard coming to us from the year 416, B.C., the first proof, the first edition, of the identical debate between Belgium and Germany, which was republished under other names and at various times between 1860 and 1914: but never so closely to the original as in 1914' (Hutton 1916: 241). Hutton believed that Thucydides warms to Cleon as a Tory but dislikes him as a democrat, an imperialist and a man. The sympathy is intellectual. The dislike is personal.

11 On Glover's biography during the war, see Wood (2015: 94–221).
12 'Since I sent the manuscript to the publisher, many months have passed; the delay was inevitable; and as I have read the proofs I have found new links of sympathy with the men of whom I wrote. Their experience is strangely like what ours has been and will be – the strain of a long war, the readjustment of all life to conditions that raise question and doubt, the endeavour to re-found society and to find a new a base from which the soul can make all its own again. Much that I wrote has been given for me a new meaning; some allusions, so quick in these last months has been the march of events, seem out of date already. But a true record of human experience is never irrelevant, and the period from Pericles to Philip had above all other great natures and master intellects to interpret it.'
13 Throughout his book, Abbott draws parallels and distinctions between the Peloponnesian War and the Great War. For example, when discussing Thucydides' literary art, he notes that, 'The Gallipoli Expedition – a disaster on a vastly larger scale – for want of such a master [Thucydides]has already become, even to those who took part in it, a bewildering blur of motive and action, while the Sicilian Expedition – a comparatively petty event of a remote past – thanks to Thucydides, lives in our imaginations as of one of the greatest tragedies in the history of the world' (Abbott 1925: 205).
14 A view of Thucydides that was already common among nineteenth-century German scholars such as Barthold Georg Niebuhr, Leopold von Ranke, Wilhelm Roscher and Eduard Meyer; see Pires (2006), Morley (2012, 2013), Wendt (2017).
15 Thucydides' literary art is taken by Abbott to be grave and masculine. He draws a lengthy comparison between Thucydides' style and the imposing nature of ancient buildings: 'After most of the incidents with which the History is concerned have faded from our minds, we retain an indelible impression of it as a whole. This impression might perhaps be summed up in the term applied by the Greeks to the Doric order of architecture – masculine. In it nothing is sacrificed to mere grace. Its lines are robust; its ornamentation sober; the general effect is one of power and

austere simplicity. True, it lacks the smoothness and symmetry of a Doric temple, reminding us rather of those massive fabrics of irregular blocks anterior to the appearance of the orders in architecture... And thus it is with the fabric which Thucydides has raised. The real secret of its strength is its antique honesty. Not a line is perfunctorily done, is less than it claims to be... Into the labour of composition Thucydides bought the same self-imposed rule which he followed with such scrupulous diligence in his investigations. That faithfulness which lay within him and commanded that every relevant fact and circumstance, even the smallest, should be carefully collected and ascertained, also compelled that they should be arranged and fitted together to the best possible advantage. He took for himself and offered to others the lowest, from a literary point of view, estimate of his business – usefulness. Yet he worked up to the highest literary standard within his reach; and performed the task of a chronicler in the spirit of an artist' (Abbott 1925: 205–6).

16 This distinction is drawn out in rather flowery prose in the final two paragraphs of the book, when Abbott describes his return to 'civilisation' (Abbott 1912: 329):

Yet, I must own, as soon as I reached Europe I began to long for Africa. The edge of my craving for cleanliness and comfort and decent cooking had been taken off at Ben Gardane. By the time I set foot at Marseilles, the commonplace advantages of civilization had lost their charm. Civilization, it is said, has a few other points in its favour. Perhaps. But when those points are summed up, what does it all amount to? At best it is a narrow, and paltry, and mean, and timid thing, when compared with the limitless grandeur of the desert and the gallant simplicity of its children.

On landing in Europe, I felt as if I had left a great part of myself behind me. But I consoled myself with the reflection that I returned the richer by a great memory – the memory of large free spaces and of large free hearts – the hearts of men who do not mind dying.

17 On the same page, Sahlins quotes Kaplan (2002: 45–6): 'While Thucydides' persistent focus on self-interest may be offensive to some, his notion that self-interest gives birth to effort, effort to options, makes his 2,400 year-old history of the Peloponnesian War a corrective of the extreme fatalism basic to Marxism and medieval Christianity.'

18 Connor continues (1984: 15): 'Thucydides' history is unquestionably aimed at an audience that values cleverness, sophistication, intellect, and self-interest, but it does not simply affirm and reinforce those values. Rather it is prepared, at least from time to time, to exploit uncertainties or inconsistencies in the attitudes of its readers, explore the ambiguities and limits of values, and challenge, perhaps even subvert, expectations and apparent certainties.'

19 In support of this assertion, Abbott quotes the following lines from Hume's essay on the *Balance of Power*: 'In all the politics of Greece, the anxiety with regard to the

balance of power is apparent, and is expressly pointed to by the ancient historians. Thucydides represents the league which was formed against Athens, and which produced the Peloponnesian war, as entirely owing to this principle' (Hume: 1994: 135).

20 In a footnote, Abbott (1925: 58) writes, 'A French historian explains the cause of the rupture of the peace of Amiens (1803) in the same words [as Thucydides 1.23]: "Dans le parlement anglaise la cause de la rupture s'avouait hautement: c'était le trop grande puissance de la France," and he goes on to quote Fox: "cet accroisement extraordinaire, qui vous surprend, qui vous effraye..." Gustave Ducoudray, *Histoire Contemporaine* (1892), p. 275. An English writer explains the alliances and counter-alliances which heralded in the Great War as due to each country's fear of its neighbour's growing power. See the Times *Lit. Suppl.*, April 26th, 1923.'

21 The founders of League never intended it to act purely as a legal system capable of arbitrating international disputes. Rather, their goal was to create a forum in which a common international 'consciousness' might arrive (Wertheim 2012).

Chapter 5

1 After a brief stint as the inaugural Koreas Chair in Byzantine studies at King's College London (Clogg 2013).

2 The *Survey* does not feature prominently in this chapter for the simple reason it rarely mentions Thucydides. There is no mention of the Greek historian in the index of the work drawn up in 1930 by Malcolm Neil and my own searches of the work have only yielded a solitary reference, to the funeral speech, in the *Survey* of the years 1920–3 (Toynbee 1927: 61–2, footnote 2). Ian Hall, however, does note that Toynbee could not resist inserting many ancient historical parallels into the *Survey*, which, in his view, were often lengthy and unneeded (2014: 28, referencing Toynbee 1927: 62–3).

3 A volume of maps and a volume responding to critics titled 'reconsiderations' would later be published in 1959 and 1961 respectively.

4 Aron cited Toynbee and the French commentator Thibaudet, 'who had linked the Thucydidean past to the grim present of the early twentieth century' (Keene 2015: 364; Aron 2003: 145). Halle quoted extensively from Toynbee's reminiscence of his feeling of the contemporaneity of Thucydides in 1914 (Halle 1955: 264).

5 Published between 1934 and 1961.

6 Even Thucydides' contemporaneity was not unique. Cf. the following statement: 'If we search now for Thucydides and Xenophon and Polybius and Josephus and Ibn Khaldin and Machiavelli and Clarendon the historians, we shall find each one of them just as much alive and just as effectively in action in his ethereal communion

with posterity as ever was in his "short and narrow verged" life in the flesh' (Toynbee 1948c: 290).

7 There is little agreement among scholars on the question of how to best to label Toynbee's thought on international relations (Brewin 1995; Lang 2011). Thompson (1955) and Ivascu (2017) identify both realist and idealist strands to his thought, while Castellin (2015) argues for an evolution in Toynbee's thought from a youthful idealist to a religiously inspired utopian in his later years. Hall (2012) points to Toynbee's campaign against imperialism and aggression in international affairs without labelling him an idealist. As we shall see below, it is no easy task to situate Toynbee's Thucydides in either the traditional idealist or realist camps. Toynbee is certainly aware of the literary realism of the text, but he does not emphasize this aspect. Neither, however, does he present Thucydides as an idealist offering concrete solutions to the problems of his age. Instead, I shall argue that Toynbee saw Thucydides as a forlorn historian surveying the breakdown of his civilization – a figure whom Toynbee felt was particularly relevant in 1914 and 1939.

8 This volume is introduced in Chapter 3.

9 McNeill (1989a: 111) points out that already in the early 1920s Toynbee appears to have sketched out the skeleton that would become his monumental work *A Study of History* in rough notes and other scribblings. These early essays on Greek history, therefore, should be thought of as an early iteration of the project that would come to dominate Toynbee's life. Toynbee's idea of a civilization, while it remained relatively static over the course of his life, also developed. In particular, his thought on history and international relations began to be increasingly influenced by Christian, particularly medieval Christian, thought over time (McIntire and Perry 1989; Perry 1989).

10 Toynbee named twenty-one civilizations in the first six volumes, but would later identify twenty-six.

11 I found McDougall (1986: 21) most useful in summarizing Toynbee's ideas and situating them in broader historiographical debates. Other useful summaries of Toynbee's arguments are found in Stromberg (1972) and Winetrout (1975).

12 It is interesting to note that Toynbee considers Sparta to be an 'arrested' civilization. Sparta departed from the normal run of Hellenic civilization because following her conquest of Messina 'the conquered environment now takes its audacious conqueror captive'. Sparta disavows her political role in Greece until the rise of Athens forces her to confront the reality of her position (Toynbee 1948c: 70–8).

13 Note that Toynbee will later downgrade the Minoan civilization to a society in the *Study*.

14 Rusten (2015) translates *kinesis* as mobilization; cf. Meier (2005), who views it is a fundamental category of Thucydidean analysis.

15 Thucydides himself is depicted by Toynbee as withdrawing from the trauma of the Peloponnesian War only to 'return' through his discovery of historiography (Morley 2017: 200–1).

16 The translation runs:

> So the class-war at Korkyra grew more and more savage, and it made a particular impression because it was the first outbreak of an upheaval that spread in time through almost the whole of Greek society. In every state there were conflicts of class, and the leaders of the respective parties now procured the intervention of the Athenians of the Lakedaimonians on their side. In peace-time they would have had neither the opportunity nor the inclination to call in the foreigner, but now there was the war, and it was easy for any party of violence to get their opponents crushed and themselves into power by an alliance with one of the belligerents. This recrudescence of class-war brought one calamity after another upon the states of Greece – calamities that occur and will continue to occur as long as human nature remains what it is, however they may be modified or occasionally mitigated by changes of circumstance. Under the favourable conditions of peace-time, communities and individuals do not have their hands forced by the logic of events, and can therefore act up to a higher standard. But war strips away all the margins of ordinary life and breaks in character to circumstance by its brutal training. So the states were torn by the class-war, and the sensation made by each outbreak had a sinister effect on the next – in fact, there was something like a competition in perfecting the fine art of conspiracies and atrocities . . .
>
> Thus the class-war plunged the Greek society into every kind of moral evil, and honesty, which is the chief constituent of idealism, was laughed out of existence in the prevailing atmosphere of hostility and suspicion. No argument was cogent enough and no pledge solemn enough to reconcile opponents. The only argument that appealed to the party momentarily in power was the unlikelihood of their remaining there long and the consequent advisability of taking no risks with their enemies. And the stupider the combatants, the greater their chances of survival, just because they were terrified at their deficiencies, expected to be outwitted and outmanoeuvred by their opponents, and therefore plunged recklessly into action, while their superiors in intellect, who trusted their wits to protect them and disdained practical precautions, were often caught defenceless and brought to destruction.
>
> Toynbee 1921a: 27–9; 3.82–3

Note that the translation was slightly amended for clarity in the *Legacy of Greece* essay (cf. Toynbee 1921b: 310–11) and is noticeably different from Toynbee's translation of the same passage produced in 1922 (cited in the bibliography as Toynbee 1959a).

17 The translation runs, 'So death is nothing to us and matters nothing to us, since we have proved that the soul is not immortal. And as in time past we felt no ill, when the Phoenicians were pouring in to battle on every front, when the world rocked with the shock and tumult of war and shivered from centre to firmament, when all mankind on sea and land must fall under the victor's empire and victory was in doubt – so, when we have ceased to be, when body and soul, whose union is our being, have been parted, then nothing can touch us – we shall not be – and nothing can make us feel, none, not if earth is confounded with sea and sea with heaven' (Toynbee 1921b: 315; Luc. 3.830–42).

18 Cf. Crane (1998: 282), who points out that it is not a particularly prominent concept in the *History*.

19 In volume 10, Toynbee points to a number of modern writers who clearly shaped the way he thought of the ancient past. He speaks of the eminent German historian Edward Meyer as demonstrating that Graeco-Roman history was a unity and Zimmern as showing that 'all true history is contemporary history', suggesting that it was from modern historians that Toynbee gained the idea of the contemporaneity of Thucydides (Toynbee 1954d: 232–3). Elsewhere in volume 10, Toynbee speaks of the influence of Thucydides on his thought. However, Thucydides is mentioned in the same breath as four other historians – Clarendon, Procopius, Josephus and Rhodes – who each described war as an instrument of change. Thucydides' depiction of change is very important. He describes the breakdown of a promising civilization, but he is certainly not singled out as being more important than the other historians named. Moreover, this depiction of Thucydides does not mention the 'personification' of forces in history. Rather, Thucydides is simply an historian of decline. Toynbee's depiction of Thucydides is important, but far from unique, and is in accordance with his treatment of Thucydides in the earlier volumes of the *Study*. For example, in the first volume we find praise for Thucydides' honesty in using his speeches. His *obiter recta* are recognized as more interesting, engaging and true than that which is found in modern historians (Toynbee 1949a: 443). Or in volume 9, Thucydides' depiction of the *stasis* on Corcyra is used as a warning that a balance of power is often likely to be upset (1954c: 530), and the Peloponnesian War as evidence that Athens and Sparta were willing to sacrifice Hellenic political unity (1954c: 554).

20 On this point, see Chapter 7.

Chapter 6

1 It is interesting to note that Powell, who was born in 1912, would have had little direct experience of the Great War. However, he seems to have discussed the conflict

and its relationship to Thucydides with those old enough to remember the war and, indeed, veterans of the fighting. In the talk, he claims that many pocket editions of the *History* went into the trenches (cf. Schelske 2015) and that Montagu Butler, master of Trinity, had written to his son comparing Prussia to Athens and Melos to Belgium (Churchill archives 1/6/19: 7, 9). This is information that Powell surely got by speaking to his older peers.

2 Powell here draws a comparison between Thucydides and a hypothetical English historian. Powell asks his listeners to suppose that in 1925 a young English historian turns to write a history of the Great War as a 'tragic whole'. He begins by tracing the roots of German imperialism in the Napoleonic Wars before tracing the story down to 1918. He makes progress before realizing in the late 1920s that the events of 1914–18 are only part of a much larger conflict. In 1935, at thirty-six years old, he occupies himself with outlining the events that are leading to the re-emergence of hostilities. He is then either a passive spectator or an active participant in the second greater contest. It is only in 1950, as an elderly man, that he can sit down to depict this greater whole and begin to explain the decline and fall of the British Empire and justify the 'humane policy' which caused the whole catastrophe: 'How little of his original draft would remain in the finished work! And how great would be the contrast of tone between one stratum and another. This is not a very different situation from that which we meet in the history of Thucydides, and particularly in the first two books' (Churchill archives 1/6/19: 4–5). Remember that Powell wrote this account three years before the outbreak of the Second World War.

3 Cf. Stahl (2003: 18, 20), who argues that Schwartz in fact resurrected the *Thukydidesfrage* under the influence of contemporary events, thereby condemning scholarship to play out old debates.

4 There is an interesting parallel here to Morley's (2018a) study of the development of the reception of Thucydides from an empirical to a doctrinal realist. Powell suggests here that it is not enough to merely recognize Thucydides' realism; one must also embrace it, before the true political import of the text can be properly understood.

5 Murray was a noted pacifist and Powell would later cite Murray's address to the Classical Association in 1932 in just such a way (Churchill archives 1/6/24: 60). I have not been able to locate a copy of this address. However, Murray's references to Thucydides in his 1913 work, *Euripides and his Age*, point to his anti-war and anti-imperialist interpretation. Murray argues that by the beginning of the Peloponnesian War Athens had become a 'tyrant city' and the 'League' had become an 'Empire'. For Murray, Thucydides associates the conflict with a 'progressive degradation' in public life (1913: 107). Murray also argues that Thucydides presented Pericles (2.63) and Cleon (3.37, 3.40) as possessing the same vision of empire and something new and unique in the Greek system of interstate relations, namely an empire that controls fellow Greeks (1913: 108). Murray's anti-war depiction of

Thucydides re-emerges later in the book when he discusses the Melian dialogue (1913: 129–30): 'As I read this Melian Dialogue, as it is called, again and again, I feel more clearly the note of deep and angry satire. Probably the Athenian war-party would indignantly have repudiated the reasoning put into the mouths of their leaders. After all they were a democracy and, as Thucydides fully recognizes, a great mass of men, if it does commit infamies, likes first to be drugged and stimulated with lies: it seldom, like the wicked man in Aristotle's Ethics, "calmly sins." But in any case the massacre of Melos produced on the minds of men like Thucydides and Euripides – and we might probably add almost all the great writers who were anywise touched by the philosophic spirit – this peculiar impression. It seemed like a revelation of naked and triumphant sin. And we cannot but feel the intention with which Thucydides continues his story.'

6   While it is true that Cochrane saw the *History* as an indictment of war, Powell is being somewhat unfair here. Cochrane's larger point was that in Thucydides there is a failure of morality and principle in Greek interstate relations. He argues that the Peace of Callias marks 'the triumph of humanistic principles in international law'. The *Thirty Years Peace* marks the death of the self-sufficing city state, cooperation was now at last appreciated and the *poleis* gravitated towards either the Peloponnesian League or the Athenian Empire (1929: 70–1). This expansion meant that Cochrane saw the Peloponnesian War as a world war. The settlement of 445 BC allowed for arbitration through an appeal to a court acceptable to both parties. Sparta ignored this clause (1.88) and Athens appealed to it (1.140). Therefore, Thucydides' account of the outbreak of the war focuses on conflicting interpretations of the treaty, but behind these negotiations lay the subterranean forces – economic, moral and spiritual – either against or for Hellenism. From Thucydides' scientific analysis of these various forces at work in the Greek city-states, Cochrane argues, 'Thucydides draws no moral from the failure of the treaty to save Hellenism from the horrors of the Peloponnesian war; but, if a moral is to be drawn, it is surely this. The treaty failed to hold because of the infirmity of human wisdom and human will. On all sides, men allowed their sense of common welfare to be blinded by their own partial interest, and obscured by their fears and passions. Instead, therefore, of holding fast to the procedure which humanism had dictated, and compromising such interests as they could not reconcile, they reverted to the ancient and suicidal policy of brute force, which destroys all interests, including those which it seeks to protect, and leaves all parties to share a common fate of poverty and distress' (1929: 76). For Cochrane, therefore, commentators are wrong to attempt to correct Thucydides' account of the causes of the war from second-rate accounts. We should trust Thucydides' depiction of the causes of the war rooted in conflicting ideas of the interpretation and meaning of key clauses in international treaties. Where clauses appeared vague, conflict inevitably arose. Subject to this limitation, Athens, and

others, felt no compunction in advancing their own interest at every possible opportunity. In this chapter, we see Cochrane attempting to wrestle with the conflict between international law in Thucydides and the 'realist' recognition that each state was driven by its own interests. He is not a realist, however, because he does not reduce Greek interstate relations to the pursuit of power in an anarchic system, but rather focuses on the pursuit of Hellenism, even though that project proved forlorn.

7 This work was translated into English in 1939. The first volume included a final short chapter on 'Thucydides: Political Philosopher' where it is claimed that Thucydides created political history (Jaeger 1944: 383): 'Athens, while concentrated earnestly and exclusively on the present, had suddenly reached a crisis in which serious political thinkers were compelled to develop a historical consciousness, although now in a new sense and with different content. They were forced, in fact, to discover the *historical* necessity of the crisis to which the nation's development had led. That is the real nature of the intellectual revolution reflected in Thucydides' history – historical writing had not become political but political thinking had become historical.'

8 As far as I am aware, both the speech and the dissertation have been entirely forgotten by later scholarship. The only mentions of these texts that I have found is in Heffer's biography of Powell, where the speech is cited in support of Powell's fixation on the upcoming war, and his belief that he could understand German culture through his reading of Nietzsche (Heffer 1998: 28).

9 Although it should be noted that Camilla Schoefield (2013: 30) has suggested that Powell's readings of Herodotus and Thucydides coloured his later views of international relations. Schoefield's arguments are convincing but I will not engage with them here, as I am concerned solely with Powell's thoughts as contained in his Thucydidean scholarship and not in his later post-Second World War life as a politician and MP.

10 It should be noted that at Cambridge, Powell was something of a prodigy who famously passed his entrance exams in half the allotted time (Heffer 1998: 12–13). However, Powell was a reluctant academic, who felt trapped by college life and the life of teaching and research that was unfolding before him. He even seriously debated whether he should accept his fellowship to Trinity, an institution which compounded his feeling of confinement and suffocation (Heffer 1998: 25).

11 Although cf. Orwin (1994), who argues that there is a notion of justice behind every appeal to advantage in Thucydides.

12 Powell does not engage with Cochrane's view of the effect of evolutionary thinking on Thucydides' portrayal of international relations, but the arguments are so novel that I believe it is worth recapitulating them here. Cochrane makes this argument in Chapter 5 of his book. There he contends that Thucydides, alone among ancient commentators, realized that the *polis* was not the final stage of Greek political

development. Rather, the forces that existed on the outskirts of the Greek world would make further organizations of power inevitable. Herodotus describes how Greeks were willing to sell out their countrymen (1929: 57–8) and how ultimately it was only fortune that saved Greece (59). '[T]o the realist, as has been said, such an answer must have been anything but reassuring.' Thucydides saw clearly that the Persian threat had not receded and, indeed, that other threats were looming, i.e. the Macedonians to the north (1929: 60) and the Thracians (1929: 61). Thucydides offers a far more accurate account of the causes, and extent, of power in the north and its relationship to the Greek settlers there. Therefore, we see that for Cochrane, Thucydides' prowess as an international relations scholar rests on his ability to see beyond the *polis* as the primary unit of politics and to delineate exactly the evolving relationship between the Greeks and their neighbours (1929: 65).

13 On this point, cf. Shanske (2013), who argues that in fact morality, particularly in a legal sense, survives in important ways in Athenian politics even at the worst of times, which serves as a reminder that Powell's bleak vision of Thucydides is shocking even today.

14 Heffer (1998: 22–3) quotes the following from Powell's correspondence: 'In my early twenties I read all Nietzsche – not just the main works but the minor works as well all of them, and every scrap of published correspondence. Nietzsche alone of men out of books has a share in the loyalty and affectionate gratitude which otherwise belongs only to living teachers.' Powell, therefore, had clearly read Nietzsche's comments on Thucydides even if he does not cite them in the dissertation.

15 Many modern scholars would agree with Powell that the dialogue represents a key articulation of Thucydidean Realpolitik. However, it is more conventional to see the speech as representing the decline of Athenian morality to a nadir of democratic imperialism. Crane (1998: 237) writes that 'The extreme point of Athenian *Realpolitik* in Thucydides, the Melian Dialogue is often analyzed as the climax of a process within the *History* that begins with the blunt analysis of the Athenian delegation at Sparta and evolves through the cool assessments of Perikles' first and final speeches, and the Mytilenean debate.' In support of this assertion, Crane cites Euben (1990), Deininger (1939), White (2012), Strauss (1978), Meiggs (1972), Cogan (1981), Pouncey (1980) and Connor (2013).

16 Morgenthau, a key figure in the history of American International Relations, similarly argues that Realpolitik requires rational thinking (Morgenthau 1948: 8, 14). However, unlike Powell, he contends that rationality is rarely present in the actions of states. Certain governments and leaders act more rationally than others do because of intellectual capabilities, legal constraints or available information. Morgenthau even goes so far as to suggest that rationality is the exception rather than the rule in politics, an assertion recently reinforced by Rathbun (2018; cf. Forde 2004).

17 As mentioned in a printed card, held in Powell's papers in the Churchill College Archives, which contains all his references for the position.

Chapter 7

1 Thucydides is not mentioned by E. H. Carr (1939), a key figure in the emergence of political realism in Britain. Neither is Thucydides discussed in Hedley Bull's seminal 1977 work, *The Anarchical Society* (cited in the Bibliography as Bull 2012). However, cf. Geoff Hawthorne's (Political Scientist, Cambridge) recent reassessment of Thucydides' politics (2014). It is beyond the scope of this book to analyse why post-Second World War British International Relations and Political Science never turned to Thucydides. Carr, as a modern historian, focused on more recent events and Bull explored medieval history in depth.
2 Strauss even wrote a critical review of *Man in his Pride* (Strauss 1951).
3 I have also found Orwin (2015b) and Jaffe (2015) very helpful.

Bibliography

Abbott, G. F. (1900), *Songs of Modern Greece*, Cambridge: Cambridge University Press.
Abbott, G. F. (1909), *Turkey in Transition*, London: Edward Arnold.
Abbott, G. F. (1912), *The Holy War in Tripoli*, Longmans, Green & Co.
Abbott, G. F. (1916), *Turkey, Greece and the Great Powers: A Study in Friendship and Hate*, London: Robert Scott.
Abbott, G. F. (1917), *The Truth about Greece: I. The Greco-Servian Treaty; II. The Landing at Salonica: A Queer Story; III. The Expedition to Servia and Its Results*, London: Voice of Greece.
Abbott, G. F. (1922), *Greece and the Allies, 1914–1922*, London: Methuen.
Abbott, G. F. (1925), *Thucydides: A Study in Historical Reality*, London: Russell & Russell.
Ackerman, R. (1991), 'The Cambridge Group: Origins and Composition', in W. Calder III (ed.), *The Cambridge Ritualists Reconsidered*, 1–20. Alpharetta, GA: Illinois Classical Studies, Supplement 2.
Adcock, F. E. (1927), 'The Archidamian War: 431–421 B.C.', in J. B. Bury, S. A. Cook and F. E. Adcock (eds), *The Cambridge Ancient History Volume 5: Athens, 478–404 BC*, 193–253, Cambridge: Cambridge University Press.
Adcock, F. E. (1963), *Thucydides and His History*, Cambridge: Cambridge University Press.
Ahrensdorf, P. J. (1997), 'Thucydides' Realistic Critique of Realism', *Polity* 30, no. 2: 231–65.
Ahrensdorf, P. J. (2000), 'The Fear of Death and the Longing for Immortality: Hobbes and Thucydides on Human Nature and the Problem of Anarchy', *American Political Science Review* 94, no. 3: 579–93.
Alford, E. M. (1998), 'Thucydides and the Plague in Athens: The Roots of Scientific Writing', *Written Communication* 15, no. 3: 361–83.
Allison, G. T. (2012), 'Thucydides's trap has been sprung in the Pacific', *Financial Times*, https://www.ft.com/content/5d695b5a-ead3-11e1-984b-00144feab49a.
Allison, G. T. (2015), 'The Thucydides Trap: Are the U.S. and China Headed for War?', *The Atlantic*, 24 September, https://www.theatlantic.com/international/archive/2015/09/united-states-china-war-thucydides-trap/406756/.
Allison, G. T. (2017a), 'The Thucydides Trap', *Foreign Policy*, 9 June, https://foreignpolicy.com/2017/06/09/the-thucydides-trap/.
Allison, G. T. (2017b), *Destined for War? Can America and China Escape Thucydides's Trap*, London: Scribe.
Allison, J. W. (1997), *Word and Concept in Thucydides*, Atlanta, GA: Scholars Press.

Andrewes, A. (1960), 'The Melian Dialogue and Perikles' Last Speech (Thucydides V, 84–113, II, 60–4)', *Proceedings of the Cambridge Philological Society* 6, no. 186: 1–10.

Anon. (1907a), 'Review: Thucydides Mythistoricus', *Hermathena* 14, no. 33: 542–3.

Anon. (1907b), 'Review: Thucydides Mythistoricus', *Journal of Hellenic Studies / the Society for the Promotion of Hellenic Studies* 27: 307.

Anon. (1947), 'Notes and News', *Classical Review* 61, no. 2: 37–9.

Arieti, J. A. (2005), *Philosophy in the Ancient World: An Introduction*, New York: Rowman & Littlefield Publishers.

Armitage, D. (2000), *The Ideological Origins of the British Empire*, Cambridge: Cambridge University Press.

Arnold, T. (2010), *Thucydides: History of the Peloponnesian War: The Text According to Bekker's Edition with Some Alterations*, Cambridge: Cambridge University Press.

Aron, R. (2003), *Peace and War: A Theory of International Relations*, New Brunswick, NJ: Transaction.

Aubrey, M. E. (1953), 'T. R. Glover Review and Reminiscence', *Baptist Quarterly* 15, no. 4: 175–82.

Auden, W. H. (2007), *Another Time*, London: Faber & Faber.

Bagby, L. M. J. (1994), 'The use and abuse of Thucydides in International Relations', *International Organization* 48: 131–53.

Bagby, L. M. J. (1995), 'Thucydidean Realism: Between Athens and Melos', *Security Studies* 5, no. 2: 169–93.

Bagby, L. M. J. (2000), 'Fathers of International Relations? Thucydides as a Model for the Twenty-First Century', in L. Gustafson (ed.), *Thucydides' Theory of International Relations: A Lasting Possession*, 17–41, Baton Rouge: Louisiana State University Press.

Baji, T. (2016), 'Zionist Internationalism? Alfred Zimmern's Post-Racial Commonwealth', *Modern intellectual History* 13, no. 3: 623–51.

Balot, R. K. (2001), *Greed and Injustice in Classical Athens*, Princeton, NJ: Princeton University Press.

Balot, R. K. (2017), 'Was Thucydides a Political Philosopher?', in S. Forsdyke, E. Foster and R. Balot (eds), *The Oxford Handbook to Thucydides*, Oxford: Oxford University Press.

Barker, E. (1955), 'Dr Toynbee's Study of History: A Review', *International Affairs* 31, no. 1: 5–16.

Beard, M. (2000), *The Invention of Jane Harrison*, Cambridge, MA: Harvard University Press.

Bedford, D. and T. Workman (2001), 'The Tragic Reading of the Thucydidean Tragedy', *Kokusaigaku Revyu = Obirin Review of International Studies* 27, no. 1: 51–67.

Beiser, F. C. (1993), 'Hegel's Historicism', in F. C. Beiser (ed.), *The Cambridge Companion to Hegel*, 270–300, Cambridge: Cambridge University Press.

Bell, D. (2007), *The Idea of Greater Britain: Empire and the Future of World Order, 1860–1900*, Princeton, NJ: Princeton University Press.

Bell, D. (2016), *Reordering the World: Essays on Liberalism and Empire*, Princeton, NJ: Princeton University Press.

Bew, J. (2016), *Realpolitik: A History*, Oxford: Oxford University Press.

Bloxham, J. (2018), *Ancient Greece and American Conservatism: Classical Influence on the Modern Right*, London: I.B. Tauris.

Bluhm, W. T. (1962), 'Causal Theory in Thucydides' Peloponnesian War', *Political Studies* 10, no. 1: 15–35.

Boak, A. E. R. (1921), 'Greek interstate Associations and the League of Nations', *American Journal of International Law* 15, no. 3: 375–83.

Boldt, A. D. (2019), *Leopold Von Ranke: A Biography*, London: Routledge.

Bosworth, A. B. (1993), 'The Humanitarian Aspect of the Melian Dialogue', *Journal of Hellenic Studies / the Society for the Promotion of Hellenic Studies*, 113: 30–44.

Boucher, D. (1998), *Political Theories of International Relations: From Thucydides to the Present*, Oxford: Oxford University Press.

Bradley, M., ed. (2010), *Classics and Imperialism in the British Empire*, Oxford: Oxford University Press.

Brewin, C. (1995), 'Arnold Toynbee, Chartham House, and Research in a Global Context', in D. Long and P. Wilson (eds), *Thinkers of the Twenty Years' Crisis: Inter-War Idealism Reassessed*, 277–301, Oxford: Clarendon Press.

Bull, H. (1969), 'The Twenty Years Crisis Thirty Years On', *International Journal* 24, no. 4: 625–38.

Bull, H. (1972), 'The Theory of International Politics 1919–1969', in B. Porter (ed.), *The Aberystwyth Papers: International Politics, 1919–1969*, 30–50, Oxford: Oxford University Press.

Bull, H. (2012), *The Anarchical Society: A Study of Order in World Politics*, London: Red Globe Press.

Burns, T. (2010), 'Marcellinus' Life of Thucydides, translated, with an introductory essay', *Interpretation: A Journal of Political Philosophy* 38, no. 1: 3–26.

Bury, J. B. (1900), *A History of Greece to the Death of Alexander the Great*, London: Macmillan and Co.

Bury, J. B. (1909), *The Ancient Greek Historians (Harvard Lectures)*, n.p.p.: Dover Books, Macmillan.

Butler, S. (2012), *Britain and Its Empire in the Shadow of Rome: The Reception of Rome in Socio-Political Debate from the 1850 to 1920s*, London: Bloomsbury.

Caldeb, W. M. (1989), 'Ulrich von Wilamowitz-Moellendorff to Sir Alfred Zimmern on the Reality of Classical Athens', *Philologus* 133, no. 1–2: 303–9.

Calder, W. III. (1991a), 'The Cambridge Group: Origins and Composition', in W. Calder III (ed.), *The Cambridge Ritualists Reconsidered*, Illinois Classical Studies, Supplement 2, 21–35, Atlanta, GA: Scholars Press.

Calder, W. III. (1991b), 'Jane Harrison's Failed Candidacies for the Yates Professorship (1888, 1896): What Did Her Colleagues Think of Her?', in W. Calder III (ed.), *The*

Cambridge Ritualists Reconsidered, Illinois Classical Studies, Supplement 2, 37–60, Atlanta, GA: Scholars Press.

Callander, T. (1961), *The Athenian Empire and the British*, London: Weidenfeld and Nicolson.

Campbell, R. (1951), 'How Democracy Died', *Life*, 1 January, 88–96.

Canfora, L. (2006), 'Thucydides in Rome and Late Antiquity', in A. Rengakos and A. Tsakmakis (eds), *Brill's Companion to Thucydides*, 721–53, Leiden: Brill.

Carr, E. H. (1939), *The Twenty Years' Crisis, 1919–1939: An Introduction to the Study Of International Relations*, London: Macmillan.

Castellin, L. (2015), 'Arnold J. Toynbee's Quest for a New World Order: A Survey', *The European Legacy, toward New Paradigms: Journal of the International Society for the Study of European Ideas* 20, no. 6: 619–35.

Chambers, M. (1991), 'Cornford's Thucydides Mythistoricus', in W. Calder III (ed.), *The Cambridge Ritualists Reconsidered*, Illinois Classical Studies, Supplement 2, 61–78, Atlanta, GA: Scholars Press.

Chan, S. (2019), 'More Than One Trap: Problematic interpretations and Overlooked Lessons from Thucydides', *Journal of Chinese Political Science* 24, no. 1: 11–24.

Chance, A. (2013), 'Realpolitik, Punishment and Control: Thucydides on the Moralization of Conflict', *Journal of Military Ethics* 12, no. 3: 263–77.

Clogg, R. (2013), *Politics and the Academy: Arnold Toynbee and the Koraes Chair*, London: Taylor & Francis.

Cochrane, C. N. (1929), *Thucydides and the Science of History*, Oxford: Oxford University Press.

Cochrane, C. N. and D. Beer (2017), *Augustine and the Problem of Power: The Essays and Lectures of Charles Norris Cochrane*, Eugene, OR: Cascade.

Cogan, M. (1981), *The Human Thing: The Speeches and Principles of Thucydides' History*, Chicago: University of Chicago Press.

Connor, W. R. (1977), 'A Post-Modernist Thucydides', *Classical Journal* 72: 289–98.

Connor, W. R. (2013), *Thucydides*, Princeton, NJ: Princeton University Press.

Constant, B. (1988), *Constant: Political Writings*, Cambridge: Cambridge University Press.

Cornford, F. M. (1907), *Thucydides Mythistoricus*, London: Edward Arnold.

Cornford, F. M. (1931), *The Laws of Motion in Ancient Thought*, Cambridge: Cambridge University Press.

Cornford, F. M. (1967), *The Unwritten Philosophy and Other Essays*, Cambridge: Cambridge University Press.

Cornford, F. M. (2018), *From Religion to Philosophy: A Study in the Origins of Western Speculation*, Princeton, NJ: Princeton University Press.

Cornford, F. M. and A. W. Verrall (1913), 'Memoir', in M. A. Bayfield and M. A. Duff (eds), *Collected Literary Essays, Classical and Modern*, xxxiv–xlviii, Cambridge: Cambridge University Press.

Crane, G. (1996), *The Blinded Eye: Thucydides and the New Written Word*, London: Rowman & Littlefield Publishers.

Crane, G. (1998), *Thucydides and the Ancient Simplicity: The Limits of Political Realism*, Berkeley: University of California Press.

Crane, G. (2015), 'Everywhere Monuments of Good and Evil: Thucydides in the Twenty-First Century', in C. Lee and N. Morley (eds), *A Handbook to the Reception of Thucydides*, 568–78, Chichester, UK: Wiley and Blackwell.

Deininger, G. (1939), *Der Melier-Dialog*, Erlangen: Krahl.

Demetriou, K. N. (1999), *George Grote on Plato and Athenian Democracy: A Study in Classical Reception*, Bern: Peter Lang.

Desmond, W. (2006), 'Lessons of Fear: A Reading of Thucydides', *Classical Philology* 101, no. 4: 359–79.

Dickins, G. (1911), 'The True Cause of the Peloponnesian War', *Classical Quarterly* 5, no. 4: 238–48.

Donnelly, J. (2000), *Realism and International Relations*, Cambridge: Cambridge University Press.

Doyle, M. W. (1990), 'Thucydidean Realism', *Review of International Studies* 16: 223–37.

Dunlap, P. T. (2015), *Awakening Our Faith in the Future: The Advent of Psychological Liberalism*, London: Taylor & Francis.

Earley, B. (2015), '"L'historien Des Politiques": Universalism and Contextualism in the Abbé de Mably's Reception of Thucydides', in C. Lee and N. Morley (eds), *A Handbook to the Reception of Thucydides*, 261–77, Chichester, UK: John Wiley & Sons Ltd.

Earley, B. (2016), 'Commerce, Militarism and Luxury: Eighteenth-Century French Depictions of the Athenian Empire', *Classical Receptions Journal* 8, no. 1: 11–31.

Eckstein A. (2017), 'Thucydides, International Law, and International Anarchy', in S. Forsdyke, E. Foster and R. Balot (eds), 491–514, Oxford: Oxford University Press.

Edmunds, L. (1975a), *Chance and Intelligence in Thucydides*, Cambridge, MA: Harvard University Press.

Edmunds, L. (1975b), 'Thucydides' Ethics as Reflected in the Description of Stasis', *Harvard Studies in Classical Philology* 79: 73–92.

Eliot, T. S. (2012), *The Letters of T.S. Eliot: 1926–1927*, ed. Valerie Eliot and John Haffenden, New Haven, CT: Yale University Press.

Euben, P. J. (1990), *The Tragedy of Political Theory: The Road Not Taken*, Princeton, NJ: Princeton University Press.

Finlay, R. (1904), 'International Arbitration', *North American Review* 179, no. 576: 659–70.

Finley Jr, J. H. (1942), *Thucydides*, Harvard, MA: Harvard University Press.

Finley Jr, J. H. (1967), *Three Essays on Thucydides*, Harvard, MA: Harvard University Press.

Fitzsimons, M. A. (1980), 'Ranke: History as Worship', *Review of Politics* 42, no. 4: 533–55.

Fliess, P. J. (1959), 'Political Disorder and Constitutional Form: Thucydides' Critique of Contemporary Politics', *Journal of Politics* 21, no. 4: 592–623.

Forde, S. (1995), 'International Realism and the Science of Politics: Thucydides, Machiavelli, and Neorealism', *International Studies Quarterly* 39, no. 2: 141–60.

Forde, S. (2004), 'Thucydides on Ripeness and Conflict Resolution', *International Studies Quarterly* 48, no. 1: 177–95.

Forde, S. (2012), 'Thucydides and "Realism" among the Classics of International Relations', in K. Harloe and N. Morley (eds), *Thucydides and the Modern World: Reception, Reinterpretation and Influence from the Renaissance to the Present*, 178–96, Cambridge: Cambridge University Press.

Foster, D. J. (1912), 'The Four Corner-Stones of the Temple of International Justice. Address of Hon. David J. Foster at the Public Mass Meeting Held in the Hall of the Americas, Washington, D. C., Friday Evening, December 8', *Advocate of Peace* 74, no. 1: 5–7.

Foster, E. (2010), *Thucydides, Pericles, and Periclean Imperialism*, Cambridge: Cambridge University Press.

Fragoulaki, M. (2013), *Kinship in Thucydides: Intercommunal Ties and Historical Narrative*, Oxford: Oxford University Press.

Fragoulaki, M. (2016), 'Emotion, Persuasion and Kinship in Thucydides: The Plataian Debate (3.52–68) and the Melian Dialogue (5.85–113)', in E. Sanders and M. Johncock (eds), *Emotion and Persuasion in Classical Antiquity*, 113–32, Stuttgart: Franz Steiner Verlag.

Frankel, B. (2013), *Roots of Realism*, London: Routledge.

Freyberg Inan, A. (2004), *What Moves Man: The Realist Theory of International Relations and Its Judgment of Human Nature*, Albany: State University of New York Press.

Fromentin, V. and S. Gotteland (2015), 'Thucydides' Ancient Reputation', in C. Lee and N. Morley (eds), *A Handbook to the Reception of Thucydides*, 11–25, Chichester, UK: John Wiley & Sons Ltd.

Garst, D. (1989), 'Thucydides and Neorealism', *International Studies Quarterly* 33, no. 1: 3–27.

Gerson, G. (1998), 'Liberals and the Carnivalesque: Gilbert Murray and Francis Cornford on Trial', *History of European Ideas* 24, no. 4–5: 331–54.

Gerson, G. (2004), *Margins of Disorder: New Liberalism and the Crisis of European Consciousness*, Albany: State University of New York Press.

Geyl, P. (1955), 'Toynbee the Prophet', *Journal of the History of Ideas* 16, no. 2: 260–74.

Geyl, P. (1956a), 'Toynbee's System of Civilizations', in A. Montagu (ed.), *Toynbee and History: Critical Essays and Reviews*, 39–72, Boston: Porter Sargent.

Geyl, P. (1956b), 'Toynbee as a Prophet', in A. Montagu (ed.), *Toynbee and History: Critical Essays and Reviews*, 360–77, Boston: Porter Sargent.

Geyl, P., A. J. Toynbee and P. A. Sorokin. (1949), *The Pattern of the Past: Can We Determine It?*, Boston: Beacon Press.

Gillies, J. (1786), *The History of Ancient Greece, Its Colonies and Conquests: From the Earliest Accounts Till the Division of the Macedonian Empire in the East. Including the History of Literature, Philosophy, and the Fine Arts*, 3 vols, Dublin: Burnett, Colles, Moncrieffe.

Gilpin, R. (1981), *War and Change in World Politics*, Cambridge: Cambridge University Press.

Glover, T. R. (1917), *From Pericles to Philip*, New York: Macmillan.

Gomme, A. W. (1930), 'Review: Thucydides and Science – Thucydides and the Science of History. By Charles Norris Cochrane. Pp. 180. London: Oxford University Press, Humphrey Milford, 1929. 10s. Net', *Classical Review* 44, no. 4: 123–4.

Gomperz, T. (1896–1909), *Griechische Denker, Eine Geschichte Der Antiken Philosophie*, 3 vols, Leipzig: Veit.

Grant, W. L. (1929), 'Review: Thucydides and the Science of History by Charles Norris Cochrane', *Canadian Historical Review* 10, no. 4: 343–5.

Greenwood, E. (2008), 'Fictions of Dialogue in Thucydides', in S. Goldhill (ed.), *The End of Dialogue in Antiquity*, 15–28, Cambridge: Cambridge University Press.

Greenwood, E. (2015), *Thucydides and the Shaping of History*, London: Bloomsbury Publishing.

Grene, D. (1951), *Man in His Pride: A Study in the Political Philosophy of Thucydides and Plato*, Chicago: University of Chicago Press.

Grote, G. (2010), *A History of Greece*, 12 vols, Cambridge: Cambridge University Press.

Grundy, G. B. (1911), *Thucydides and the History of His Age*, London: J. Murray.

Grundy, G. B. (1917). 'Political psychology: A science which has yet to be created', *Nineteenth Century* 8, no. 155: 155–70.

Grundy, G. B. (1948), *Thucydides and the History of His Age*, Vol. 2, Oxford: Basil Blackwell.

Grundy, G. B. and G. Dickins. (1913), 'The True Cause of the Peloponnesian War', *Classical Quarterly* 7, no. 1: 59–62.

Guthrie, W. K. C. (1967), 'Memoir', in *The Unwritten Philosophy and Other Essays*, vii–xix, Cambridge: Cambridge University Press.

Hackforth, R. and D. Gill. (2004), 'Cornford, Francis Macdonald (1874–1943), classical scholar', *Oxford Dictionary of National Biography*, https://www.oxforddnb.com/view/10.1093/ref:odnb/9780198614128.001.0001/odnb-9780198614128-e-32571.

Hagerman, C. (2013), *Britain's Imperial Muse: The Classics, Imperialism, and the Indian Empire, 1784–1914*, Basingstoke, UK: Palgrave Macmillan.

Hall, I. (2003), 'Challenge and Response: The Lasting Engagement of Arnold J. Toynbee and Martin Wight', *International Relations* 17, no. 3: 389–404.

Hall, I. (2012), '"The Toynbee Convector": The Rise and Fall of Arnold J. Toynbee's Anti-Imperial Mission to the West', *The European Legacy, toward New Paradigms: Journal of the International Society for the Study of European* 17, no. 4: 455–69.

Hall, I. (2014), '"Time of Troubles": Arnold J. Toynbee's Twentieth Century', *International Affairs* 90, no. 1: 23–36.

Halle, L. (1955), *Civilization and Foreign Policy: An Enquiry For Americans*, New York: Harper.

Hamilton, E. (1942), *The Greek Way*, New York: W. W. Norton.

Hammond, M., trans., and P. J. Rhodes (2009), *Thucydides: The Peloponnesian War*, Oxford: Oxford University Press.

Harloe, K. and N. Morley (2012), 'Introduction: The Modern Reception of Thucydides', in K. Harloe and N. Morley (eds), *Thucydides and the Modern World: Reception, Reinterpretation and Influence from the Renaissance to the Present*, 1–24, Cambridge: Cambridge University Press.

Harrison, J. E. (1906), *Primitive Athens as Described by Thucydides*, Cambridge: Cambridge University Press.

Harrison, J. E. (2010), *Themis: A Study of the Social Origins of Greek Religion*, Cambridge: Cambridge University Press.

Hawthorn, G. (2012), 'Receiving Thucydides Politically', in K. Harloe and N. Morley (eds), *Thucydides and the Modern World: Reception, Reinterpretation and Influence from the Renaissance to the Present*, 212–28, Cambridge: Cambridge University Press.

Hawthorn, G. (2014), *Thucydides on Politics: Back to the Present*, Cambridge: Cambridge University Press.

Hawthorn, G. (2015), 'Receiving the Reception', in C. Lee and N. Morley (eds), *A Handbook to the Reception of Thucydides*, 579–88, Chichester, UK: Wiley and Blackwell.

Heffer, S. (1998), *Like the Roman: The Life of Enoch Powell*, London: Weidenfeld & Nicolson.

Heinburg, J. G. (1926), 'History of the Majority Principal', *American Political Science Review* 20, no. 1: 52–68.

Hesk, J. (2015), 'Thucydides in the Twentieth and Twenty-First Centuries', in C. Lee and N. Morley (eds), *A Handbook to the Reception of Thucydides*, 218–38, Chichester, UK: Wiley and Blackwell.

Hobbes, T., trans., and D. Grene (1989), *The Peloponnesian War*, Chicago: University of Chicago Press.

Hoekstra, K. (2012), 'Thucydides and the Bellicose Beginnings of Modern Political Theory', in K. Harloe and N. Morley (eds), *Thucydides and the Modern World: Reception, Reinterpretation and Influence from the Renaissance to the Present*, 24–54, Cambridge: Cambridge University Press.

Hoekstra, K. (2016), 'Hobbes's Thucydides', in A. P. Martinish and K. Hoekstra (eds), *The Oxford Handbook of Hobbes*, 547–74, Oxford: Oxford University Press.

Hoekstra, K. and M. Fisher (2017), 'Thucydides and the Politics of Necessity', in S. Forsdyke, E. Foster and R. Balot (eds), *The Oxford Handbook to Thucydides*, 373–90, Oxford: Oxford University Press.

Holladay, A. J. and J. C. F. Poole (1979), 'Thucydides and the Plague of Athens', *Classical Quarterly* 29, no. 2: 282–300.

Hornblower, S. (1991), *A Commentary on Thucydides*, Vol 1, Oxford: Oxford University Press.

Hornblower, S. (1992), 'The Religious Dimension to the Peloponnesian War, Or, What Thucydides Does Not Tell Us', *Harvard Studies in Classical Philology* 94: 169–97.

Hornblower, S. (2004), *Thucydides and Pindar: Historical Narrative and the World of Epinikian Poetry*, Oxford: Oxford University Press.

Hornblower, S. (2010), *Thucydidean Themes*, Oxford: Oxford University Press.
Horsley, G. H. R. (2008), 'Cornford Mythistoricus', *Antichthon*, 42: 121–41.
Hume, D. (1994), *Hume: Political Essays*, Cambridge: Cambridge University Press.
Hunter, V. J. (1973), *Thucydides: The Artful Reporter*, Toronto: Hakkert.
Hunter, V. J. (1986), 'Thucydides, Gorgias, and Mass Psychology', *Hermes* 114, no. 4: 412–29.
Huth, C. F. (1912), 'Review: The Greek Commonwealth: Politics and Economics in Fifth-Century Athens', *Journal of Political Economy* 20, no. 5: 516–20.
Hutton, M. (1910), 'Notes on Herodotus and Thucydides', *Transactions and Proceedings of the American Philological Association* 41: 11–17.
Hutton, M. (1911), 'The Mind of Herodotus', *Transactions and Proceedings of the American Philological Association* 42: 33–43.
Hutton, M. (1916), 'Thucydides and History', *Transactions of the Royal Society of Canada = Memoires de La Société Royale Du Canada* 10, no. 3: 225–48.
Iglesias-Zoido, J. C. (2011), *El Legado de Tucídides En La Cultura Occidental: Discursos E Historia*, Humanitas Supplementum, 10, Coimbra: Centro de Estudos Clássicos e Humanísticos da Universidade de Coimbra.
Innis, H. A. (1946), 'Obituaries: Charles Norris Cochrane, 1889–1945', *Canadian Journal of Economics and Political Science / Revue canadienne d'Economique et de Science politique* 12, no. 1, 95–7.
Ivascu, B. (2017), 'Toynbee's Study of History: An "Abortive" Idealist Philosophy of History?', *Collingwood and British Idealism Studies* 23, no. 2: 197–224.
J. S. (1913), 'From Religion to Philosophy: A Criticism of Mr. Cornford', *Studies: An Irish Quarterly Review* 2, no. 5: 835–45.
Jaeger, W. (1944), *Paideia: The Ideals of Greek Culture*, 3 vols, trans. Gilbert Highet, Oxford: Basil Blackwell.
Jaffe, S. N. (2015), 'The Straussian Thucydides', in C. Lee and N. Morley (eds), *A Handbook to the Reception of Thucydides*, 278–95, Chichester, UK: Wiley and Blackwell.
Jaffe, S. N. (2017a), *Thucydides on the Outbreak of War: Character and Contest*, Oxford: Oxford University Press.
Jaffe, S. N. (2017b), 'The Regime (Politeia) in Thucydides', in S. Forsdyke, E. Foster and R. Balot (eds), *The Oxford Handbook to Thucydides*, 391–408, Oxford: Oxford University Press.
Jebb, R. C. (1907), *Essays and Addresses*, Cambridge: Cambridge University Press.
Johnson, G. (2008), *University Politics: F.M. Cornford's Cambridge and His Advice to the Young Academic Politician*, Cambridge: Cambridge University Press.
Johnson, L. M. (2015), 'Thucydides the Realist?', in C. Lee and N. Morley (eds), *The Blackwell Handbook to the Reception of Thucydides*, 391–405, Chichester, UK: Wiley and Blackwell.
Joho, T. (2017), 'Thucydides, Epic, and Tragedy', in S. Forsdyke, E. Foster and R. Balot (eds), *The Oxford Handbook of Thucydides*, 587–604, Oxford: Oxford University Press.

Jordan, B. (1986), 'Religion in Thucydides', *Transactions and Proceedings of the American Philological Association*, 116: 119–47.
Kagan, D. (1969), *The Outbreak of the Peloponnesian War*, Ithaca, NY: Cornell University Press.
Kagan, D. (1974), *The Archidamian War*, Ithaca, NY: Cornell University Press.
Kagan, D. (1981), *The Peace of Nicias and the Sicilian Expedition*, Ithaca, NY: Cornell University Press.
Kagan, D. (1987), *The Fall of the Athenian Empire*, Ithaca, NY: Cornell University Press.
Kallet, L. (2006), 'Thucydides' Workshop of History and Utility Outside the Text', in A. Tsakmakis and A. Rengagkos (eds), *Brill's Companion to Thucydides*, 335–68, Leiden: Brill.
Kaplan, R. D. (2002), *Warrior Politics: Why Leadership Demands a Pagan Ethos*, New York: Vintage Books.
Keedus, L. (2016), 'Leo Strauss's Thucydides and the Meaning of Politics', in C. Thauer and C. Wendt (eds), *Thucydides and Political Order: Lessons of Governance and the History of the Peloponnesian War*, 75–93. New York: Palgrave Macmillan US.
Keene, E. (2015), 'The Reception of Thucydides in the History of International Relations', in *A Handbook to the Reception of Thucydides*, 355–72, Chichester, UK: Wiley and Blackwell.
Kellog Wood, D. (1990), 'F.M. Cornford', in W. W. Briggs and W. Calder III (eds), *Classical Scholarship: A Biographical Encyclopedia*, New York: Garland Publishing.
Kendle, J. (1975), *The Round Table Movement and Imperial Union*, Toronto: University of Toronto Press.
Kierstead, J. (2014), 'Grote's Athens: The Character of Democracy', in K. N. Demetriou (ed.), *Brill's Companion to George Grote and the Classical Tradition*, 161–210, Leiden: Brill.
Kirshner, J. (2018), 'Handle Him with Care: The Importance of Getting Thucydides Right', *Security Studies* 28, no. 1: 1–24.
Knutsen, T. L. (1997), *History of International Relations Theory*, Manchester: Manchester University Press.
Koditschek, T. (2011), *Liberalism, Imperialism, and the Historical Imagination: Nineteenth-Century Visions of a Great Britain*, Cambridge: Cambridge University Press.
Kopp, H. (2016), 'The "Rule of the Sea": Thucydidean Concept or Periclean Utopia?', in C. Thauer and C. Wendt (eds), *Thucydides and Political Order: Concepts of Order and the History of the Peloponnesian War*, 129–49, London: Palgrave Macmillan.
Kopp, H. (2017), *Das Meer als Versprechen: Bedeutung und Funktion von Seeherrschaft bei Thukydides*, Göttingen: Vandenhoeck & Ruprecht.
Krebs, P. M. (2004), *Gender, Race, and the Writing of Empire: Public Discourse and the Boer War*, Cambridge: Cambridge University Press.
Kumar, K. (2014), 'The Return of Civilization – and of Arnold Toynbee?', *Comparative Studies in Society and History* 56, no. 4: 815–43.

Lamb, W. (1914), *Clio Enthroned*, Cambridge: Cambridge University Press.
Lamb, W. (1926), 'Thucydides: A Study in Historical Reality [review]', *Classical Review* 40, no. 6: 199–200.
Lang, M. (2011), 'Globalization and Global History in Toynbee', *Journal of World History: Official Journal of the World History Association* 22, no. 4: 747–83.
Laqua, D. (2011), 'Translational Intellectual Cooperation, the League of Nations, and the Problem of Order', *Journal of Global History* 6, no. 2: 223–47.
Lebow, R. N. (2001), 'Thucydides the Constructivist', *American Political Science Review* 95, no. 3: 547–60.
Lebow, R. N. (2003), *The Tragic Vision of Politics: Ethics, Interests and Orders*, Cambridge: Cambridge University Press.
Lebow, R. N. (2012), 'International Relations and Thucydides', in K. Harloe and N. Morley (eds), *Thucydides and the Modern World: Reception, Reinterpretation and Influence from the Renaissance to the Present*, 197–211, Cambridge: Cambridge University Press.
Lebow, R. N. (2016), 'Thucydides and Order', in C. Thauer and C. Wendt (eds), *Thucydides and Political Order: Lessons of Governance and the History of the Peloponnesian War*, 21–54, London: Palgrave Macmillan.
Lebow, R. N. and D. Tomkins (2016), 'The Thucydides Claptrap', *Washington Monthly*, 28 June, https://washingtonmonthly.com/thucydides-claptrap.
Lebow, R. N. and B. Strauss, eds (1991), *Hegemonic Rivalry: From Thucydides To The Nuclear Age*, New York: Avalon Publishing.
Leddy, J. F. (1957), 'Toynbee and the History of Rome', *Phoenix* 11: 139–52.
Lee, C. (2016), 'The Power and Politics of Ontology', in C. Thauer and C. Wendt (eds), *Thucydides and Political Order: Lessons of Governance and the History of the Peloponnesian War*, 95–130, London: Palgrave Macmillan.
Levesque, P. Ch., trans. (1795), *L'Histoire De Thucydide, Fils D'Olorus*, 4 vols, Paris: Aubin.
Lianeri, A. (2015), 'On Historical Time and Method: Thucydides' Contemporary History in Nineteenth-Century Britain', in C. Lee and N. Morley (eds), *The Blackwell Handbook to the Reception of Thucydides*, 176–96, Chichester, UK: John Wiley & Sons Ltd.
Lingelbach, W. E. (1930), 'Commercial Policies as Causes of International Friction', *Annals of the American Academy of Political and Social Science* 150: 117–25.
Liotsakis, V. (2017), *Redeeming Thucydides' Book VIII: Narrative Artistry in the Account of the Ionian War*, Berlin: Walter de Gruyter.
Livingstone, R. W. (1921), 'Preface', in R. W. Livingstone (ed.), *The Legacy of Greece*, unnumbered preface, Oxford: Clarendon Press.
Londey, P. (2007), 'A Possession for Ever: Charles Bean, the Ancient Greeks, and Military Commemoration in Australia', *Australian Journal of Politics and History* 51, no. 3: 344–59.
Loraux, N. (1986), 'Thucydides et La Sedition Dans Les Mots', *Quaderni Di Storia Della Medicina E Della Scienza / Cattedra Di Storia Della Medicina Della Facolta Di Medicina E Chirurgia dell'Universita Degli Studi Di Roma 'La Sapienza'* 23: 95–134.

Low, P. (2007), *International Relations in Classical Greece: Morality and Power*, Cambridge: Cambridge University Press.

Lubenow, W. C. (2010), *Liberal Intellectuals and Public Culture in Modern Britain, 1815-1914: Making Words Flesh*, Woodbridge, UK: Boydell & Brewer.

Luginbill, R. D. (1999), *Thucydides on War and National Character*, Boulder, CO: Westview Press.

Mably, G. B. de (1769), *Phocion's Conversations: Or, the Relation between Morality and Politics. Originally Translated by Abbe Mably, From a Greek Manuscript of Nicocles; with Notes by William Macbean, A. M. and Master of a Boarding-School at Newmarket. Inscribed to the Friends of Morality and Just Politics*, London: Dodsley.

Machen, A. (1915), *The Angels of Mons: The Bowmen, and Other Legends of the War*, New York: Knickerbocker Press.

MacKay, J. and C. D. LaRoche (2017), 'The Conduct of History in International Relations: Rethinking Philosophy of History in IR Theory', *International Theory* 9, no. 2: 203-36.

MacKenzie, C. (1930), *Gallipoli Memories*, New York: Doubleday, Doran, and Company.

Macleod, C. W. (1974), 'Form and Meaning in the Melian Dialogue', *Historia: Zeitschrift Für Alte Geschichte* 23, no. 4: 385-400.

Macleod, C. W. (1983), 'Thucydides and Tragedy', in C. W. Macleod, *Collected Essays*, 140-58, Oxford: Clarendon Press.

Mahaffy, J. P. (1874), *Social Life in Greece from Homer to Menander*, London: Macmillan.

Mali, J. (2003), *Mythistory: The Making of a Modern Historiography*, Chicago: University of Chicago Press.

Mara, G. M. (2008), *The Civic Conversations of Thucydides and Plato: Classical Political Philosophy and the Limits of Democracy*, Albany, NY: State University of New York Press.

Marinatos, N. (1981), *Thucydides and Religion*, Meisenheim: Verlag Anton Hain.

Markwell, D. J. (1986), 'Sir Alfred Zimmern Revisited: Fifty Years On', *Kokusaigaku Revyu = Obirin Review of International Studies* 12, no. 4: 279-92.

Markwell, D. J. (2004), 'Zimmern, Sir Alfred Eckhard (1879-(1957), Internationalist', *Oxford Dictionary of National Biography*, https://www.oxforddnb.com/view/10.1093/ref:odnb/9780198614128.001.0001/odnb-9780198614128-e-37088.

Martindale, C. (1993), *Redeeming the Text: Latin Poetry and the Hermeneutics of Reception*, Cambridge: Cambridge University Press.

Martindale, C. (2013), 'Reception - a New Humanism? Receptivity, Pedagogy, the Transhistorical', *Classical Receptions Journal* 5, no. 2: 169-83.

Mazower, M. (2007), 'Alfred Zimmern and the Empire of Freedom', in M. Mazower (ed.), *No Enchanted Palace: The End of Empire and the Ideological Origins of the United States*, Princeton, NJ: Princeton University Press.

McDougall, W. A. (1986), '"Mais Ce N'est Pas L'histoire!": Some Thoughts on Toynbee, McNeill, and the Rest of Us', *Journal of Modern History* 58, no. 1: 19-42.

McIntire, C. T. and M. Perry (1989), 'Toynbee's Achievement', in C. T. McIntire and M. Perry (eds), *Toynbee: Reappraisals*, 3–31, Toronto: University of Toronto Press.

McManus, B. S. (2007), '"Macte nova virtute, puer!": Gilbert Murray as Mentor and Friend to J. A. K. Thomson', in C. Stray (ed.), *Gilbert Murray Reassessed: Hellenism, Theatre, and International Politics*, 167–80, Oxford: Oxford University Press.

McNeill, W. H. (1989a), *Arnold J. Toynbee: A Life*, Oxford: Oxford University Press.

McNeill, W. H. (1989b), 'Toynbee's Life and Thought: Some Unresolved Questions', in C. T. McIntire and M. Perry (eds), *Toynbee: Reappraisals*, 32–49, Toronto: University of Toronto Press.

Mehta, U. S. (1999), *Liberalism and Empire: A Study in Nineteenth-Century British Liberal Thought*, Chicago: University of Chicago Press.

Meier, M. (2005), '"Die Größte Erschütterung Für Die Griechen" – Krieg Und Naturkatastrophen Im Geschichtswerk Des Thukydides', *Klio* 87: 329–45.

Meiggs, R. (1972), *The Athenian Empire*, Oxford: Clarendon Press.

Meineke, S. (2006), 'Thucydidism', in H. Cancik, H. Schneider and C. Salazar (eds), *Brill's New Pauly: Classical Tradition*, Leiden: Brill.

Meister, K. (2013), *Thukydides als Vorbild der Historiker: von der Antike bis zur Gegenwart*, Paderborn: Ferdinand Schöningh.

Meister, K. (2015), 'Thucydides in Nineteenth-Century Germany', in C. Lee and N. Morley (eds), *The Blackwell Handbook to the Reception of Thucydides*, 197–217, Chichester, UK: Wiley and Blackwell.

Meuss, H. (1892), 'Thukydides Und Die Religiöse Aufklärung', *Classische Philologie* 38, 225–33.

Millet, P. (2007), 'Alfred Zimmern's The Greek Commonwealth Revisited', in C. Stray (ed.), *Oxford Classics: Teaching and Learning, 1800–2000*, 168–207, London: Duckworth.

Milner, H. (1991), 'The Assumption of Anarchy in International Relations Theory: A Critique', *Review of International Studies* 17, no. 1: 67–85.

Mitford, W. (2010), *The History of Greece*, 5 vols, Cambridge: Cambridge University Press.

Mitrany, D. (1925), 'Thucydides and Aggression', *Manchester Guardian*, 14 March.

Momigliano, A. (1966), 'Time in Ancient Historiography', *History and Theory*, 6: 1–23.

Monoson, S. and M. Loriaux (1998), 'The Illusion of Power and the Disruption of Moral Norms: Thucydides' Critique of Periclean Policy', *American Political Science Review* 92, no. 2: 285–97.

Montagu, A. (1956), *Toynbee and History: Critical Essays and Reviews*, Boston: Porter Sargent.

Monten, J. (2006), 'Thucydides and Modern Realism', *International Studies Quarterly* 50, no. 1: 3–25.

Montgomery, H. (1942), 'Thucydides and Geopolitics', *Classical Journal* 38, no. 2: 93–6.

Morefield, J. (2005), *Covenants Without Swords: Idealist Liberalism and the Spirit of Empire*, Princeton, NJ: Princeton University Press.

Morefield, J. (2007), '"An Education to Greece": The Round Table, Imperial Theory and the Uses of History', *History of Political Thought* 28, no. 2: 328–61.

Morefield, J. (2014), *Empires Without Imperialism: Anglo-American Decline and the Politics of Deflection*, Oxford: Oxford University Press.

Morgenthau, H. (1948), *Politics Among Nations: The Struggle for Power and Peace*, New York: Alfred A. Knopf.

Morley, F. (1937), 'How Can the United States Aid in Maintaining Peace?', *Annals of the American Academy of Political and Social Science* 192: 113–22.

Morley, N. (2004), 'Nietzsche and Antiquity: His Reaction and Response to the Classical Tradition', in P. Bishop (ed.), *'Unhistorical Greeks': Myth, History, and the Uses of Antiquity*, 27–39, Woodbridge, UK: Camden House.

Morley, N. (2012), 'Thucydides, History and Historicism in Wilhelm Roscher', in K. Harloe and N. Morley (eds), *Thucydides and the Modern World: Reception, Reinterpretation and Influence from the Renaissance to the Present*, 115–39, Cambridge: Cambridge University Press.

Morley, N. (2013), *Thucydides and the Idea of History*, London: I.B. Tauris.

Morley, N. (2015), 'The Idea of Thucydides in the Western Tradition', in C. Lee and N. Morley (eds), *A Handbook to the Reception of Thucydides*, 589–604, Chichester, UK: John Wiley & Sons Ltd.

Morley, N. (2016a), 'Contextualism and Universalism in Thucydidean Thought', in C. Thauer and C. Wendt (eds), *Thucydides and Political Order: Concepts of Order and the History of the Peloponnesian War*, 23–40, London: Palgrave Macmillan.

Morley, N. (2016b), 'The Anti-Thucydides: Herodotus and the Development of Modern Historiography', in J. Priestley and V. Zali (eds), *Brill's Companion to the Reception of Herodotus in Antiquity and Beyond*, 143–68, Leiden: Brill.

Morley, N. (2017), 'Thucydides and the Historiography of Trauma', *KTÈMA Civilisations de l'Orient, de La Grèce et de Rome Antiques* 42: 195–206.

Morley, N. (2018a), 'Thucydides: The Origins of Realism?', in M. Hollingsworth and R. Schuett (eds), *The Edinburgh Companion to Political Realism*, Edinburgh: Edinburgh University Press.

Morley, N. (2018b), 'Legitimizing War and Defending Peace: Thucydides in the First World War and After', *Classical Receptions Journal* 10, no. 4: 415–34.

Muhlack, U. (2011), 'Herodotus and Thucydides in the View of Nineteenth-Century German Historians', in A. Lianeri (ed.), *The Western Time of Ancient History: Historiographical Encounters with the Greek and Roman Pasts*, 179–209, Cambridge: Cambridge University Press.

Murphy, J. M. (1912), 'Athenian Imperialism', *Studies: An Irish Quarterly Review* 1, no. 1: 97–113.

Murray, G. (1903), *A History of Greek Literature*, London: D. Appleton and Company.

Murray, G. (1907), 'History and Tragedy', *Albany Review* 1, no. 4: 467–70.

Murray, G. (1913), *Euripides and His Age*, London: H. Holt.

Murray, G. (1919), *Aristophanes and the War Party: A Study in the Contemporary Criticism of the Peloponnesian War*, London: Allen and Unwin.

Murray, G. (1920), *Our Great War and the Great War of the Ancient Greeks*, New York: Thomas Seltzer.

Murray, G. (1921), 'The Value of Greece to the Future of the World', in R. W. Livingstone (ed.), *The Legacy of Greece*, 1–24, Oxford: Clarendon Press.

Murray, G. (2012), *Five Stages of Greek Religion*, Mineola and New York: Dover Publications.

Murray, G. (2015a), 'Why Teach Thucydides Today? (And If We're At It, How?)', in C. Lee and N. Morley (eds), *A Handbook to the Reception of Thucydides*, 560–67, Chichester, UK: Wiley and Blackwell.

Murray, G. (2015b), 'Reading Thucydides with Leo Strauss', in T. W. Burns (ed.), *Brill's Companion to Leo Strauss' Writings on Classical Political Thought*, 50–75, Leiden: Brill.

Murray, G. (2017), 'Thucydides on Nature and Human Conduct', in S. Forsdyke, E. Foster and R. Balot (eds), *The Oxford Handbook to Thucydides*, Oxford: Oxford University Press.

Neill, M. (1932), *Consolidated Index to the Survey of International Affairs and Supplementary Volumes*, London: Oxford University Press.

Nietzsche, F. (1997), *Twilight of the Idols*, trans. Richard Polt, Indianapolis: Hackett Publishing.

Ober, J. (1998), *Political Dissent in Democratic Athens: Intellectual Critics of Popular Rule*, Princeton, NJ: Princeton University Press.

Ober, J. (2001), 'Thucydides Theoretikos/Thucydides Histor: Realist Theory and the Challenge of History', in D. R. McCann and B. Strauss (eds), *Democracy and War: A Comparative Study of the Korean War and the Peloponnesian War*, 273–306, Armonk, NY: M.E. Sharp.

Ober, J. (2006), 'Thucydides and the Invention of Political Science', in A. Rengagkos and A. Tsakmakis (eds), *Brill's Companion to Thucydides*, 131–59, Leiden: Brill.

Ober, J. and T. J. Perry (2014), 'Thucydides as a Prospect Theorist, *Polis: The Journal for Ancient Greek Political Thought* 31, no. 2: 206–32.

Oost, S. I. (1975), 'Thucydides and the Irrational: Sundry Passages', *Classical Philology* 70, no. 3: 186–96.

Organski, A. F. K. (1958), *World Politics*, New York: Knopf.

Orwin, C. (1994), *The Humanity of Thucydides*, Princeton, NJ: Princeton University Press.

Orwin, C. (2015a), 'Why Teach Thucydides Today? (And If We're At It, How?)', in C. Lee and N. Morley (eds), *A Handbook to the Reception of Thucydides*, 560–7, Chichester, UK: Wiley and Blackwell.

Orwin, C. (2015b), 'Reading Thucydides with Leo Strauss', in T. W. Burns (ed.), *Brill's Companion to Leo Strauss' Writings on Classical Political Thought*, 50–75, Leiden: Brill.

Orwin, C. (2017), 'Thucydides on Nature and Human Conduct', in S. Forsdyke, E. Foster and R. Balot (eds), *The Oxford Handbook to Thucydides*, Oxford: Oxford University Press.

Osiander, A. (1998), 'Rereading Early Twentieth-Century IR Theory: Idealism Revisited', *International Studies Quarterly: A Publication of the International Studies Association* 42, no. 3: 409–32.

Ostwald, M. (1988), *ANAΓKH in Thucydides*, Atlanta, GA: Scholars Press.

Page, D. L. (1953), 'Thucydides' Description of the Great Plague at Athens', *Classical Quarterly* 3, no. 3–4: 97–119.

Palmer, M. (1992), *Love of Glory and the Common Good: Aspects of the Political Thought of Thucydides*, London: Rowman & Littlefield Publishers.

Palmer, M. (2017), 'Stasis in the War Narrative', in S. Forsdyke, E. Foster and R. Balot (eds), *The Oxford Handbook of Thucydides*, 409–26, Oxford: Oxford University Press.

Parry, A. (1981), *Logos and Ergon in Thucydides*, New York: Arno Press.

Payen, P. (2015), 'The Reception of Thucydides in Eighteenth- and Nineteenth-Century France', in C. Lee and N. Morley (eds), *The Blackwell Handbook to the Reception of Thucydides*, 158–75, Chichester, UK: John Wiley & Sons Ltd.

Peacock, S. J. (1988), *Jane Ellen Harrison*, New Haven, CT: Yale University Press.

Perrin, B. (1908), 'Review: Thucydides Mythistoricus', *American Historical Review* 13, no. 2: 314–16.

Perry, M. (1989), 'Toynbee and the Meaning of Athens and Jerusalem', in C. T. Mcintire and M. Perry, *Toynbee: Reappraisals*, Toronto: University of Toronto Press.

Petersen, R. and E. Liaras (2006), 'Countering Fear in War: The Strategic Use of Emotion', *Journal of Military Ethics* 5, no. 4: 317–33.

Pires, F. M. (2006), 'Thucydidean Modernities: History between Science and Art', in A. Rengagkos and A. Tsakmakis (eds), *Brill's Companion to Thucydides*, 811–37, Leiden: Brill.

Pires, F. M. (2007), *Modernidades Tucidideanas: Ktema Es Aei*, São Paulo: Editora da Universidade de São Paulo.

Pitt, W. (1840), *Correspondence of William Pitt, Earl of Chatham*, vol. 4, London: Murray.

Pohlenz, M. (1919, 1920), *Thukydidesstudien I. II.*, Göttingen: Göttingische Nachrichten.

Polansky, D. (2015), 'Nietzsche on Thucydidean Realism', *Review of Politics* 77, no. 3: 425–48.

Postgate, J. P. (1907), 'Thucydides the Mythistorian', *Classical Quarterly* 1, no. 4: 308–18.

Potter, E. (2012), 'The Education Offered by Athens: Thucydides and the Stirrings of Democracy in Britain', in K. Harloe and N. Morley (eds), *Thucydides and the Modern World: Reception, Reinterpretation and Influence from the Renaissance to the Present*, 93–114. Cambridge: Cambridge University Press.

Pouncey, P. R. (1980), *The Necessities of War: A Study of Thucydides' Pessimism*, New York: Columbia University Press.

Powell, J. E. (1933), 'Studies on the Greek Reflexive – Herodotus', *Classical Quarterly* 27, no. 3–4: 208–21.

Powell, J. E. (1936a), 'The Bâle and Leyden Scholia to Thucydides', *Classical Quarterly* 30, no. 2: 80–93.

Powell, J. E. (1936b), 'The Aldine Scholia to Thucydides', *Classical Quarterly* 30, no. 3–4: 146–50.

Powell, J. E. (1938a), 'The Archetype of Thucydides', *Classical Quarterly* 32, no. 2: 75–9.

Powell, J. E. (1938b), 'The Cretan Manuscripts of Thucydides', *Classical Quarterly* 32, no. 2: 103–8.

Price, J. J. (2001), *Thucydides and Internal War*, Cambridge: Cambridge University Press.

Pritchett, W. K., trans. (1975), *On Thucydides*, Berkeley: University of California Press.

Rachman, G. (2018), 'Destined for War? China, America and the Thucydides Trap', *Financial Times*, 19 December, https://www.ft.com/content/0e4ddcf4-fc78-11e8-aebf-99e208d3e521.

Rahe, P. A. (1995), 'Thucydides' Critique of Realpolitik', *Security Studies* 5, no. 2: 105–41.

Rathbun, B. (2018), 'The Rarity of Realpolitik: What Bismarck's Rationality Reveals about International Politics', *International Security* 43, no. 1: 7–55.

Rawlings, H. R. (2015), 'Why We Need to Read Thucydides – Even When "We" Are Only a Few', in C. Lee and N. Morley (eds), *The Blackwell Handbook to the Reception of Thucydides*, 551–9, Chichester, UK: Wiley and Blackwell.

Rich, P. (1995), 'Alfred Zimmern's Cautious Idealism: The League of Nations, International Education, and the Commonwealth', in D. Long and P. Wilson (eds), *Thinkers of the Twenty Years' Crisis: Inter-War Idealism Reassessed*, 79–99. Oxford: Clarendon Press.

Rich, P. (2002), 'Reinventing Peace: David Davies, Alfred Zimmern and Liberal Internationalism in Interwar Britain', *International Relations* 16, no. 1: 117–33.

Roberts, J. T. (1997), *Athens on Trial: The Antidemocratic Tradition in Western Thought*, Princeton, NJ: Princeton University Press.

Robinson, A. (2002), *The Life and Work of Jane Ellen Harrison*, Oxford: Oxford University Press.

Rodgers, W. L. (1942), 'Guarantees of Peace', *World Affairs Institute* 105, no. 1: 37–9.

Romilly, J. de (1956), *Histoire et Raison Chez Thucydide*, Paris: Les Belles lettres.

Romilly, J. de (1963), *Thucydides and Athenian Imperialism*, trans. Philip Thody, Oxford: Blackwell.

Romilly, J. de (1977), *The Rise and Fall of States according to Greek Authors*, Ann Arbor: University of Michigan Press.

Romilly, J. de (2012), *The Mind of Thucydides*, trans. Elizabeth Trapnell Rawlings, Ithaca, NY: Cornell University Press.

Rood, T. (1998), *Thucydides : Narrative and Explanation*, Oxford: Oxford University Press,

Rood, T. (2006), 'Objectivity and Authority: Thucydides' Historical Method', in A. Tsakmakis and A. Rengakos (eds), *Brill's Companion to Thucydides*, 225–50, Leiden: Brill.

Ruback, T. (2015), 'Thucydides Our Father, Thucydides Our Shibboleth: The History of the Peloponnesian War as a Marker of Contemporary International Relations Theory', in C. Lee and N. Morley (eds), *A Handbook to the Reception of Thucydides*, 406-24, Chichester, UK: John Wiley & Sons Ltd.

Ruback, T. (2016), 'Ever Since The Days of Thucydides: The Quest for Textual Origins of IR Theory', in S. G. Nelson and S. Nevzat (eds), *Modern Theory, Modern Power, World Politics*, Critical Investigations, 17-34, Farnham, UK: Ashgate.

Rule, J. C., and B. Stevens Crosby (1965), 'Bibliography of Works on Arnold J. Toynbee, 1946-1960', *History and Theory* 4, no. 2: 212-33.

Rusten, J. (2015), 'Kinesis in the Preface to Thucydides', in C. Clark, E. Foster and J. Hallett (eds), *Kinesis: The Ancient Depiction of Gesture, Motion, and Emotion*, 27-40, Ann Arbor: University of Michigan Press.

Sachs, J. (2016), 'The Ends of Empire: Romantic interpretations of Greek Decline', *Classical Receptions Journal* 8, no. 1: 32-53.

Sahlins, M. (2004), *Apologies to Thucydides: Understanding History as Culture and Vice Versa*, Chicago: University of Chicago Press.

Salomon, A. (1942), 'On Humanistic Writings', *Social Research* 9, no. 3: 405-10.

Sawyer, E. (2013), 'The Reception of Thucydides in Contemporary America', Unpublished PhD thesis, Oxford University.

Sawyer, E. (2015), 'Thucydides in Modern Political Rhetoric', in C. Lee and N. Morley (eds), *The Blackwell Handbook to the Reception of Thucydides*, 529-48, Chichester, UK: Wiley and Blackwell.

Saxonhouse, A. W. (1995), *Fear of Diversity: The Birth of Political Science in Ancient Greek Thought*, Chicago: University of Chicago Press.

Saxonhouse, A. W. (2017), 'Kinēsis, Navies, and the Power Trap in Thucydides', in S. Forsdyke, E. Foster and R. Balot (eds), *The Oxford Handbook to Thucydides*, 339-54, Oxford: Oxford University Press.

Scanlon, T. F. (2002), '"The Clear Truth" in Thucydides 1.22.4', *Historia: Zeitschrift Für Alte Geschichte* 51, no. 2: 131-48.

Schadewaldt, W. (1929), *Die Geschichtsschreibung Des Thukydides*, Berlin: Weidmannsche Buchhandlung.

Schelske, O. (2015), 'Thucydides as an Educational Text', in C. Lee and N. Morley (eds), *The Blackwell Handbook to the Reception of Thucydides*, 75-90, Chichester, UK: Wiley and Blackwell.

Schoefield, C. (2013), *Enoch Powell and the Making of Postcolonial Britain*, Cambridge: Cambridge University Press.

Schwartz, E. (1919), *Das Geschichtswerk Des Thukydides*, Bonn: F. Cohen.

Scott J. (2011), 'What Does Nietzsche Owe Thucydides?', *Journal of Nietzsche Studies* 42, no. 1: 32-50.

Scott, J. B. (1936), 'Justice – the Bond of Commonwealths', *World Affairs* 99, no. 1: 21-4.

Sears, R. (1977), 'Thucydides and the Scientific Approach to International Politics', *Australian Journal of Politics and History* 23, no. 1: 28-40.

Shanske, D. (2006), *Thucydides and the Philosophical Origins of History*, Cambridge: Cambridge University Press.

Shanske, D. (2013), 'Thucydides and Law: A Response to Leiter', *Legal Theory* 19, no. 3: 282–306.

Shimko, K. L. (1992), 'Realism, Neorealism, and American Liberalism', *Review of Politics* 54, no. 2: 281–301.

Shorey, P. (1893), 'On the Implicit Ethics and Psychology of Thucydides', *Transactions and Proceedings of the American Philological Association* 24: 66–88.

Shorey, P. (1907), 'A Dramatic History', *The Dial*: 43.

Shorey, P. (1930), 'Thucydides and the Science of History [review]', *Classical Philology* 25, no. 3: 290–2.

Sinclair, T. A. (2010), *A History of Greek Political Thought*, London: Routledge.

Sluga, G. (2006), *Nation, Psychology, and International Politics, 1870–1919*, London: Palgrave Macmillan.

Smail, R. (2004), *Verrall, Arthur Woollgar (1851–1912), Classical Scholar*, Oxford: Oxford University Press.

Smith, C. F. (1903), 'Character-Drawing in Thucydides', *American Journal of Philology* 24, no. 4: 369–87.

Spengler, O. (1991), *The Decline of the West*, ed. H. Werner, H. S. Hughes, C. F. Atkinson and A. Helps, New York: Oxford University Press.

Stahl, H. (2003), *Thucydides: Man's Place in History*, Swansea: Classical Press of Wales.

Stanyan, T. (1751), *The Grecian History: From the Original of Greece, to the End of the Peloponnesian War. Containing the Space of about 1684 Years*, 2 vols, London: Tonson.

Stapleton, J. (2001), *Political Intellectuals and Public Identities in Britain Since 1850*, Manchester: Manchester University Press.

Stapleton, J. (2007), 'The Classicist as Liberal Intellectual: Gilbert Murray and Alfred Eckhard Zimmern', in C. Stray (ed.), *Gilbert Murray Reassessed: Hellenism, Theatre, and International Politics*, 261–92, Oxford: Oxford University Press.

Ste Croix, G. E. M. de (1972), *The Origins of the Peloponnesian War*, Ithaca, NY: Cornell University Press.

Stewart, J. (1959), *Jane Ellen Harrison: A Portrait from Letters*, London: Merlin Press.

Stradis, A. (2015), 'Thucydides in the Staff College', in C. Lee and N. Morley (eds), *The Blackwell Handbook to the Reception of Thucydides*, 426–46, Chichester, UK: Wiley and Blackwell.

Strauss, L. (1951), 'Man in His Pride: A Study in the Political Philosophy of Thucydides and Plato by David Grene [review]', *Social Research* 18, no. 3: 394–7.

Strauss, L. (1978), *The City and Man*, Chicago: University of Chicago Press.

Stray, C. (1997), '"Thucydides or Grote?" Classical Disputes and Disputed Classics in Nineteenth-Century Cambridge', *Transactions and Proceedings of the American Philological Association* 127: 363–71.

Stray, C. (2013), *Oxford Classics: Teaching and Learning 1800–2000*, London: Bloomsbury.

Stray, C. (2018), 'From odium to bellum: classical scholars at war in Europe and America, 1800–1924', *Classical Receptions Journal* 10, no. 4: 356–75.
Stromberg, R. N. (1972), *Arnold J. Toynbee: Historian for an Age in Crisis*, Carbondale: Southern Illinois University Press.
Stromberg, R. N. (1989), 'A Study of History and a World at War: Toynbee's Two Great Enterprises', in C. T. McIntire and M. Perry (eds), *Toynbee: Reappraisals*, 141–59. Toronto: University of Toronto Press.
Süßmann, J. (2012), 'Historicising the Classics: How Nineteenth-Century German Historiography Changed the Perspective on Historical Tradition', in K. Harloe and N. Morley (eds), *Thucydides and the Modern World: Reception, Reinterpretation and Influence from the Renaissance to the Present*, 77–92, Cambridge: Cambridge University Press.
Taylor, A. J. P. (1956), 'Much Learning', in A. Montagu, *Toynbee and History: Critical Essays and Reviews*, 115–17, Boston: Porter Sargent.
Taylor, M. (2010), *Thucydides, Pericles, and the Idea of Athens in the Peloponnesian War*, Cambridge: Cambridge University Press.
Thauer, C. (2016), 'It's Time for History! Thucydides in International Relations: Toward a Post-"Westphalian" Reading of a Pre-"Westphalian" Author', in C. Thauer and C. Wendt (eds), *Thucydides and Political Order: Concepts of Order and the History of the Peloponnesian War*, 41–58, London: Palgrave Macmillan.
Thauer, C. and C. Wendt. (2016), 'Thucydides and Political Order', in C. Thauer and C. Wendt (eds), *Thucydides and Political Order: Concepts of Order and the History of the Peloponnesian War*, 3–20. London: Palgrave Macmillan.
Thibaudet, A. (1922), *La Campagne Avec Thucydide*, Paris: Éditions de la Nouvelle revue française.
Thomas, R. (2006), 'Thucydides' Intellectual Milieu and the Plague', in A. Tsakmakis and A. Rengagkos (eds), *Brill's Companion to Thucydides*, 87–108, Leiden: Brill.
Thomas, R. (2017), 'Thucydides and His Intellectual Milieu', in R. Balot, S. Forsdyke and E. Foster (eds), *The Oxford Handbook of Thucydides*, 567–86, Oxford: Oxford University Press.
Thompson, K. (1955), 'Toynbee's Approach to History Reviewed', *Ethics* 63, no. 4: 287–303.
Thompson, K. (1956), 'Toynbee and the Theory of International Politics', *Political Science Quarterly* 71, no. 3: 365–86.
Thomson, J. A. K. (1913), *The Greek Tradition: Essays in the Reconstruction of Ancient Thought*, London: Allen and Unwin.
Thorpe, W. A. (1926), 'Thucydides and the Discipline of Detachment', *New Criterion* 4 (October): 630–44.
Toye, J. and R. Toye (2010), 'One World, Two Cultures? Alfred Zimmern, Julian Huxley and the Ideological Origins of UNESCO', *History* 95.
Toynbee, A. J. (1921a), *The Tragedy of Greece: A Lecture Delivered for the Professor of Greek to Candidates for Honours in Literae Humaniores at Oxford in May 1920*, Oxford: Clarendon Press.

Toynbee, A. J. (1921b), 'History', in R. W. Livingstone (ed.), *The Legacy of Greece*, 289–320, Oxford: Clarendon Press.

Toynbee, A. J. (1927), *A Survey of International Affairs 1920–1923*, London: Oxford University Press.

Toynbee, A. J. (1948a), *A Study of History*, Vol. I, London: Oxford University Press.

Toynbee, A. J. (1948b), *A Study of History*, Vol. II, London: Oxford University Press.

Toynbee, A. J. (1948c), *A Study of History*, Vol. III, London: Oxford University Press.

Toynbee, A. J. (1948d), *A Study of History*, Vol. IV, London: Oxford University Press.

Toynbee, A. J. (1948e), *A Study of History*, Vol. V, London: Oxford University Press.

Toynbee, A. J. (1948f), *A Study of History*, Vol. VI, London: Oxford University Press.

Toynbee, A. J. (1948g.), *Civilization on Trial*, London: Oxford University Press.

Toynbee, A. J. (1950), *Greek Civilisation and Character: The Self Revelation of Ancient Greek Society*, Boston: Beacon Press.

Toynbee, A. J. (1954a), *A Study of History*, Vol. VII, London: Oxford University Press.

Toynbee, A. J. (1954b), *A Study of History*, Vol. VIII, London: Oxford University Press.

Toynbee, A. J. (1954c), *A Study of History*, Vol. IX, London: Oxford University Press.

Toynbee, A. J. (1954d), *A Study of History*, Vol. X, London: Oxford University Press.

Toynbee, A. J. (1954e), *A Study of History*, Vol. XI, London: Oxford University Press.

Toynbee, A. J. (1954f), *A Study of History*, Vol. XII, London: Oxford University Press.

Toynbee, A. J. (1959a), *Greek Historical Thought*, New York: Mentor.

Toynbee, A. J. (1959b), *Hellenism: The History of a Civilization*, Oxford: Oxford University Press.

Trevor-Roper, H. (1956), 'Testing the Toynbee System', in A. Montagu (ed.), *Toynbee and History: Critical Essays and Reviews*, 122–4, Boston: Porter Sargent.

Tritle, L. (2006), 'Thucydides and Power Politics', in A. Tsakmakis and A. Rengagkos (eds), *Brill's Companion to Thucydides*, 469–91, Leiden: Brill.

Ulrici, H. (1833), *Charakteristik Der Antiken Historiographie*, Berlin: Reimer.

Vandiver, E. (2010), *Stand in the Trench, Achilles: Classical Receptions in British Poetry of the Great War*, Oxford: Oxford University Press.

Vasunia, P. (2013), *The Classics and Colonial India*, Oxford: Oxford University Press.

Verrall, A. W. (1913), *Euripides the Rationalist: A Study in the History of Art and Religion*, Cambridge: Cambridge University Press.

Vidal-Naquet, P. (1986), *The Black Hunter: Forms of Thought and Forms of Society in the Greek World*, trans. A. Szegedy-Maszak, Baltimore, MD: Johns Hopkins University Press.

Visvardi, E. (2015), *Emotion in Action: Thucydides and the Tragic Chorus*, Leiden: Brill.

Volney, C. F. (1800), *Lectures on History, Delivered in the Normal School of Paris*, London: Oriental Press.

Wallas, G. (1908), *Human Nature in Politics*, London: Archibald Constant.

Waltz, K. N. (2010), *Theory of International Politics*, Long Grove, IL: Waveland Press.

Waltz, K. N. (2018), *Man, the State, and War: A Theoretical Analysis*, ed. S. M. Walt, New York: Columbia University Press.

Weinstock, H. (1934), *Polis, Der Greichische Beitrag Zu Einer Deutschen Bildung Heute, an Thukydides Erläut*, Berlin: Runde.

Welch, D. (2003), 'Why International Relations Theorists Should Stop Reading Thucydides', *Kokusaigaku Revyu = Obirin Review of International Studies* 29: 301–19.

Wendt, C. (2016), 'Thucydides as a "Statesmen's Manual"?', in C. Thauer and C. Wendt (eds), *Thucydides and Political Order: Lessons of Governance and the History of the Peloponnesian War*, 151–67. London: Palgrave Macmillan.

Wendt, C. (2017), 'Spree-Athen nach dem Untergang. Eduard Meyer zur Parallelität von Geschichte', *KTÈMA Civilisations de l'Orient, de la Grèce et de Rome antiques* 42: 151–66.

Wertheim, S. (2012), 'The League of Nations: A Retreat from International Law?', *Journal of Global History* 7, no. 2: 210–32.

Whibley, L. (1889), *Political Parties in Athens During the Peloponnesian War*, Cambridge: Cambridge University Press.

White, J. B. (2012), *When Words Lose Their Meaning: Constitutions and Reconstitutions of Language, Character, and Community*, Chicago: University of Chicago Press.

Williams, A. J., A. Hadfield and J. S. Rofe (2012), *International History and International Relations*, London: Routledge.

Williams, M. (1998), *Ethics in Thucydides: The Ancient Simplicity*, Lanham, MD: University Press of America.

Williams, O. (1919), 'Some treasured books of an English soldier', originally published in the *New Statesman*, reprinted in *The Living Age* (May): 468–71.

Wills, D. (2009), *The Mirror of Antiquity: 20th Century British Travellers in Greece*, Newcastle upon Tyne: Cambridge Scholars Publishing.

Wilson, G. G. (1941), 'Grotius: Law of War and Peace', *American Journal of International Law* 35, no. 2: 205–26.

Winetrout, K. (1975), *Arnold Toynbee: The Ecumenical Vision*, Boston: Twayne.

Wohl, V. (2017), 'Thucydides on the Political Passions', in S. Forsdyke, E. Foster and R. Balot (eds), *The Oxford Handbook to Thucydides*, 443–58, Oxford: Oxford University Press.

Wood, H. G. (2015), *Terrot Reaveley Glover*, Cambridge: Cambridge University Press.

Workman, T. (2015), 'Thucydides, Science, and Late Modern Philosophy', in Lee, C. and N. Morley (eds), *A Handbook to the Reception of Thucydides*, 512–28, Chichester, UK: Blackwell.

Zimmern, A. E. (1911), *The Greek Commonwealth*, Oxford: Clarendon Press.

Zimmern, A. E. (1921), 'Political Thought', in R. W. Livingstone (ed.), *The Legacy of Greece*, 321–52. Oxford: Clarendon Press.

Zimmern, A. E. (1922), *Europe in Convalescence*, London: Mills and Boon.

Zimmern, A. E. (1928), *Solon and Croesus and Other Greek Essays*, Oxford: Oxford University Press.

Zimmern, A. E. (1929), *The Prospects of Democracy, and Other Essays*, London: Chatto & Windus.

Zimmern, A. E. (1938), 'The Decline of International Standards', *International Affairs* 17, no. 1: 3–31.

Zumbrunnen, J. (2002), '"Courage in the Face of Reality": Nietzsche's Admiration for Thucydides', *Polity* 35, no. 2: 237–63.

Zumbrunnen, J. (2010), *Silence and Democracy: Athenian Politics in Thucydides' History*, University Park: Pennsylvania State University Press.

Zumbrunnen, J. (2015), 'Realism, Constructivism, and Democracy in the History', in C. Lee and N. Morley (eds), *The Blackwell Handbook to the Reception of Thucydides*, 296–312, Chichester, UK: Wiley and Blackwell.

Index

Abbott, George Frederick 12, 18, 81–6, 91, 173
  American scholars 160
  empire 140
  fear 103–6
  Great War, the 85–6, 91–2, 98
  Greece and the Allies 100
  historical realism of Thucydides 92–7
  Holy War In Tripoli, The 97
  human nature 97–100, 105
  influence 170
  Melian dialogue 146–7
  political realism of Thucydides 97–100, 141
  self-interest in Thucydides 101–3
  Thucydides: A Study in Historical Reality 81, 91, 107–8, 133
  Turkey, Greece and the Great Powers: A Study in Friendship and Hate 100
Adcock, F. E. 148
advantage (*ophelimos*, ὠφέλιμος) 150
Aegina 150
Aeschylean drama 26
Aeschylus 26, 27, 38, 39, 51, 52
aitia (αἰτία) 37
Alcibiades 36, 37, 38–9, 69
Allison, Graham
  Destined for War? Can America and China Escape Thucydides's Trap 1–2
  Thucydides trap, the 1–4, 68, 79, 104, 112, 139, 172–3
America 2, 3, 14–15, 172–3
American scholarship 159–62, 164–5, 167–70
Amphictyonic Council, the 106
anangke (necessity, ἀνάγκη) 168, 169
Anarchical Society, The (Bull, Hedley) 195 n. 1
ancient Greece 25, 26, 28
  foreign relations 67
  history 117–22

literature 66
political scale 67
political thought 63–9
politics 69
psychology 69
realism 69
science 66
tragedy 51–2
writing 51
ancient world
  parallels with modern world 160, 161–2, 165–6
apprehension (*deos*, δέος) 103–6, 150
Archidamus, king of Sparta 36
Arieti, J. A. 50
Aristides 51–2
Aristophanes and the War Party: A Study in the Contemporary Criticism of the Peloponnesian War (Murray, Gilbert) 87, 181 n. 7
Aristotle 66, 69
  Poetics 115
Arnold, Edward 23
Arnold, Thomas 100, 132
Aron, Raymond 110
asebeia (impiety, ἀσέβεια) 147
ate (blindness, ἄτη) 26, 38, 71
Athenian Empire and the British, The (Callander, Thomas) 166–7
Athens 34–40, 44–5, 69, 132, 149–50,
  future plans 184 n. 7
  imperialism 57, 60–2, 101, 146–8, 152, 156
  Lord, Louis 162
  Murray, Gilbert 181 n. 4
  political psychology 74
  war party/spirit 58–9, 60
  Zimmern, Alfred Eckhard 56–7, 58–9, 181 n. 4
Atticism 6
Auden, W. H. 3

Bailey, S. H. 54
Balot, R. K. 50
Bannon, Steve 1
Barker, Ernst 113–14
Beer, George Louis 76
Bew, J. 141, 142
blindness (*ate*, ἄτη) 26, 38, 71
Boak, A. E. K. 161
Boer Wars 36, 44–5, 57–8
Britain 9–10, 12–13, 132–3
   Boer Wars 36, 44–5, 57–8
   Cornford, Francis Macdonald 26, 44
   education 13–14
   imperialism 13, 36, 45, 57–8, 60, 152
   political psychology 70
   political scale 67
British scholarship 164, 165–7, 170–3
Bull, Hedley 195 n. 1
   Anarchical Society, The 195 n. 1
Bury, J. B. 48, 146, 164
   History of Greece 34
Busolt, G.
   Griechische Geschichte 34
Butler, H. M. 87
Butler, G. K. M. 87

Callander, Thomas 166
   Athenian Empire and the British, The 166–7
Cambridge Ancient History 119
Cambridge ritualists 30
Campagne avec Thucydides, La Thibaudet, Albert 133
Campbell, George 129
Campbell-Bannerman, Henry (Prime Minister) 36
Carr, E. H. 99, 195 n. 1
   Twenty Years' Crisis, The 54, 111
Chambers, M. 34, 47
Chance, Alek 142
Charakteristik de antiken Historiographie (Ulrici, Hermann) 39
Chatham, Lord (William Pitt) 8
Chicago, University of 167–8
China 2, 3
Churchill, Winston 87
Cicero 6
City and Man, The (Strauss, Leo) 168, 169

civilizations 110–12
   cyclical history of 113–22, 126–7
   equivalences in 115, 120–2
   Graeco-Roman 119–20
   Hellenic 114
   personification 123–5
   stages of 117–19
   states of 114–15, 117–18
   Toynbee, Arnold 113–22
class war (*stasis*) 121–2
Classen 92, 100
Classical Association, the 131
classical history 117–22
classical realists 16, 105, 137
Classics, the 13–14, 18, 29, 64, 171, 172
   Cornford, Francis Macdonald 43, 44
   influence 67
   Murray, Gilbert 180 n. 4
Cleon 36, 37, 38, 51, 148–9
   imperialism 61, 148–9
   war spirit 59–60
Clio Enthroned (Lamb, Walter) 48–9
Cochrane, Charles 12, 49, 50, 140, 141, 150–1
   Thucydides and the Science of History 49, 134
Cold War, the 169–70, 172
Connor, W. R. 101, 129
Constant, Benjamin 9, 68–9
Cook, A. B. 30, 31
Corcyrean debate 150
Cornford, Francis Macdonald 26, 27–34, 43–52, 65, 141
   American scholars 160
   From Religion to Philosophy 25
   Greek Religious Thought from Homer to Alexander 25–6
   influence 170
   'Mysticism and science in the Pythagorean tradition' 25
   Origin of Attic Comedy, The 25
   Peloponnesian War causes 93
   political psychology 71–2, 150
   Powell, Enoch 133, 150
   Thucydides Mythistoricus. See *Thucydides Mythistoricus*
   Toynbee, Arnold 122–5
   Unconscious Element in Literature and Philosophy, The 46

Coulange, Fustel de 69
Courtney, Catherine 89
Cousin, Victor 12
Crane, Gregory 16, 78, 101, 137, 138, 183 n. 2
    Realpolitik 142–3
Cratylus (Plato) 29

democracy 84, 96, 152
deos (fear, δέος) 103–6, 150
desire (*eros*, ἔρος) 38, 71, 74
Desmond, W. 79
Destined for War? Can America and China Escape Thucydides's Trap (Allison, Graham) 1–2
destiny 42
Dietzfelbinger 134
dikaion (justice, δίκαιον) 168, 169
Diodotus 148, 149, 150
Dionysius of Halicarnassus 96, 146
Dionysius of Thrace 66
doctrinal realism 11
Donnelly, J. 183 n. 3
doom (*nemesis*, νέμεσις) 26, 38, 39, 47, 123, 125, 146
Dörpfeld, Wilhelm 30
drama 39, 51
dunamis (greatness, δύναμις) 62

Edmunds, Lowell 51
elpis (hope, ἐλπίς) 38, 40
emotions 18, 26, 40, 51, 71–2, 103–5, 150
empirical realism 10–11
envy of the Gods (*phthonos*, φθόνος) 123, 125
eros (desire, ἔρος) 38, 71, 74
Euben, Peter 51–2
Euclid 66
euergesia (good deeds, εὐεργεσία) 150
Euripides 29, 51, 52
    Trojan Women 62
Euripides the Rationalist: A Study in the History of Art and Religion (Verrall, Arthur Woollgar) 28–9
Europe 2, 7–8
    political psychology 70, 74
    war 103–4 (*see also* Great War, the *and* Second World War)
Europe in Convalescence (Zimmern, Alfred Eckhard) 74

evolution 44, 140, 151
expansionism 145

fear (*phobos*, φόβος) 71, 104
fear/apprehension (*deos*, δέος) 103–6, 150
Finley, J. H. 51, 164
    Thucydides 164–5
First World War. *See* Great War, the
Fisher, M. 73
Forde, Steven 16
foresight (*gnome*, γνώμη) 38
fortune (*tuche*, τύχη) 38
Foster, David J. 161
Fragoulaki, M. 138
France 132–3, 152
    political psychology 70
Frankel, Benjamin 113
French Revolution, the 83
Freyburg-Inan, Annette 183 n. 4
From Pericles to Philip (Glover, Terrot Reaveley) 88, 89–91
From Religion to Philosophy (Cornford, Francis Macdonald) 25

Gardner, Arthur 30
Garst, Daniel 16, 143
German scholarship 9, 132, 134–5, 163–4
Germany 9, 134–5, 163
Gerson, Gal 43–4
Geyl, Pieter 111
Gillies, John 119
Gilpin, R. 112
Glover, T. R. 12
Glover, Terrot Reaveley 88–91
    From Pericles to Philip 88, 89–91
gnome (γνώμη, foresight) 38
Gomperz, Theodor 31–2, 47
    Greek Thinkers 31
good deeds (*euergesia*, εὐεργεσία) 150
Great War, the 13–14, 83, 84, 85–91, 172–3
    Abbott, George Frederick 83, 106
    Grundy, G. B. 73
    Lord, Louis 162
    parallels with Peloponnesian War 87–8, 120–1, 125–8, 133, 152–3
    Powell, Enoch 131–3
    Schwartz, Eduard 132
    Toynbee, Arnold 109, 114, 120–2, 125–8
    Zimmern, Alfred Eckhard 63, 70, 72

greatness (*dunamis*, δύναμις) 62
Greece. *See* ancient Greece
Greece and the Allies (Abbott, George Frederick) 100
greed (*pleonexia*, πλεονεξία) 150
Greek Classics. *See* Classics
Greek Commonwealth, The (Zimmern, Alfred Eckhard) 53, 55, 56, 58, 60, 65, 78, 164
Greek drama 38–9
Greek Historical Thought (Toynbee, Arnold) 123
Greek literature 66
Greek political thought 63–9
Greek Political Thought (Zimmern, Alfred Eckhard) 55
Greek religion 123
Greek Religious Thought from Homer to Alexander (Cornford, Francis Macdonald) 25–6
Greek science 66
Greek Thinkers (Gomperx, Theodor) 31
Greek thought 25, 26, 28–31, 66, 123
Greek Tradition, The (Thomson, J. A. K.) 51
Greek tragedy 51–2
Greek writing 51
Greenwood, E. 147
Grene, David 167
  Man in his Pride: A Study in the Political Thought of Thucydides and Plato 167–8
Griechische Geschichte (Busolt, G.) 34
Grote, George 9–10, 65, 84, 96
  History of Greece 119
Grundsätze der Realpolitik angewendet auf die staatlichen Zustände Deutschlands (Rochau, Ludwig von) 141
Grundy, G. B. 12, 140, 146, 164
  political psychology 72
  Political psychology: A science which has yet to be created 73
  Thucydides and the History of his Age 73, 165–7
Guarantees of Peace (Rodgers, W. L.) 162
Guthrie, W. K. C. 26, 43

Halle, Louis J. 15, 110, 137
  Message from Thucydides, A 129

Harrison, Jane Ellen 29–31
  Primitive Athens as described by Thucydides 12, 30–1
Headlam, Arthur 27
Hegel, Georg 9
Heinberg, John Gilbert 161
Hellenic civilization 114
Hermocrates 145
Herodotus 9, 31–4, 117
  reputation 33
Hesiod 51
Hippocrates 49–50, 66
historicism 9, 168
history 77
  causation 37
  contemporaneity 109, 110, 111–13, 125–9
  cycles of 3, 6, 97–9, 112–22, 126–8, 139, 151
  equivalences 115, 120–2
  Graeco-Roman 119–20
  historical change 151–2, 155
  impersonal forces of 123–5
  personification 123–5
  stages of classical 117–19
  tragedy in 122
History of Greece (Bury, J. B.) 34
History of Greece (Grote, George) 119
History of Greece (Mitford, William) 8
History of Greek Literature, A (Murray, Gilbert) 84
History of Greek Political Thought, A (Sinclair, T. A.) 154
History of the Peloponnesian War (Thucydides) 1–2, 4–6, 13
  dating debate 92, 132, 145
  as drama 38–9
  Great War, the 85–92
  historical change in 151–2
  Hobbes, Thomas 7
  literary style 32, 46, 48, 96, 107–8, 147, 185 n. 15
  Melian dialogue 95–6, 146–7, 149, 192 n. 5
  Mytilene debate 148–9
  Pericles' funeral speech 56, 58, 61, 69, 85
  political passions 59
  practical applicability 140

readership 138–9, 153
speeches, verisimilitude of 94–6
speeches as political thought 145–9
stasis passage 120–1
Thomson, J. A. K. 51
Zimmern, Alfred Eckhard 68
Hitler, Adolf 142 (*see also* Nazism)
Hobbes, Thomas 2–3, 7, 37, 68, 108, 129
  Leviathan 7
Hobson, J. A.
  Psychology of Jingoism 58
Hoekstra, Kinch 6–7, 74
Holy War In Tripoli, The (Abbott, George Frederick) 97
Homer 51
hope (*elpis*, ἐλπίς) 38, 40
Hornblower, S. 37
Horsley, G. H. R. 36
hubris (pride, ὕβρις) 26, 38, 44, 47, 123, 125, 147
human nature (*phusis anangkaia* φύσις ἀνάγκαια) 18, 41, 97–100, 104–5, 136, 140
  Athenians 147–8
  emotions 18, 26, 40, 51, 71–2, 103–5, 150
  morality 155–6
  Powell, Enoch 144, 150–1
  war 155
Human Nature in Politics (Wallas, Graham) 56
humanities, the 76
Hunter, Virginia 72, 112
Hutton, William 12, 88

idealism 54, 77, 170, 180 n. 2
imperialism 13, 36, 45, 144–5, 149, 152–4
  Athens 57, 60–2, 101, 146–8, 152, 156
  Britain 13, 36, 45, 57–8, 60, 152
  Callander, Thomas 166
  Classics, and the 180 n. 3
  Cleon 61, 148–9
  Hermocrates 145
  morality 156
  Zimmern, Alfred Eckhard 56–8, 60–3
impiety (*asebeia*, ἀσέβεια) 147
individuality 68–9
international politics 105, 106

International Relations 3, 4, 14–16, 171
  fear 103–6
  history, cycles of 112–13
  Toynbee, Arnold 111

Jackson, Henry 27, 29
Jaeger, Werner
  Paideia 134
Jaffe, Seth 17, 78
Jebb, Richard Claverhouse 25, 32–3, 39–40, 146
jingoism 58–9
justice (*dikaion*, δίκαιον) 168, 169

Kagan, Donald 169–70
Kallet, L. 139
Keedus, Liisi 168
Keene, Edward 110, 169

Lamb, Walter 12, 48–9, 81
  Clio Enthroned 48–9
League of Nations 54, 63–4, 106
Lebow, Ned 16–17, 72, 112, 137
Legacy of Greece, The (Livingstone, R. W.) 64, 65–6, 114
Levesque, Pierre Charles 8
Leviathan (Hobbes, Thomas) 7
Lingelbach, William 161
literary realism 18
literature 66
Livingstone, R. W. 78
  Legacy of Greece, The 64, 65–6, 114
Loraux, Nicole 51
Lord, Louis 159, 162–5, 167
  Thucydides and the World War 159–60, 162–4
Low, P. 78
Lucretius 122
Luginbill, R. D. 79

Mably, abbé Gabriel Bonnot de 7–8
  Two dialogues, concerning the manner of writing history 7
MacKay, Joseph and Christopher David LaRoche 113
MacKenzie, Compton 87
MacLeod, Colin 51, 147
McNeill, William 117
Mahaffy, J. P. 83–4, 100, 132

Man in his Pride: A Study in the Political Thought of Thucydides and Plato (Grene, David) 167–8
Manuscripts of Thucydides in Cambridge and Venice (Powell, Enoch) 143
Marshall, George 129
Mayfield, A. L. 154–6
Maynard, J. D. 89–91
Megarian decrees 34, 35, 36
Meineke, Stefan 72
Melian dialogue 95–6, 146–7, 149, 192 n. 5
Melos 136, 147, 149–50
Message from Thucydides, A (Halle, Louis J.) 129
Meyer, Edward 163, 164, 190 n. 19
  Thucydides und die Entstehung der Wissenschaftlichen Geschichtsschreibung 164
militarism 58–9
Mill, John Stuart 9, 84
Mitford, William 84, 96, 119
  History of Greece 8
Mitrany, David 13, 54
modern world
  parallels with ancient world 160, 161–2, 165–6
modernity 63–9
Momigliano, Arnaldo 112
Monten, Jonathan 16
Moral and Political Principles of Thucydides and their Influence on Later Antiquity, The (Powell, Enoch) 135, 138, 154–6
Morefield, Jeanne 56–7, 58, 78
Morgenthau, Hans 105, 137, 194 n. 16
  Politics Among Nations 169
Morley, Felix 161
Morley, n. 10, 82, 87, 176 n. 3, 191 n. 4
Muhlack, Hans 83
Muhlack, Ulrich 9
Murray, Gilbert 60, 100, 140, 180 n. 4
  Aristophanes and the War Party: A Study in the Contemporary Criticism of the Peloponnesian War 87, 181 n. 7
  Cambridge ritualism 30
  Cornford, Francis Macdonald 31, 43, 44, 47, 123
  History of Greek Literature, A 84
  pacifism 134
  Value of Greece to the Modern World, The 66
'Mysticism and science in the Pythagorean tradition' (Cornford, Francis Macdonald) 2
Mytilene 140
Mytilene debate 148–9

nation states 16, 67, 70–1, 73–5 (see also *polis*, the)
  Glover, Terrot Reaveley 88
  Great War, the 86
  morality 155–6
  Powell, Enoch 144, 150
  Realpolitik 155–6
national character 152
Nationality and Government (Zimmern, Alfred Eckhard) 65
nature (*phusis*, φύσις) 16–17, 155 (see also human nature)
Nazism 134–5, 142
necessity (*anangke*, ἀνάγκη) 168, 169
nemesis (doom, νέμεσις)) 26, 38, 39, 47, 123, 125, 146
Neus Thukidideshild (Wassermann, Felix) 134
Nietzsche, Friederich 10–11, 77, 142, 183 n. 4
  Twilight of the Idols 10
neorealists 16
Nicias (Athenian commander) 45
Noel-Baker, Philip 54
nomos 16

On the Implicit Ethics and Psychology of Thucydides (Shorey, Paul) 41, 164
ophelimos (advantage, ὠφέλιμος) 150
Organski, A. F. K.
  World Politics 4
Origin of Attic Comedy, The (Cornford, Francis Macdonald) 25
Orwin, Clifford 16, 78, 138, 147
Osiander, A. 54
Oxford University 14

pacifism 134
Paideia (Jaeger, Werner) 134
Palmer, M. 50, 121
Parry, A. 147

party of the Piraeus 34, 35
peitho (persuasion, πείθω) 38, 71
Peloponnesian War, the 93, 162
  Battle of Pylos 38, 40
  causes of 1–2, 3, 34–7, 48, 93, 104, 106
  class war (stasis) 121
  Cochrane, Charles 192 n. 6
  parallels with Second World War 159
  parallels with the Great War 87–8,
    120–1, 125–8, 133, 152–3
  Zimmern, Alfred Eckhard 58
Pericles 35–6, 37, 38, 51, 58, 69
  funeral speech 61, 69, 85, 134
  imperialism 60–2
  war spirit 59
personification 123–5
persuasion (peitho, πείθω) 38, 71
Petersen, R. and E. Liaras 79
philology 143
philonekia (tenacity, φιλονικία) 150
philosophy 77
phobos (fear, φόβος) 71, 104
phthonos (envy of the Gods, φθόνος) 123, 125
phusis (nature, φύσις) 16–17, 155 (see also human nature)
phusis anangkaia (human nature, φύσις νάγκαια). See human nature
Piraeus 34, 35, 106
Pitt, William (the Elder), 1st Earl of Chatham 8
Pitt, William (the Younger) 8
Plataea 59
Plato 51–2, 66–7, 69, 142
  Cratylus 29
  Grene, David 167–8
pleonexia (greed, πλεονεξία) 150
Poetics (Aristotle) 115
Pohlenz, Max 132, 148
polis, the 56, 72, 150 (see also nation states)
Polis, der greichische Beitrag zu einer deutschen Bildung heute, an Thukydides erläut (The Greek Contribution to German Education To-day, Illustrated from Thucydides) (Weinstock, Heinrich) 134–5
political order 68
political psychology 64, 69–75, 149–51
  definition 73

Political psychology: A science which has yet to be created (Grundy, G. B.) 73
political realism 100
political scale 67
Political Science 3
political theory 16
Political Thought (Zimmern, Alfred Eckhard) 64, 65, 67
politics 69, 73
Politics Among Nations (Morgenthau, Hans) 169
Powell, Enoch 12, 42–3, 87, 131–5, 136, 137, 138
  American scholars 160
  British imperialism 152
  Great War, the 131–3
  historical change 150–1
  imperialism of Thucydides 152–4
  influence 170
  Manuscripts of Thucydides in Cambridge and Venice 143
  moral and political principals of Thucydides 135–41, 142, 173
  Moral and Political Principles of Thucydides and their Influence on Later Antiquity, The 135, 138, 154–6
  Nazism 135
  philology 143
  political psychology 149–51
  Realpolitik 141–5, 156
  speeches as political thought 145–9
power 105–6, 130, 136, 137–8, 151, 155 (see also Realpolitik)
  Athens 106, 136, 147–8, 150
power politics 74, 141 (see also Realpolitik)
power transition theory 4
Price, J. J. 121
pride (hubris, ὕβρις) 26, 38, 44, 47, 123, 125
Primitive Athens as described by Thucydides (Harrison, Jane Ellen) 12, 30
prophasis (πρόφασις) 37
psychology 17–18, 51, 150
Psychology of Jingoism (Hobson, J. A.) 58

Rahe, Paul 16, 74, 142
Ranke, Leopold von 9, 12, 144

Rathbun, Brian 143
rationality 150
realism 10–11, 15–16, 18, 69
   international politics 105
   Realpolitik 143
   types 82
Realpolitik 73, 136–7, 140–5, 155–6
religion 116–17, 123
republicanism 7
rhetoric 6, 146
Rochau, Ludwig von 141
   Grundsätze der Realpolitik angewendet auf die staatlichen Zustände Deutschlands 141
Rodgers, W. L. 161–2
   Guarantees of Peace 162
Rome 6, 122
Romilly, J. de 78–9
Roscher, William 12
Round Table association 60
Ruback, T. 15

Sawyer, Elizabeth 78, 129
Scanlon, T. F. 139
Schadewelt, W. 132, 148
Schoefield, Camilla 193 n. 9
Scholar in Public Affairs, The (Zimmern, Alfred Eckhard) 55, 76
scholarship 12–13, 43, 75–7, 172
   American 159–62, 164–5, 167–70
   British scholarship 164, 165–7, 170–3
   German 9, 132, 134–5, 163–4
Schwartz, Eduard 92, 132, 133–4, 135, 140
   Lord, Louis 164
   Melian dialogue 147
   Mytilene debate 148, 149
science 50, 66
scientific history 24
Sears, R. 50
Second World War 127–8, 159, 161–3
self-interest 101, 105
Shorey, Paul 25, 41–2, 48
   On the Implicit Ethics and Psychology of Thucydides 41, 164
Sinclair, T. A.
   History of Greek Political Thought, A 154
social class 121
Solon (Athenian politician) 56
Sophocles 52

Sparta 104, 105, 106, 132, 150, 162, 188 n. 12
Spengler, Oswald 116
   Untergang des Abendlandes, Der 116
Stahl, H. 135, 139
Stanyon, Temple 119
stasis (class war) 121–2
Ste Croix, G. E. M. de 50
Strauss, B. 17
Strauss, Leo 15, 160, 168–9
   City and Man, The 168, 169
Study of History, A (Toynbee, Arnold) 110–11, 188 n. 9

Taylor, A. J. P. 111
tenacity (*philonekia*, φιλονικία) 150
Thaur, C. and C. Wendt 17
Thibaudet, Albert
   Campagne avec Thucydides, La 133
Thomas, Rosalind 49–50
Thomson, J. A. K. 12, 50–1
   Greek Tradition, The 51
Thorpe, W. A.
   Thucydides and the Disciple of Detachment 85, 97
Thucydidean turn, the 5, 12, 167–70
   British 171–3
   scholarship 17–18 (*see also* scholarship)
Thucydides 2, 86, 89, 153
   academic readings of 12–13, 43 (*see also* scholarship)
   class war (*stasis*) 121
   collective psychology 72
   constructivist 72–3
   contemporaneity 109, 110, 111–13, 125–30, 141
   cycle of civilizations 113–22
   cycle of history 112–13
   didactic aims 155
   drama 39, 40, 48, 147
   dramatic characters 38–9
   exile 89, 126
   fear 78–9, 103–6
   foresight (*gnome*, γνώμη) 38
   fortune (*tuche*, τύχη) 38
   greatness (*dunamis*, δύναμις) 62
   Greek thought 31–2
   as historian 77–8
   historical change 151–2, 155

historical realism 91–7
History of the Peloponnesian War. See *History of the Peloponnesian War*
history, cycles of 112–13
hope (*elpis*, ἐλπίς) 40
human nature 41–2, 64, 70, 77, 97–100, 104, 140–1, 144–5, 150–1
humanity 62–3
as idealist 75
imperialism 60–3, 144–5, 152–4
influences of 51
International Relations 3, 4, 170
iterations of 4
justice 160, 168, 169
labelling 4, 5–14, 15–17, 23, 24, 171
literary style 32, 46, 48, 96, 107–8, 147, 185 n. 15
mass psychology 72
Melian dialogue 95–6, 146–7, 149, 192 n. 5
as monarchist 7, 68
moral and political principals of 133–4, 135–41, 142, 149, 156
myth 23–4, 32
Mytilene debate 148–9
nation states 144–5
National Socialist (Nazi) reading of 134–5
necessity 168, 169
Peloponnesian War 34–5
Pericles' funeral speech 56, 58, 61, 69, 85, 134
personal feelings 154
personification, use of 123–5
philosophy 46–7, 99, 146, 155
as political analyst 81
as political historian 139, 143–4
as political philosopher 21, 139, 155, 160, 172
political psychology 64, 69–75, 78, 151, 173
as political realist 15–16, 97–100
political science 3, 24
political thought 4–5, 32, 42, 65–7, 147
political views 84
power politics 74
as psychologist 53, 77, 141, 150–1
as public scholar 75–8
as rationalist 23–4, 32–4

readership 139
as realist 53, 55, 64, 70, 75–6, 77, 81–2, 89, 141
as Realpolitiker 136–7, 140–5, 146, 155–6
red/black interpretations 7
religion 23, 33
reputation 33
rhetoric 6, 146
science 93–5
as scientific historian 23, 24, 37, 49–50, 83
as scientist 49–50, 81–2, 97, 141
self-interest 99, 101–3
as soldier 86, 89
speeches as political thought 145–9
speeches, verisimilitude of 94–6
as tragedian 24, 32, 38–40, 48, 141
Trojan War 94
works 4
Thucydides (Finley, J. H.) 164–5
Thucydides: A Study in Historical Reality (Abbott, George Frederick) 81, 91, 107–8, 133
Thucydides and the Disciple of Detachment (Thorpe, W. A.) 85, 97
Thucydides and the History of his Age (Grundy, G. B.) 73, 165–7
Thucydides and the Science of History (Cochrane, Charles) 49, 134
Thucydides and the World War (Lord, Louis) 159–60, 162
Thucydides Mythistoricus (Cornford, Francis) 12, 23–8, 31–3, 34–40
  Boer Wars 60
  influence 47–52
  political psychology 71
  politics and ethics 40–7
  Powell, Enoch 133
  reception 47–52
  Toynbee, Arnold 122–3
Thucydides the Imperialist (Zimmern, Alfred Eckhard) 55, 60–3, 78, 164
Thucydides trap, the 1–4, 68, 79, 104, 112, 139, 172–3
Thucydides und die Entstehung der Wissenschaftlichen Geschichtsschreibung (Meyer, Edward) 164

Thukydidesfrage 92, 132, 145
Toynbee, Arnold 12, 109–13, 126, 128, 141
   American scholars 160
   contemporaneity of Thucydides 109, 110, 111–13, 125–30, 173
   Cornford, Francis Macdonald 122–5
   criticism 111
   cycle of civilizations 113–22, 126–8
   Great War, the 114, 120–2, 125–6
   Graeco-Roman history 119–20
   Greek Historical Thought 123
   historical equivalences 115, 120–2
   influence 170
   personification 123–5
   religion 116–17, 123
   stages of classical history 117–19
   stasis passage 120–2
   Study of History, A 110–11, 188 n. 9
tragic passions 71
Trevor-Roper, Hugh 111
Trojan Women (Euripides) 62
Trump, Donald 1
tuche (τύχη, fortune) 38
Turkey, Greece and the Great Powers: A Study in Friendship and Hate (Abbott, George Frederick) 100
Turnball, Malcolm 1
Twenty Years' Crisis, The (Carr, E. H.) 54, 111
Twilight of the Idols (Nietzsche, Friederich) 10
Two dialogues, concerning the manner of writing history (Mably, abbé Gabriel Bonnot de) 7

Ullrich, F. W. 92
Ulrici, Hermann
   Charakteristik de antiken Historiographie 39
Unconscious Element in Literature and Philosophy, The (Cornford, Francis Macdonald) 46
University of Chicago 167–8
Untergang des Abendlandes, Der (Spengler, Oswald) 116
US. *See* America

Valla, Lorenzo 6
Value of Greece to the Modern World, The (Murray, Gilbert) 66

Verrall, Arthur Woollgar 28–9
   Euripides the Rationalist: A Study in the History of Art and Religion 28–9
Vidal-Naquet, Pierre 112
Visvardi, E. 72
Volney, C. F. 9, 83

Wallas, Graham
   Human Nature in Politics 56
war 155 (*see also* Great War, the *and* Peloponnesian War, the)
   causes of 1–2, 114
   Cold War, the 169–70, 172
   cycle of 128
   fear 103–5
   geographical proximity 152
   as instrument of change 117
   Lord, Louis 162
   Second World War 127–8, 159, 161–3
   Toynbee, Arnold 114, 128
war party/spirit 58–9, 60
Wassermann, Felix
   Neus Thukididesbild 134
Weinstock, Heinrich
   Polis, der greichische Beitrag zu einer deutschen Bildung heute, an Thukydides erläut (*The Greek Contribution to German Education To-day, Illustrated from Thucydides*) 134–5
Welch, David 16, 183 n. 4
Wendt, C. 17, 139
Williams, Orlo 85–7
Wilson, Thomas Woodrow (President) 142
World Politics (Organski, A. F. K.) 4

Xenophon 121
Xi Jinping 1

Zimmern, Alfred Eckhard 12, 18, 42, 53, 55–6, 84, 123, 141
   American scholars 160
   Athens 56–7, 58–9, 181 n. 4
   contemporaneity 190 n. 19
   Europe in Convalescence 74
   funeral speech translation 56, 58, 61, 65, 69, 78
   Great War, the 63

Greek Commonwealth, The 53, 55, 56, 58, 60, 65, 78, 164
Greek Political Thought 55
Greek political thought 63–9
imperialism 56–8, 60–3
influence 170
International Relations 53–5, 65
League of Nations 63–4
liberalism 64
Low, P. 78
Melian dialogue 149
modernity 63–9
Nationality and Government 65
political order 68
political psychology 64, 69–75, 78, 151, 173
Political Thought 64, 65, 67
Scholar in Public Affairs, The 55, 76
Thucydides as public scholar 76–8
Thucydides the Imperialist 55, 60–3, 78, 164
war party/spirit 58–9, 60

www.ingramcontent.com/pod-product-compliance
Lightning Source LLC
Chambersburg PA
CBHW072147290426
44111CB00012B/1996